The Poet at the Breakfast Table by Oliver Wendell Holmes

Oliver Wendell Holmes, Sr. was born on August 29th 1809.

Among his many talents were those of physician, poet, professor, lecturer, and author.

Here we concentrate on his writing. He was regarded by many of his peers – including such luminaries as Ralph Waldo Emerson, Henry Wadsworth Longfellow and James Russell Lowell – as one of the finest writers of their times. A great compliment indeed.

As a poet he is considered to be one of the Fireside Poets and indeed his poems are works of real talent and quality. As a writer he is perhaps best known for his 'Breakfast Table' series.

In this collection we publish his medical essays and show just why he was seen as an important reformer in that field.

Born in Cambridge, Massachusetts, his education was at Phillips Academy followed by Harvard College. After graduating in 1829, he was to study law briefly before turning to the medical profession.

At tis time he also began to write poetry and one of his most famous "Old Ironsides", was published in 1830.

Following training at the prestigious medical schools of Paris, Holmes was granted his M.D. from Harvard Medical School in 1836. He taught for a time at Dartmouth Medical School before returning to teach at Harvard and, for a time, served as dean there.

As a writer, many of his works were published in The Atlantic Monthly, a magazine that he also named. He was, over the years, the recipient of many honorary degrees from Universities around the world for his many literary achievements and other accomplishments. His writing style was often humorous and conversational and often reflected his native Boston area.

Holmes retired from Harvard in 1882 but continued to write poetry, novels and essays until his death on October 7th 1894.

Table of Contents
PREFACE
PREFACE TO THE NEW EDITION
CHAPTER I
CHAPTER II
CHAPTER III
CHAPTER IV
CHAPTER V
CHAPTER VI
CHAPTER VII
CHAPTER VIII
CHAPTER IX
CHAPTER X
CHAPTER XI
CHAPTER XII

PREFACE

In this, the third series of Breakfast-Table conversations, a slight dramatic background shows off a few talkers and writers, aided by certain silent supernumeraries. The machinery is much like that of the two preceding series. Some of the characters must seem like old acquaintances to those who have read the former papers. As I read these over for the first time for a number of years, I notice one character; presenting a class of beings who have greatly multiplied during the interval which separates the earlier and later Breakfast-Table papers, I mean the scientific specialists. The entomologist, who confines himself rigidly to the study of the coleoptera, is intended to typify this class. The subdivision of labor, which, as we used to be told, required fourteen different workmen to make a single pin, has reached all branches of knowledge. We find new terms in all the Professions, implying that special provinces have been marked off, each having its own school of students. In theology we have many curious subdivisions; among the rest eschatology, that is to say, the geography, geology, etc., of the "undiscovered country;" in medicine, if the surgeon who deals with dislocations of the right shoulder declines to meddle with a displacement on the other side, we are not surprised, but ring the bell of the practitioner who devotes himself to injuries of the left shoulder.

On the other hand, we have had or have the encyclopaedic intelligences like Cuvier, Buckle, and more emphatically Herbert Spencer, who take all knowledge, or large fields of it, to be their province. The author of "Thoughts on the Universe" has something in common with these, but he appears also to have a good deal about him of what we call the humorist; that is, an individual with a somewhat heterogeneous personality, in which various distinctly human elements are mixed together, so as to form a kind of coherent and sometimes pleasing whole, which is to a symmetrical character as a breccia is to a mosaic.

As for the Young Astronomer, his rhythmical discourse may be taken as expressing the reaction of what some would call "the natural man" against the unnatural beliefs which he found in that lower world to which he descended by day from his midnight home in the firmament.

I have endeavored to give fair play to the protest of gentle and reverential conservatism in the letter of the Lady, which was not copied from, but suggested by, one which I received long ago from a lady bearing an honored name, and which I read thoughtfully and with profound respect.

December, 1882.

PREFACE TO THE NEW EDITION.

It is now nearly twenty years since this book was published. Being the third of the Breakfast-Table series, it could hardly be expected to attract so much attention as the earlier volumes. Still, I had no reason to be disappointed with its reception. It took its place with the others, and was in some points a clearer exposition of my views and feelings than either of the other books, its predecessors. The poems "Homesick in Heaven" and the longer group of passages coming from the midnight reveries of the Young Astronomer have thoughts in them not so fully expressed elsewhere in my writings.

The first of these two poems is at war with our common modes of thought. In looking forward to rejoining in a future state those whom we have loved on earth, as most of us hope and many of us believe we shall, we are apt to forget that the same individuality is remembered by one relative as a babe, by another as an adult in the strength of maturity, and by a third as a wreck with little left except its infirmities and its affections. The main thought of this poem is a painful one to some persons. They have so closely associated life with its accidents that they expect to see their departed friends in the costume of the time in which they best remember them, and feel as if they should meet the spirit of their grandfather with his wig and cane, as they habitually recall him to memory.

The process of scientific specialization referred to and illustrated in this record has been going on more actively than ever during these last twenty years. We have only to look over the lists of the Faculties and teachers of our Universities to see the subdivision of labor carried out as never before. The movement is irresistible; it brings with it exactness, exhaustive knowledge, a narrow but complete self-satisfaction, with such accompanying faults as pedantry, triviality, and the kind of partial blindness which belong to intellectual myopia. The specialist is idealized almost into sublimity in Browning's "Burial of the Grammarian." We never need fear that he will undervalue himself. To be the supreme authority on anything is a satisfaction to self-love next door to the precious delusions of dementia. I have never pictured a character more contented with himself than the "Scarabee" of this story.

BEVERLY FARMS, MASS., August 1, 1891. O. W. H.

CHAPTER I

The idea of a man's "interviewing" himself is rather odd, to be sure. But then that is what we are all of us doing every day. I talk half the time to find out my own thoughts, as a school-boy turns his pockets inside out to see what is in them. One brings to light all sorts of personal property he had forgotten in his inventory.

You don't know what your thoughts are going to be beforehand? said the "Member of the Haouse," as he calls himself.

Why, of course I don't. Bless your honest legislative soul, I suppose I have as many bound volumes of notions of one kind and another in my head as you have in your Representatives' library up there at the State House. I have to tumble them over and over, and open them in a hundred places, and sometimes cut the leaves here and there, to find what I think about this and that. And a good many people who flatter themselves they are talking wisdom to me, are only helping me to get at the shelf and the book and the page where I shall find my own opinion about the matter in question.

The Member's eyes began to look heavy.

It 's a very queer place, that receptacle a man fetches his talk out of. The library comparison does n't exactly hit it. You stow away some idea and don't want it, say for ten years. When it turns up at last it has got so jammed and crushed out of shape by the other ideas packed with it, that it is no more like what it was than a raisin is like a grape on the vine, or a fig from a drum like one hanging on the tree. Then, again, some kinds of thoughts breed in the dark of one's mind like the blind fishes in the Mammoth Cave. We can't see them and they can't see us; but sooner or later the daylight gets in and we find that some cold, fishy little negative has been spawning all over our beliefs, and the brood of blind questions it has given birth to are burrowing round and under and butting their blunt noses against the pillars of faith we thought the whole world might lean on. And then, again, some of our old beliefs are dying out every year, and others feed on them and grow fat, or get poisoned as the case may be. And so, you see, you can't tell what the thoughts are that you have got salted down, as one may say, till you run a streak of talk through them, as the market people run a butterscoop through a firkin.

Don't talk, thinking you are going to find out your neighbor, for you won't do it, but talk to find out yourself. There is more of you and less of you, in spots, very likely than you know.

The Member gave a slight but unequivocal start just here. It does seem as if perpetual somnolence was the price of listening to other people's wisdom. This was one of those transient nightmares that one may have in a doze of twenty seconds. He thought a certain imaginary Committee of Safety of a certain imaginary Legislature was proceeding to burn down his haystack, in accordance with an Act, entitled an Act to make the Poor Richer by making the Rich Poorer. And the chairman of the committee was instituting a forcible exchange of hats with him, to his manifest disadvantage, for he had just bought him a new beaver. He told this dream afterwards to one of the boarders.

There was nothing very surprising, therefore, in his asking a question not very closely related to what had gone before.

Do you think they mean business?

I beg your pardon, but it would be of material assistance to me in answering your question if I knew who "they" might happen to be.

Why, those chaps that are setting folks on to burn us all up in our beds. Political firebugs we call 'em up our way. Want to substitoot the match-box for the ballot-box. Scare all our old women half to death.

Oh, ah, yes, to be sure. I don't believe they say what the papers put in their mouths any more than that a friend of mine wrote the letter about Worcester's and Webster's Dictionaries, that he had to disown the other day. These newspaper fellows are half asleep when they make up their reports at two or three o'clock in the morning, and fill out the speeches to suit themselves. I do remember some things that sounded pretty bad, about as bad as nitro-glycerine, for that matter. But I don't believe they ever said 'em, when they spoke their pieces, or if they said 'em I know they did n't mean 'em. Something like this, wasn't it? If the majority didn't do something the minority wanted 'em to, then the people were to burn up our cities, and knock us down and jump on our stomachs. That was about the kind of talk, as the papers had it; I don't wonder it scared the old women.

The Member was wide awake by this time.

I don't seem to remember of them partickler phrases, he said.

Dear me, no; only levelling everything smack, and trampling us under foot, as the reporters made it out. That means FIRE, I take it, and knocking you down and stamping on you, whichever side of your person happens to be uppermost. Sounded like a threat; meant, of course, for a warning. But I don't believe it was in the piece as they spoke it, could n't have been. Then, again, Paris wasn't to blame, as much as to say, so the old women thought, that New York or Boston would n't be to blame if it did the same thing. I've heard of political gatherings where they barbecued an ox, but I can't think there's a party in this country that wants to barbecue a city. But it is n't quite fair to frighten the old women. I don't doubt there are a great many people wiser than I am that would n't be hurt by a hint I am going to give them. It's no matter what you say when you talk to yourself, but when you talk to other people, your business is to use words with reference to the way in which those other people are like to understand them. These pretended inflammatory speeches, so reported as to seem full of combustibles, even if they were as threatening as they have been represented, would do no harm if read or declaimed in a man's study to his books, or by the sea-shore to the waves. But they are not so wholesome moral entertainment for the dangerous classes. Boys must not touch off their squibs and crackers too near the powder-magazine. This kind of speech does n't help on the millennium much.

It ain't jest the thing to grease your ex with ile o' vitrul, said the Member.

No, the wheel of progress will soon stick fast if you do. You can't keep a dead level long, if you burn everything down flat to make it. Why, bless your soul, if all the cities of the world were reduced ashes, you'd have a new set of millionnaires in a couple of years or so, out of the trade in potash. In the mean time, what is the use of setting the man with the silver watch against the man with the gold watch, and the man without any watch against them both?

You can't go agin human natur', said the Member

You speak truly. Here we are travelling through desert together like the children of Israel. Some pick up more manna and catch more quails than others and ought to help their hungry neighbors more than they do; that will always be so until we come back to primitive Christianity, the road to which does not seem to be via Paris, just now; but we don't want the incendiary's pillar of a cloud by day and a pillar of fire by night to lead us in the march to civilization, and we don't want a Moses who will smite rock, not to bring out water for our thirst, but petroleum to burn us all up with.

It is n't quite fair to run an opposition to the other funny speaker, Rev. Petroleum V. What 's-his-name, spoke up an anonymous boarder.

You may have been thinking, perhaps, that it was I, I, the Poet, who was the chief talker in the one-sided dialogue to which you have been listening. If so, you were mistaken. It was the old man in the spectacles with large round glasses and the iron-gray hair. He does a good deal of the talking at our table, and, to tell the truth, I rather like to hear him. He stirs me up, and finds me occupation in various ways, and especially, because he has good solid prejudices, that one can rub against, and so get up and let off a superficial intellectual irritation, just as the cattle rub their backs against a rail (you remember Sydney Smith's contrivance in his pasture) or their sides against an apple-tree (I don't know why they take to these so particularly, but you will often find the trunk of an apple-tree as brown and smooth as an old saddle at the height of a cow's ribs). I think they begin rubbing in cold blood, and then, you know, l'appetit vient en mangeant, the more they rub the more they want to. That is the way to use your friend's prejudices. This is a sturdy-looking personage of a good deal more than middle age, his face marked with strong manly furrows, records of hard thinking and square stand-up fights with life and all its devils. There is a slight touch of satire in his discourse now and then, and an odd way of answering one that makes it hard to guess how much more or less he means than he seems to say. But he is honest, and always has a twinkle in his eye to put you on your guard when he does not mean to be taken quite literally. I think old Ben Franklin had just that look. I know his great-grandson (in pace!) had it, and I don't doubt he took it in the straight line of descent, as he did his grand intellect.

The Member of the Haouse evidently comes from one of the lesser inland centres of civilization, where the flora is rich in checkerberries and similar bounties of nature, and the fauna lively with squirrels, wood-chucks, and the like; where the leading sportsmen snare patridges, as they are called, and "hunt" foxes with guns; where rabbits are entrapped in "figgery fours," and trout captured with the unpretentious earth-worm, instead of the gorgeous fly; where they bet prizes for butter and cheese, and rag-carpets executed by ladies more than seventy years of age; where whey wear dress-coats before dinner, and cock their hats on one side when they feel conspicuous and distinshed; where they say Sir to you in their common talk and have other Arcadian and bucolic ways which are highly unobjectionable, but are not so much admired in cities, where the people are said to be not half so virtuous.

There is with us a boy of modest dimensions, not otherwise especially entitled to the epithet, who ought be six or seven years old, to judge by the gap left by his front milk teeth, these having resigned in favor of their successors, who have not yet presented their credentials. He is rather old for an enfant terrible, and quite too young to have grown into the bashfulness of adolescence; but he has some of the qualities of both these engaging periods of development, The member of the Haouse calls him "Bub," invariably, such term I take to be an abbreviation of "Beelzeb," as "bus" is the short form of "omnibus." Many eminently genteel persons, whose manners make them at home anywhere, being evidently unaware of true derivation of this word, are in the habit of addressing all unknown children by one of the two terms, "bub" and "sis," which they consider endears them greatly to the young people, and recommends them to the acquaintance of their honored parents, if these happen to accompany them. The other boarders commonly call our diminutive companion That Boy. He is a sort of expletive at the table, serving to stop gaps, taking the same place a washer does that makes a loose screw fit, and contriving to get driven in like a wedge between any two chairs where there is a crevice. I shall not call that boy by the monosyllable referred to, because, though he has many impish traits at present, he may become civilized and humanized by being in good company. Besides, it is a term which I understand is considered vulgar by the nobility and gentry of the Mother Country, and it is not to be found in Mr. Worcester's Dictionary, on which, as is well known, the literary men of this metropolis are by special statute allowed to be sworn in place of the Bible. I know one, certainly, who never takes his oath on any other dictionary, any advertising fiction to the contrary, notwithstanding.

I wanted to write out my account of some of the other boarders, but a domestic occurrence, a somewhat prolonged visit from the landlady, who is rather too anxious that I should be comfortable broke in upon the continuity of my thoughts, and occasioned in short, I gave up writing for that day.

"I wonder if anything like this ever happened. Author writing, jacks?"

"To be, or not to be: that is the question Whether 't is nobl"

"William, shall we have pudding to-day, or flapjacks?"

"Flapjacks, an' it please thee, Anne, or a pudding, for that matter; or what thou wilt, good woman, so thou come not betwixt me and my thought."

Exit Mistress Anne, with strongly accented closing of the door and murmurs to the effect: "Ay, marry, 't is well for thee to talk as if thou hadst no stomach to fill. We poor wives must swink for our masters, while they sit in their arm-chairs growing as great in the girth through laziness as that ill-mannered fat man William hath writ of in his books of players' stuff. One had as well meddle with a porkpen, which hath thorns all over him, as try to deal with William when his eyes be rolling in that mad way."

William, writing once more, after an exclamation in strong English of the older pattern,

"Whether 't is nobler, nobler, nobler"

To do what? O these women! these women! to have puddings or flapjacks! Oh!

"Whether 't is nobler in the mind to suffer
The slings and arrows of"

Oh! Oh! these women! I will e'en step over to the parson's and have a cup of sack with His Reverence for methinks Master Hamlet hath forgot that which was just now on his lips to speak.

So I shall have to put off making my friends acquainted with the other boarders, some of whom seem to me worth studying and describing. I have something else of a graver character for my readers. I am talking, you know, as a poet; I do not say I deserve the name, but I have taken it, and if you consider me at all it must be in that aspect. You will, therefore, be willing to run your eyes over a few pages read, of course by request, to a select party of the boarders.

THE GAMBREL-ROOFED HOUSE AND ITS OUTLOOK.

A PANORAMA, WITH SIDE-SHOWS.

My birthplace, the home of my childhood and earlier and later boyhood, has within a few months passed out of the ownership of my family into the hands of that venerable Alma Mater who seems to have renewed her youth, and has certainly repainted her dormitories. In truth, when I last revisited that familiar scene and looked upon the flammantia mœnia of the old halls, "Massachusetts" with the dummy clock-dial, "Harvard" with the garrulous belfry, little "Holden" with the sculptured unpunishable cherub over its portal, and the rest of my early brick-and-mortar acquaintances, I could not help saying to myself that I had lived to see the peaceable establishment of the Red Republic of Letters.

Many of the things I shall put down I have no doubt told before in a fragmentary way, how many I cannot be quite sure, as I do not very often read my own prose works. But when a man dies a great deal is said of him which has often been said in other forms, and now this dear old house is dead to me in one sense, and I want to gather up my recollections and wind a string of narrative round them, tying them up like a nosegay for the last tribute: the same blossoms in it I have often laid on its threshold while it was still living for me.

We Americans are all cuckoos, we make our homes in the nests of other birds. I have read somewhere that the lineal descendants of the man who carted off the body of William Rufus, with Walter Tyrrel's arrow sticking in it, have driven a cart (not absolutely the same one, I suppose) in the New Forest, from that day to this. I don't quite understand Mr. Ruskin's saying (if he said it) that he couldn't get along in a country where there were no castles, but I do think we lose a great deal in living where there are so few permanent homes. You will see how much I parted with which was not reckoned in the price paid for the old homestead.

I shall say many things which an uncharitable reader might find fault with as personal. I should not dare to call myself a poet if I did not; for if there is anything that gives one a title to that name, it is that his inner nature is naked and is not ashamed. But there are many such things I shall put in words, not because they are personal, but because they are human, and are born of just such experiences as those who hear or read what I say are like to have had in greater or less measure. I find myself so much like other people that I often wonder at the coincidence. It was only the other day that I sent out a copy of verses about my great-grandmother's picture, and I was surprised to find how many other people had portraits of their great-grandmothers or other progenitors, about which they felt as I did about mine, and for whom I had spoken, thinking I was speaking for myself only. And so I am not afraid to talk very freely with you, my precious reader or listener. You too, Beloved, were born somewhere and remember your birthplace or your early home; for you some house is haunted by recollections; to some roof you have bid farewell. Your hand is upon mine, then, as I guide my pen. Your heart frames the responses to the litany of my remembrance. For myself it is a tribute of affection I am rendering, and I should put it on record for my own satisfaction, were there none to read or to listen.

I hope you will not say that I have built a pillared portico of introduction to a humble structure of narrative. For when you look at the old gambrel-roofed house, you will see an unpretending mansion, such as very possibly you were born in yourself, or at any rate such a place of residence as your minister or some of your well-to-do country cousins find good enough, but not at all too grand for them. We have stately old Colonial palaces in our ancient village, now a city, and a thriving one, square-fronted edifices that stand back from the vulgar highway, with folded arms, as it were; social fortresses of the time when the twilight lustre of the throne reached as far as our half-cleared settlement, with a glacis before them in the shape of a long broad gravel-walk, so that in King George's time they looked as formidably to any but the silk-stocking gentry as Gibraltar or Ehrenbreitstein to a visitor without the password. We forget all this in the kindly welcome they give us to-day; for some of them are still standing and doubly famous, as we all know. But the gambrel-roofed house, though stately enough for college dignitaries and scholarly clergymen, was not one of those old Tory, Episcopal-church-goer's strongholds. One of its doors opens directly upon the green, always called the Common; the other, facing the south, a few steps from it, over a paved foot-walk, on the other side of which is the miniature front yard, bordered with lilacs and syringas. The honest mansion makes no pretensions. Accessible, companionable, holding its hand out to all, comfortable, respectable, and even in its way dignified, but not imposing, not a house for his Majesty's Counsellor, or the Right Reverend successor of Him who had not where to lay his head, for something like a hundred and fifty years it has stood in its lot, and seen the generations of men come and go like the leaves of the forest. I passed some pleasant hours, a few years since, in the Registry of Deeds and the Town Records, looking up the history of the old house. How those dear friends of mine, the antiquarians, for whose grave councils I compose my features on the too rare Thursdays when I am at liberty to meet them, in whose human herbarium the leaves and blossoms of past generations are so carefully spread out and pressed and laid away, would listen to an expansion of the following brief details into an Historical Memoir!

The estate was the third lot of the eighth "Squadron" (whatever that might be), and in the year 1707 was allotted in the distribution of undivided lands to "Mr. ffox," the Reverend Jabez Fox of Woburn, it may be supposed, as it passed from his heirs to the first Jonathan Hastings; from him to his son, the long remembered College Steward; from him in the year 1792 to the Reverend Eliphalet Pearson, Professor of Hebrew and other Oriental languages in Harvard College, whose large personality swam into my ken when I was looking forward to my teens; from him the progenitors of my unborn self.

I wonder if there are any such beings nowadays as the great Eliphalet, with his large features and conversational basso profundo, seemed to me. His very name had something elephantine about it, and it seemed to me that the house shook from cellar to garret at his footfall. Some have pretended that he had Olympian aspirations, and wanted to sit in the seat of Jove and bear the academic thunderbolt and the aegis inscribed Christo et Ecclesiae. It is a common weakness enough to wish to find one's self in an empty saddle; Cotton Mather was miserable all his days, I am afraid, after that entry in his Diary: "This Day Dr. Sewall was chosen President, for his Piety."

There is no doubt that the men of the older generation look bigger and more formidable to the boys whose eyes are turned up at their venerable countenances than the race which succeeds them, to the same boys grown older. Everything is twice as large, measured on a three-year-olds three-foot scale as on a thirty-year-olds six-foot scale; but age magnifies and aggravates persons out of due proportion. Old people are a kind of monsters to little folks; mild manifestations of the terrible, it may be, but still, with their white locks and ridged and grooved features, which those horrid little eyes exhaust of their details, like so many microscopes not exactly what human beings ought to be. The middle-aged and young men have left comparatively faint impressions in my memory, but how grandly the procession of the old clergymen who filled our pulpit from time to time, and passed the day under our roof, marches before my closed eyes! At their head the most venerable David Osgood, the majestic minister of Medford, with massive front and shaggy over-shadowing eyebrows; following in the train, mild-eyed John Foster of Brighton, with the lambent aurora of a smile about his pleasant mouth, which not even the "Sabbath" could subdue to the true Levitical aspect; and bulky Charles Steams of Lincoln, author of "The Ladies' Philosophy of Love. A Poem. 1797" (how I stared at him! he was the first living person ever pointed out to me as a poet); and Thaddeus Mason Harris of Dorchester (the same who, a poor youth, trudging along, staff in hand, being then in a stress of sore need, found all at once that somewhat was adhering to the end of his stick, which somewhat proved to be a gold ring of price, bearing the words, "God speed thee, Friend!"), already in decadence as I remember him, with head slanting forward and downward as if looking for a place to rest in after his learned labors; and that other Thaddeus, the old man of West Cambridge, who outwatched the rest so long after they had gone to sleep in their own churchyards, that it almost seemed as if he meant to sit up until the morning of the resurrection; and bringing up the rear, attenuated but vivacious little Jonathan Homer of Newton, who was, to look upon, a kind of expurgated, reduced and Americanized copy of Voltaire, but very unlike him in wickedness or wit. The good-humored junior member of our family always loved to make him happy by setting him chirruping about Miles Coverdale's Version, and the Bishop's Bible, and how he wrote to his friend Sir Isaac (Coffin) about something or other, and how Sir Isaac wrote back that he was very much pleased with the contents of his letter, and so on about Sir Isaac, ad libitum, for the admiral was his old friend, and he was proud of him. The kindly little old gentleman was a collector of Bibles, and made himself believe he thought he should publish a learned Commentary some day or other; but his friends looked for it only in the Greek Calends, say on the 31st of April, when that should come round, if you would modernize the phrase. I recall also one or two exceptional and infrequent visitors with perfect distinctness: cheerful Elijah Kellogg, a lively missionary from the region of the Quoddy Indians, with much hopeful talk about Sock Bason and his tribe; also poor old Poor-house-Parson Isaac Smith, his head going like a China mandarin, as he discussed the possibilities of the escape of that distinguished captive whom he spoke of under the name, if I can reproduce phonetically its vibrating nasalities of "General Mmbongaparty," a name suggestive to my young imagination of a dangerous, loose-jointed skeleton, threatening us all like the armed figure of Death in my little New England Primer.

I have mentioned only the names of those whose images come up pleasantly before me, and I do not mean to say anything which any descendant might not read smilingly. But there were some of the black-coated gentry whose aspect was not so agreeable to me. It is very curious to me to look back on my early likes and dislikes, and see how as a child I was attracted or repelled by such and such ministers, a good deal, as I found out long afterwards, according to their theological beliefs. On the whole, I think the old-fashioned New England divine softening down into Arminianism was about as agreeable as any of them. And here I may remark, that a mellowing rigorist is always a much pleasanter object to contemplate than a tightening liberal, as a cold day warming up to 32 Fahrenheit is much more agreeable than a warm one chilling down to the same temperature. The least pleasing change is that kind of mental hemiplegia which now and then attacks the rational side of a man at about the same period of life when one side of the body is liable to be palsied, and in fact is, very probably, the same thing as palsy, in another form. The worst of it is that the subjects of it never seem to suspect that they are intellectual invalids, stammerers and cripples at best, but are all the time hitting out at their old friends with the well arm, and calling them hard names out of their twisted mouths.

It was a real delight to have one of those good, hearty, happy, benignant old clergymen pass the Sunday, with us, and I can remember some whose advent made the day feel almost like "Thanksgiving." But now and then would come along a clerical visitor with a sad face and a wailing voice, which sounded exactly as if somebody must be lying dead up stairs, who took no interest in us children, except a painful one, as being in a bad way with our cheery looks, and did more to unchristianize us with his woebegone ways than all his sermons were like to accomplish in the other direction. I remember one in particular, who twitted me so with my blessings as a Christian child, and whined so to me about the naked black children who, like the "Little Vulgar Boy," "had n't got no supper and hadn't got no ma," and hadn't got no Catechism, (how I wished for the moment I was a little black boy!) that he did more in that one day to make me a heathen than he had ever done in a month to make a Christian out of an infant Hottentot. What a debt we owe to our friends of the left centre, the Brooklyn and the Park Street and the

Summer street ministers; good, wholesome, sound-bodied, one-minded, cheerful-spirited men, who have taken the place of those wailing poitrinaires with the bandanna handkerchiefs round their meagre throats and a funeral service in their forlorn physiognomies! I might have been a minister myself, for aught I know, if this clergyman had not looked and talked so like an undertaker.

All this belongs to one of the side-shows, to which I promised those who would take tickets to the main exhibition should have entrance gratis. If I were writing a poem you would expect, as a matter of course, that there would be a digression now and then.

To come back to the old house and its former tenant, the Professor of Hebrew and other Oriental languages. Fifteen years he lived with his family under its roof. I never found the slightest trace of him until a few years ago, when I cleaned and brightened with pious hands the brass lock of "the study," which had for many years been covered with a thick coat of paint. On that I found scratched; as with a nail or fork, the following inscription:

E PE

Only that and nothing more, but the story told itself. Master Edward Pearson, then about as high as the lock, was disposed to immortalize himself in monumental brass, and had got so far towards it, when a sudden interruption, probably a smart box on the ear, cheated him of his fame, except so far as this poor record may rescue it. Dead long ago. I remember him well, a grown man, as a visitor at a later period; and, for some reason, I recall him in the attitude of the Colossus of Rhodes, standing full before a generous wood-fire, not facing it, but quite the contrary, a perfect picture of the content afforded by a blazing hearth contemplated from that point of view, and, as the heat stole through his person and kindled his emphatic features, seeming to me a pattern of manly beauty. What a statue gallery of posturing friends we all have in our memory! The old Professor himself sometimes visited the house after it had changed hands. Of course, my recollections are not to be wholly trusted, but I always think I see his likeness in a profile face to be found among the illustrations of Rees's Cyclopaedia. (See Plates, Vol. IV., Plate 2, Painting, Diversities of the Human Face, Fig. 4.)

And now let us return to our chief picture. In the days of my earliest remembrance, a row of tall Lombardy poplars mounted guard on the western side of the old mansion. Whether, like the cypress, these trees suggest the idea of the funeral torch or the monumental spire, whether their tremulous leaves make wits afraid by sympathy with their nervous thrills, whether the faint balsamic smell of their foliage and their closely swathed limbs have in them vague hints of dead Pharaohs stiffened in their cerements, I will guess; but they always seemed to me to give an of sepulchral sadness to the house before which stood sentries. Not so with the row of elms which you may see leading up towards the western entrance. I think the patriarch of them all went over in the great gale of 1815; I know I used to shake the youngest of them with my hands, stout as it is now, with a trunk that would defy the bully of Crotona, or the strong man whose liaison with the Lady Delilah proved so disastrous.

The College plain would be nothing without its elms. As the long hair of a woman is a glory to her, are these green tresses that bank themselves against sky in thick clustered masses the ornament and the pride of the classic green. You know the "Washington elm," or if you do not, you had better rekindle our patriotism by reading the inscription, which tells you that under its shadow the great leader first drew his sword at the head of an American army. In a line with that you may see two others: the coral fan, as I always called it from its resemblance in form to that beautiful marine growth, and a third a little farther along. I have heard it said that all three were planted at the same time, and that the difference of their growth is due to the slope of the ground, the Washington elm being lower than either of the others. There is a row of elms just in front of the old house on the south. When I was a child the one at the southwest corner was struck by lightning, and one of its limbs and a long ribbon of bark torn away. The tree never fully recovered its symmetry and vigor, and forty years and more afterwards a second thunderbolt crashed upon it and set its heart on fire, like those of the lost souls in the Hall of Eblis. Heaven had twice blasted it, and the axe finished what the lightning had begun.

The soil of the University town is divided into patches of sandy and of clayey ground. The Common and the College green, near which the old house stands, are on one of the sandy patches. Four curses are the local inheritance: droughts, dust, mud, and canker-worms. I cannot but think that all the characters of a region help to modify the children born in it. I am fond of making apologies for human nature, and I think I could find an excuse for myself if I, too, were dry and barren and muddy-witted and "cantankerous," disposed to get my back up, like those other natives of the soil.

I know this, that the way Mother Earth treats a boy shapes out a kind of natural theology for him. I fell into Manichean ways of thinking from the teaching of my garden experiences. Like other boys in the country, I had my patch of ground, to which, in the spring-time, I entrusted the seeds furnished me, with a confident trust in their resurrection and glorification in the better world of summer. But I soon found that my lines had fallen in a place where a vegetable growth had to run the gauntlet of as many foes and dials as a Christian pilgrim. Flowers would not Blow; daffodils perished like criminals in their cone demned caps, without their petals ever seeing daylight; roses were disfigured with monstrous protrusions through their very centres, something that looked like a second bud pushing through the middle of the corolla; lettuces and cabbages would not head; radishes knotted themselves until they looked like centenerians' fingers; and on every stem, on every leaf, and both sides of it, and at the root of everything that dew, was a professional specialist in the shape of grub, caterpillar, aphis, or other expert, whose business it was to devour that particular part, and help order the whole attempt at vegetation. Such experiences must influence a child born to them. A sandy soil, where nothing flourishes but weeds and evil beasts of small dimensions, must breed different qualities in its human offspring from one of those fat and fertile spots which the wit whom I have once before noted described so happily that, if I quoted the passage, its brilliancy would spoil one of my pages, as a diamond breastpin sometimes kills the social effect of the wearer, who might have passed for a gentleman without it. Your arid patch of earth should seem to the natural birthplace of the leaner virtues and the abler vices, of temperance and the domestic proprieties on the one hand, with a tendency to light weights in groceries and provisions, and to clandestine abstraction from the person on the other, as opposed to the free hospitality, the broadly planned burglaries, and the largely conceived homicides of our rich Western alluvial regions. Yet Nature is never wholly unkind. Economical as she was in my unparadised Eden, hard as it was to make some of my floral houris unveil, still the damask roses sweetened the June breezes, the bladed and plumed flower-de-luces unfolded their close-wrapped cones, and larkspurs and lupins, lady's delights, plebeian manifestations of the pansy, self-sowing marigolds, hollyhocks, the forest flowers of two seasons, and the perennial lilacs and syringas, all whispered to' the winds blowing over them that some caressing presence was around me.

Beyond the garden was "the field," a vast domain of four acres or thereabout, by the measurement of after years, bordered to the north by a fathomless chasm, the ditch the base-ball players of the present era jump over; on the east by unexplored territory; on the south by a barren enclosure, where the red sorrel proclaimed liberty and equality under its drapeau rouge, and succeeded in establishing a vegetable commune where all were alike, poor, mean, sour, and uninteresting; and on the west by the Common, not then disgraced by jealous enclosures, which make it look like a cattle-market. Beyond, as I looked round, were the Colleges, the meeting-house, the little square market-house, long vanished; the burial-ground where the dead Presidents stretched their weary bones under epitaphs stretched out at as full length as their subjects; the pretty church where the gouty Tories used to kneel on their hassocks; the district schoolhouse, and hard by it Ma'am Hancock's cottage, never so called in those days, but rather "tenfooter"; then houses scattered near and far, open spaces, the shadowy elms, round hilltops in the distance, and over all the great bowl of the sky. Mind you, this was the WORLD, as I first knew it; terra veteribus cognita, as Mr. Arrowsmith would have called it, if he had mapped the universe of my infancy:

But I am forgetting the old house again in the landscape. The worst of a modern stylish mansion is, that it has no place for ghosts. I watched one building not long since. It had no proper garret, to begin with, only a sealed interval between the roof and attics, where a spirit could not be accommodated, unless it were flattened out like Ravel, Brother, after the millstone had fallen on him. There was not a nook or a corner in the whole horse fit to lodge any respectable ghost, for every part was as open to observation as a literary man's character and condition, his figure and estate, his coat and his countenance, are to his (or her) Bohemian Majesty on a tour of inspection through his (or her) subjects' keyholes.

Now the old house had wainscots, behind which the mice were always scampering and squeaking and rattling down the plaster, and enacting family scenes and parlor theatricals. It had a cellar where the cold slug clung to the walls, and the misanthropic spider withdrew from the garish day; where the green mould loved to grow, and the long white potato-shoots went feeling along the floor, if haply they might find the daylight; it had great brick pillars, always in a cold sweat with holding up the burden they had been aching under day and night far a century and more; it had sepulchral arches closed by rough doors that hung on hinges rotten with rust, behind which doors, if there was not a heap of bones connected with a mysterious disappearance of long ago, there well might have been, for it was just the place to look for them. It had a garret; very nearly such a one as it seems to me one of us has described in one of his books; but let us look at this one as I can reproduce it from memory. It has a flooring of laths with ridges of mortar squeezed up between them, which if you tread on you will go to the Lord have mercy on you! where will you go to? the same being crossed by narrow bridges of boards, on which you may put your feet, but with fear and trembling. Above you and around you are beams and joists, on some of which you may see, when the light is let in, the marks of thé conchoidal clippings of the broadaxe, showing the rude way in which the timber was shaped as it came, full of sap, from the neighboring forest. It is a realm of darkness and thick dust, and shroud-like cobwebs and dead things they wrap in their gray folds. For a garret is like a seashore, where wrecks are thrown up and slowly go to pieces. There is the cradle which the old man you just remember was rocked in; there is the ruin of the bedstead he died on; that ugly slanting contrivance used to be put under his pillow in the days when his breath came hard; there is his old chair with both arms gone, symbol of the desolate time when he had nothing earthly left to lean on; there is the large wooden reel which the blear-eyed old deacon sent the minister's lady, who thanked him graciously, and twirled it smilingly, and in fitting season bowed it out decently to the limbo of troublesome conveniences. And there are old leather portmanteaus, like stranded porpoises, their mouths gaping in gaunt hunger for the food with which they used to be gorged to bulging repletion; and old brass andirons, waiting until time shall revenge them on their paltry substitutes, and they shall have their own again, and bring with them the fore-stick and the back-log of ancient days; and the empty churn, with its idle dasher, which the Nancys and Phoebes, who have left their comfortable places to the Bridgets and Norahs, used to handle to good purpose; and the brown, shaky old spinning-wheel, which was running, it may be, in the days when they were hinging the Salem witches.

Under the dark and haunted garret were attic chambers which themselves had histories. On a pane in the northeastern chamber may be read these names:

"John Tracy," "Robert Roberts," "Thomas Prince;" "Stultus" another hand had added. When I found these names a few years ago (wrong side up, for the window had been reversed), I looked at once in the Triennial to find them, for the epithet showed that they were probably students. I found them all under the years 1771 and 1773. Does it please their thin ghosts thus to be dragged to the light of day? Has "Stultus" forgiven the indignity of being thus characterized?

The southeast chamber was the Library Hospital. Every scholar should have a book infirmary attached his library. There should find a peaceable refuge the many books, invalids from their birth, which are sent "with the best regards of the Author"; the respected, but unpresentable cripples which have lost cover; the odd volumes of honored sets which go mourning all their days for their lost brother; the school-books which have been so often the subjects of assault and battery, that they look as if the police must know them by heart; these and still more the pictured story-books, beginning with Mother Goose (which a dear old friend of mine has just been amusing his philosophic leisure with turning most ingeniously and happily into the tongues of Virgil and Homer), will be precious mementos by and by, when children and grandchildren come along. What would I not give for that dear little paper-bound quarto, in large and most legible type, on certain pages of which the tender hand that was the shield of my infancy had crossed out with deep black marks something awful, probably about BEARS, such as once tare two-and-forty of us little folks for making faces, and the very name of which made us hide our heads under the bedclothes.

I made strange acquaintances in that book infirmary up in the southeast attic. The "Negro Plot" at New York helped to implant a feeling in me which it took Mr. Garrison a good many years to root out. "Thinks I to Myself," an old novel, which has been attributed to a famous statesman, introduced me to a world of fiction which was not represented on the shelves of the library proper, unless perhaps by Coelebs in Search of a Wife, or allegories of the bitter tonic class, as the young doctor that sits on the other side of the table would probably call them. I always, from an early age, had a keen eye for a story with a moral sticking out of it, and gave it a wide berth, though in my later years I have myself written a couple of "medicated novels," as one of my dearest and pleasantest old friends wickedly called them, when somebody asked her if she had read the last of my printed performances. I forgave the satire for the charming esprit of the epithet. Besides the works I have mentioned, there was an old, old Latin alchemy book, with the manuscript annotations of some ancient Rosicrucian, in the pages of which I had a vague notion that I might find the mighty secret of the Lapis Philosophorum, otherwise called Chaos, the Dragon, the Green Lion, the Quinta Essentia, the Soap of Sages, the Vinegar of Philosophers, the Dew of Heavenly Grace, the Egg, the Old Man, the Sun, the Moon, and by all manner of odd aliases, as I am assured by the plethoric little book before me, in parchment covers browned like a meerschaum with the smoke of furnaces and the thumbing of dead gold seekers, and the fingering of bony-handed book-misers, and the long intervals of dusty slumber on the shelves of the bouquiniste; for next year it will be three centuries old, and it had already seen nine generations of men when I caught its eye (Alchemiae Doctrina) and recognized it at pistol-shot distance as a prize, among the breviaries and Heures and trumpery volumes of the old open-air dealer who exposed his treasures under the shadow of St. Sulpice. I have never lost my taste for alchemy since I first got hold of the Palladium Spagyricum of Peter John Faber, and sought, in vain, it is true, through its pages for a clear, intelligible, and practical statement of how I could turn my lead sinkers and the weights of tall kitchen clock into good yellow gold, specific gravity 19.2, and exchangeable for whatever I then wanted, and for many more things than I was then aware of. One of the greatest pleasures of childhood found in the mysteries which it hides from the skepticism of the elders, and works up into small mythologies of its own. I have seen all this played over again in adult life, the same delightful bewilderment semi-emotional belief in listening to the gaseous praises of this or that fantastic system, that I found in the pleasing mirages conjured up for me by the ragged old volume I used to pore over in the southeast attic-chamber.

The rooms of the second story, the chambers of birth and death, are sacred to silent memories.

Let us go down to the ground-floor. I should have begun with this, but that the historical reminiscences of the old house have been recently told in a most interesting memoir by a distinguished student of our local history. I retain my doubts about those "dents" on the floor of the right-hand room, "the study" of successive occupants, said to have been made by the butts of the Continental militia's firelocks, but this was the cause to which the story told me in childhood laid them. That military consultations were held in that room when the house was General Ward's headquarters, that the Provincial generals and colonels and other men of war there planned the movement which ended in the fortifying of Bunker's Hill, that Warren slept in the house the night before the battle, that President Langdon went forth from the western door and prayed for God's blessing on the men just setting forth on their bloody expedition, all these things have been told, and perhaps none of them need be doubted.

But now for fifty years and more that room has been a meeting-ground for the platoons and companies which range themselves at the scholar's word of command. Pleasant it is to think that the retreating host of books is to give place to a still larger army of volumes, which have seen service under the eye of a great commander. For here the noble collection of him so freshly remembered as our silver-tongued orator, our erudite scholar, our honored College President, our accomplished statesman, our courtly ambassador, are to be reverently gathered by the heir of his name, himself not unworthy to be surrounded by that august assembly of the wise of all ages and of various lands and languages.

Could such a many-chambered edifice have stood a century and a half and not have had its passages of romance to bequeath their lingering legends to the after-time? There are other names on some of the small window-panes, which must have had young flesh-and-blood owners, and there is one of early date which elderly persons have whispered was borne by a fair woman, whose graces made the house beautiful in the eyes of the youth of that time. One especially you will find the name of Fortescue Vernon, of the class of 1780, in the Triennial Catalogue, was a favored visitor to the old mansion; but he went over seas, I think they told me, and died still young, and the name of the maiden which is scratched on the windowpane was never changed. I am telling the story honestly, as I remember it, but I may have colored it unconsciously, and the legendary pane may be broken before this for aught I know. At least, I have named no names except the beautiful one of the supposed hero of the romantic story.

It was a great happiness to have been born in an old house haunted by such recollections, with harmless ghosts walking its corridors, with fields of waving grass and trees and singing birds, and that vast territory of four or five acres around it to give a child the sense that he was born to a noble principality. It has been a great pleasure to retain a certain hold upon it for so many years; and since in the natural course of things it must at length pass into other hands, it is a gratification to see the old place making itself tidy for a new tenant, like some venerable dame who is getting ready to entertain a neighbor of condition. Not long since a new cap of shingles adorned this ancient mother among the village, now city, mansions. She has dressed herself in brighter colors than she has hitherto worn, so they tell me, within the last few days. She has modernized her aspects in several ways; she has rubbed bright the glasses through which she looks at the Common and the Colleges; and as the sunsets shine upon her through the flickering leaves or the wiry spray of the elms I remember from my childhood, they will glorify her into the aspect she wore when President Holyoke, father of our long since dead centenarian, looked upon her in her youthful comeliness.

The quiet corner formed by this and the neighboring residences has changed less than any place I can remember. Our kindly, polite, shrewd, and humorous old neighbor, who in former days has served the town as constable and auctioneer, and who bids fair to become the oldest inhabitant of the city, was there when I was born, and is living there to-day. By and by the stony foot of the great University will plant itself on this whole territory, and the private recollections which clung so tenaciously and fondly to the place and its habitations will have died with those who cherished them.

Shall they ever live again in the memory of those who loved them here below? What is this life without the poor accidents which made it our own, and by which we identify ourselves? Ah me! I might like to be a winged chorister, but still it seems to me I should hardly be quite happy if I could not recall at will the Old House with the Long Entry, and the White Chamber (where I wrote the first verses that made me known, with a pencil, stans pede in uno, pretty, nearly), and the Little Parlor, and the Study, and the old books in uniforms as varied as those of the Ancient and Honorable Artillery Company used to be, if my memory serves me right, and the front yard with the Star-of-Bethlehems growing, flowerless, among the grass, and the dear faces to be seen no more there or anywhere on this earthly place of farewells.

I have told my story. I do not know what special gifts have been granted or denied me; but this I know, that I am like so many others of my fellow-creatures, that when I smile, I feel as if they must; when I cry, I think their eyes fill; and it always seems to me that when I am most truly myself I come nearest to them and am surest of being listened to by the brothers and sisters of the larger family into which I was born so long ago. I have often feared they might be tired of me and what I tell them. But then, perhaps, would come a letter from some quiet body in some out-of-the-way place, which showed me that I had said something which another had often felt but never said, or told the secret of another's heart in unburdening my own. Such evidences that one is in the highway of human experience and feeling lighten the footsteps wonderfully. So it is that one is encouraged to go on writing as long as the world has anything that interests him, for he never knows how many of his fellow-beings he may please or profit, and in how many places his name will be spoken as that of a friend.

In the mood suggested by my story I have ventured on the poem that follows. Most people love this world more than they are willing to confess, and it is hard to conceive ourselves weaned from it so as to feel no emotion at the thought of its most sacred recollections, even after a sojourn of years, as we should count the lapse of earthly time, in the realm where, sooner or later, all tears shall be wiped away. I hope, therefore, the title of my lines will not frighten those who are little accustomed to think of men and women as human beings in any state but the present.

HOMESICK IN HEAVEN.

THE DIVINE VOICE.

Go seek thine earth-born sisters, thus the Voice
That all obey, the sad and silent three;
These only, while the hosts of heaven rejoice,
Smile never: ask them what their sorrows be:

And when the secret of their griefs they tell,
Look on them with thy mild, half-human eyes;
Say what thou wast on earth; thou knowest well;
So shall they cease from unavailing sighs.

THE ANGEL.
Why thus, apart, the swift-winged herald spake,
Sit ye with silent lips and unstrung lyres
While the trisagion's blending chords awake
In shouts of joy from all the heavenly choirs?

THE FIRST SPIRIT.
Chide not thy sisters, thus the answer came;
Children of earth, our half-weaned nature clings
To earth's fond memories, and her whispered name
Untunes our quivering lips, our saddened strings;

For there we loved, and where we love is home,
Home that our feet may leave, but not our hearts,
Though o'er us shine the jasper-lighted dome:

The chain may lengthen, but it never parts!

Sometimes a sunlit sphere comes rolling by,
And then we softly whisper, can it be?
And leaning toward the silvery orb, we try
To hear the music of its murmuring sea;

To catch, perchance, some flashing glimpse of green,
Or breathe some wild-wood fragrance, wafted through
The opening gates of pearl, that fold between
The blinding splendors and the changeless blue.

THE ANGEL.
Nay, sister, nay! a single healing leaf
Plucked from the bough of yon twelve-fruited tree,
Would soothe such anguish, deeper stabbing grief
Has pierced thy throbbing heart

THE FIRST SPIRIT.
Ah, woe is me!
I from my clinging babe was rudely torn;
His tender lips a loveless bosom pressed
Can I forget him in my life new born?
O that my darling lay upon my breast!

THE ANGEL.
And thou?

THE SECOND SPIRIT.
I was a fair and youthful bride,

The kiss of love still burns upon my cheek,
He whom I worshipped, ever at my side,
Him through the spirit realm in vain I seek.

Sweet faces turn their beaming eyes on mine;
Ah! not in these the wished-for look I read;
Still for that one dear human smile I pine;
Thou and none other! is the lover's creed.

THE ANGEL.
And whence thy sadness in a world of bliss
Where never parting comes, nor mourner's tear?
Art thou, too, dreaming of a mortal's kiss

Amid the seraphs of the heavenly sphere?

THE THIRD SPIRIT.
Nay, tax not me with passion's wasting fire;
When the swift message set my spirit free,
Blind, helpless, lone, I left my gray-haired sire;
My friends were many, he had none save me.

I left him, orphaned, in the starless night;
Alas, for him no cheerful morning's dawn!
I wear the ransomed spirit's robe of white,
Yet still I hear him moaning, She is gone!

THE ANGEL.
Ye know me not, sweet sisters? All in vain
Ye seek your lost ones in the shapes they wore;
The flower once opened may not bud again,
The fruit once fallen finds the stem no more.

Child, lover, sire, yea, all things loved below,
Fair pictures damasked on a vapor's fold,
Fade like the roseate flush, the golden glow,
When the bright curtain of the day is rolled.

I was the babe that slumbered on thy breast.
And, sister, mine the lips that called thee bride.
Mine were the silvered locks thy hand caressed,
That faithful hand, my faltering footstep's guide!

Each changing form, frail vesture of decay,
The soul unclad forgets it once hath worn,
Stained with the travel of the weary day,
And shamed with rents from every wayside thorn.

To lie, an infant, in thy fond embrace,
To come with love's warm kisses back to thee,
To show thine eyes thy gray-haired father's face,
Not Heaven itself could grant; this may not be!

Then spread your folded wings, and leave to earth
The dust once breathing ye have mourned so long,
Till Love, new risen, owns his heavenly birth,
And sorrow's discords sweeten into song!

CHAPTER II

I am going to take it for granted now and henceforth, in my report of what was said and what was to be seen at our table, that I have secured one good, faithful, loving reader, who never finds fault, who never gets sleepy over my pages, whom no critic can bully out of a liking for me, and to whom I am always safe in addressing myself. My one elect may be man or woman, old or young, gentle or simple, living in the next block or on a slope of Nevada, my fellow-countryman or an alien; but one such reader I shall assume to exist and have always in my thought when I am writing.

A writer is so like a lover! And a talk with the right listener is so like an arm-in-arm walk in the moonlight with the soft heartbeat just felt through the folds of muslin and broadcloth! But it takes very little to spoil everything for writer, talker, lover. There are a great many cruel things besides poverty that freeze the genial current of the soul, as the poet of the Elegy calls it. Fire can stand any wind, but is easily blown out, and then come smouldering and smoke, and profitless, slow combustion without the cheerful blaze which sheds light all round it. The one Reader's hand may shelter the flame; the one blessed ministering spirit with the vessel of oil may keep it bright in spite of the stream of cold water on the other side doing its best to put it out.

I suppose, if any writer, of any distinguishable individuality, could look into the hearts of all his readers, he might very probably find one in his parish of a thousand or a million who honestly preferred him to any other of his kind. I have no doubt we have each one of us, somewhere, our exact facsimile, so like us in all things except the accidents of condition, that we should love each other like a pair of twins, if our natures could once fairly meet. I know I have my counterpart in some State of this Union. I feel sure that there is an Englishman somewhere precisely like myself. (I hope he does not drop his h's, for it does not seem to me possible that the Royal Dane could have remained faithful to his love for Ophelia, if she had addressed him as 'Amlet.) There is also a certain Monsieur, to me at this moment unknown, and likewise a Herr Von Something, each of whom is essentially my double. An Arab is at this moment eating dates, a mandarin is just sipping his tea, and a South-Sea-Islander (with undeveloped possibilities) drinking the milk of a cocoa-nut, each one of whom, if he had been born in the gambrel-roofed house, and cultivated my little sand-patch, and grown up in "the study" from the height of Walton's Polyglot Bible to that of the shelf which held the Elzevir Tacitus and Casaubon's Polybius, with all the complex influences about him that surrounded me, would have been so nearly what I am that I should have loved him like a brother, always provided that I did not hate him for his resemblance to me, on the same principle as that which makes bodies in the same electric condition repel each other.

For, perhaps after all, my One Reader is quite as likely to be not the person most resembling myself, but the one to whom my nature is complementary. Just as a particular soil wants some one element to fertilize it, just as the body in some conditions has a kind of famine for one special food, so the mind has its wants, which do not always call for what is best, but which know themselves and are as peremptory as the salt-sick sailor's call for a lemon or a raw potato, or, if you will, as those capricious "longings," which have a certain meaning, we may suppose, and which at any rate we think it reasonable to satisfy if we can.

I was going to say something about our boarders the other day when I got run away with by my local reminiscences. I wish you to understand that we have a rather select company at the table of our boarding-house.

Our Landlady is a most respectable person, who has seen better days, of course, all landladies have, but has also, I feel sure, seen a good deal worse ones. For she wears a very handsome silk dress on state occasions, with a breastpin set, as I honestly believe, with genuine pearls, and appears habitually with a very smart cap, from under which her gray curls come out with an unmistakable expression, conveyed in the hieratic language of the feminine priesthood, to the effect that while there is life there is hope. And when I come to reflect on the many circumstances which go to the making of matrimonial happiness, I cannot help thinking that a personage of her present able exterior, thoroughly experienced in all the domestic arts which render life comfortable, might make the later years of some hitherto companionless bachelor very endurable, not to say pleasant.

The condition of the Landlady's family is, from what I learn, such as to make the connection I have alluded to, I hope with delicacy, desirable for incidental as well as direct reasons, provided a fitting match could be found. I was startled at hearing her address by the familiar name of Benjamin the young physician I have referred to, until I found on inquiry, what I might have guessed by the size of his slices of pie and other little marks of favoritism, that he was her son. He has recently come back from Europe, where he has topped off his home training with a first-class foreign finish. As the Landlady could never have educated him in this way out of the profits of keeping boarders, I was not surprised when I was told that she had received a pretty little property in the form of a bequest from a former boarder, a very kind-hearted, worthy old gentleman who had been long with her and seen how hard she worked for food and clothes for herself and this son of hers, Benjamin Franklin by his baptismal name. Her daughter had also married well, to a member of what we may call the post-medical profession, that, namely, which deals with the mortal frame after the practitioners of the healing art have done with it and taken their leave. So thriving had this son-in-law of hers been in his business, that his wife drove about in her own carriage, drawn by a pair of jet-black horses of most dignified demeanor, whose only fault was a tendency to relapse at once into a walk after every application of a stimulus that quickened their pace to a trot; which application always caused them to look round upon the driver with a surprised and offended air, as if he had been guilty of a grave indecorum.

The Landlady's daughter had been blessed with a number of children, of great sobriety of outward aspect, but remarkably cheerful in their inward habit of mind, more especially on the occasion of the death of a doll, which was an almost daily occurrence, and gave them immense delight in getting up a funeral, for which they had a complete miniature outfit. How happy they were under their solemn aspect! For the head mourner, a child of remarkable gifts, could actually make the tears run down her cheeks, as real ones as if she had been a grown person following a rich relative, who had not forgotten his connections, to his last unfurnished lodgings.

So this was a most desirable family connection for the right man to step into, a thriving, thrifty mother-in-law, who knew what was good for the sustenance of the body, and had no doubt taught it to her daughter; a medical artist at hand in case the luxuries of the table should happen to disturb the physiological harmonies; and in the worst event, a sweet consciousness that the last sad offices would be attended to with affectionate zeal, and probably a large discount from the usual charges.

It seems as if I could hardly be at this table for a year, if I should stay so long, without seeing some romance or other work itself out under my eyes; and I cannot help thinking that the Landlady is to be the heroine of the love-history like to unfold itself. I think I see the little cloud in the horizon, with a silvery lining to it, which may end in a rain of cards tied round with white ribbons. Extremes meet, and who so like to be the other party as the elderly gentleman at the other end of the table, as far from her now as the length of the board permits? I may be mistaken, but I think this is to be the romantic episode of the year before me. Only it seems so natural it is improbable, for you never find your dropped money just where you look for it, and so it is with these a priori matches.

This gentleman is a tight, tidy, wiry little man, with a small, brisk head, close-cropped white hair, a good wholesome complexion, a quiet, rather kindly face, quick in his movements, neat in his dress, but fond of wearing a short jacket over his coat, which gives him the look of a pickled or preserved schoolboy. He has retired, they say, from a thriving business, with a snug property, suspected by some to be rather more than snug, and entitling him to be called a capitalist, except that this word seems to be equivalent to highway robber in the new gospel of Saint Petroleum. That he is economical in his habits cannot be denied, for he saws and splits his own wood, for exercise, he says, and makes his own fires, brushes his own shoes, and, it is whispered, darns a hole in a stocking now and then, all for exercise, I suppose. Every summer he goes out of town for a few weeks. On a given day of the month a wagon stops at the door and takes up, not his trunks, for he does not indulge in any such extravagance, but the stout brown linen bags in which he packs the few conveniences he carries with him.

I do not think this worthy and economical personage will have much to do or to say, unless he marries the Landlady. If he does that, he will play a part of some importance, but I don't feel sure at all. His talk is little in amount, and generally ends in some compact formula condensing much wisdom in few words, as that a man, should not put all his eggs in one basket; that there are as good fish in the sea as ever came out of it; and one in particular, which he surprised me by saying in pretty good French one day, to the effect that the inheritance of the world belongs to the phlegmatic people, which seems to me to have a good deal of truth in it.

The other elderly personage, the old man with iron-gray hair and large round spectacles, sits at my right at table. He is a retired college officer, a man of books and observation, and himself an author. Magister Artium is one of his titles on the College Catalogue, and I like best to speak of him as the Master, because he has a certain air of authority which none of us feel inclined to dispute. He has given me a copy of a work of his which seems to me not wanting in suggestiveness, and which I hope I shall be able to make some use of in my records by and by. I said the other day that he had good solid prejudices, which is true, and I like him none the worse for it; but he has also opinions more or less original, valuable, probable, fanciful; fantastic, or whimsical, perhaps, now and then; which he promulgates at table somewhat in the tone of imperial edicts. Another thing I like about him is, that he takes a certain intelligent interest in pretty much everything that interests other people. I asked him the other day what he thought most about in his wide range of studies.

Sir, said he, I take stock in everything that concerns anybody. Humani nihil, you know the rest. But if you ask me what is my specialty, I should say, I applied myself more particularly to the contemplation of the Order of Things.

A pretty wide subject, I ventured to suggest.

Not wide enough, sir, not wide enough to satisfy the desire of a mind which wants to get at absolute truth, without reference to the empirical arrangements of our particular planet and its environments. I want to subject the formal conditions of space and time to a new analysis, and project a possible universe outside of the Order of Things. But I have narrowed myself by studying the actual facts of being. By and by, by and by, perhaps, perhaps. I hope to do some sound thinking in heaven, if I ever get there, he said seriously, and it seemed to me not irreverently.

I rather like that, I said. I think your telescopic people are, on the whole, more satisfactory than your microscopic ones.

My left-hand neighbor fidgeted about a little in his chair as I said this. But the young man sitting not far from the Landlady, to whom my attention had been attracted by the expression of his eyes, which seemed as if they saw nothing before him, but looked beyond everything, smiled a sort of faint starlight smile, that touched me strangely; for until that moment he had appeared as if his thoughts were far away, and I had been questioning whether he had lost friends lately, or perhaps had never had them, he seemed so remote from our boarding-house life. I will inquire about him, for he interests me, and I thought he seemed interested as I went on talking.

No, I continued, I don't want to have the territory of a man's mind fenced in. I don't want to shut out the mystery of the stars and the awful hollow that holds them. We have done with those hypaethral temples, that were open above to the heavens, but we can have attics and skylights to them. Minds with skylights, yes, stop, let us see if we can't get something out of that.

One-story intellects, two story intellects, three story intellects with skylights. All fact, collectors, who have no aim beyond their facts, are one-story men. Two-story men compare, reason, generalize, using the labors of the fact-collectors as well as their own. Three-story men idealize, imagine, predict; their best illumination comes from above, through the skylight. There are minds with large ground floors, that can store an infinite amount of knowledge; some librarians, for instance, who know enough of books to help other people, without being able to make much other use of their knowledge, have intellects of this class. Your great working lawyer has two spacious stories; his mind is clear, because his mental floors are large, and he has room to arrange his thoughts so that he can get at them, facts below, principles above, and all in ordered series; poets are often narrow below, incapable of clear statement, and with small power of consecutive reasoning, but full of light, if sometimes rather bare of furniture, in the attics.

The old Master smiled. I think he suspects himself of a three-story intellect, and I don't feel sure that he is n't right.

Is it dark meat or white meat you will be helped to? said the Landlady, addressing the Master.

Dark meat for me, always, he answered. Then turning to me, he began one of those monologues of his, such as that which put the Member of the Haouse asleep the other day.

It 's pretty much the same in men and women and in books and everything, that it is in turkeys and chickens. Why, take your poets, now, say Browning and Tennyson. Don't you think you can say which is the dark-meat and which is the white-meat poet? And so of the people you know; can't you pick out the full-flavored, coarse-fibred characters from the delicate, fine-fibred ones? And in the same person, don't you know the same two shades in different parts of the character that you find in the wing and thigh of a partridge? I suppose you poets may like white meat best, very probably; you had rather have a wing than a drumstick, I dare say.

Why, yes, said I, I suppose some of us do. Perhaps it is because a bird flies with his white-fleshed limbs and walks with the dark-fleshed ones. Besides, the wing-muscles are nearer the heart than the leg-muscles.

I thought that sounded mighty pretty, and paused a moment to pat myself on the back, as is my wont when I say something that I think of superior quality. So I lost my innings; for the Master is apt to strike in at the end of a bar, instead of waiting for a rest, if I may borrow a musical phrase. No matter, just at this moment, what he said; but he talked the Member of the Haouse asleep again.

They have a new term nowadays (I am speaking to you, the Reader) for people that do a good deal of talking; they call them "conversationists," or "conversationalists "; talksts, I suppose, would do just as well. It is rather dangerous to get the name of being one of these phenomenal manifestations, as one is expected to say something remarkable every time one opens one's mouth in company. It seems hard not to be able to ask for a piece of bread or a tumbler of water, without a sensation running round the table, as if one were an electric eel or a torpedo, and couldn't be touched without giving a shock. A fellow is n't all battery, is he? The idea that a Gymnotus can't swallow his worm without a coruscation of animal lightning is hard on that brilliant but sensational being. Good talk is not a matter of will at all; it depends, you know we are all half-materialists nowadays, on a certain amount of active congestion of the brain, and that comes when it is ready, and not before. I saw a man get up the other day in a pleasant company, and talk away for about five minutes, evidently by a pure effort of will. His person was good, his voice was pleasant, but anybody could see that it was all mechanical labor; he was sparring for wind, as the Hon. John Morrissey, M. C., would express himself. Presently,

Do you, Beloved, I am afraid you are not old enough, but do you remember the days of the tin tinder-box, the flint, and steel? Click! click! click! Al-h-h! knuckles that time! click! click! CLICK! a spark has taken, and is eating into the black tinder, as a six-year-old eats into a sheet of gingerbread.

Presently, after hammering away for his five minutes with mere words, the spark of a happy expression took somewhere among the mental combustibles, and then for ten minutes we had a pretty, wandering, scintillating play of eloquent thought, that enlivened, if it did not kindle, all around it. If you want the real philosophy of it, I will give it to you. The chance thought or expression struck the nervous centre of consciousness, as the rowel of a spur stings the flank of a racer. Away through all the telegraphic radiations of the nervous cords flashed the intelligence that the brain was kindling, and must be fed with something or other, or it would burn itself to ashes.

And all the great hydraulic engines poured in their scarlet blood, and the fire kindled, and the flame rose; for the blood is a stream that, like burning rock-oil, at once kindles, and is itself the fuel. You can't order these organic processes, any more than a milliner can make a rose. She can make something that looks like a rose, more or less, but it takes all the forces of the universe to finish and sweeten that blossom in your button-hole; and you may be sure that when the orator's brain is in a flame, when the poet's heart is in a tumult, it is something mightier than he and his will that is dealing with him! As I have looked from one of the northern windows of the street which commands our noble estuary, the view through which is a picture on an illimitable canvas and a poem in innumerable cantos, I have sometimes seen a pleasure-boat drifting along, her sail flapping, and she seeming as if she had neither will nor aim. At her stern a man was laboring to bring her head round with an oar, to little purpose, as it seemed to those who watched him pulling and tugging. But all at once the wind of heaven, which had wandered all the way from Florida or from Labrador, it may be, struck full upon the sail, and it swelled and rounded itself, like a white bosom that had burst its bodice, and

You are right; it is too true! but how I love these pretty phrases! I am afraid I am becoming an epicure in words, which is a bad thing to be, unless it is dominated by something infinitely better than itself. But there is a fascination in the mere sound of articulated breath; of consonants that resist with the firmness of a maid of honor, or half or wholly yield to the wooing lips; of vowels that flow and murmur, each after its kind; the peremptory b and p, the brittle k, the vibrating r, the insinuating s, the feathery f, the velvety v, the bell-voiced m, the tranquil broad a, the penetrating e, the cooing u, the emotional o, and the beautiful combinations of alternate rock and stream, as it were, that they give to the rippling flow of speech, there is a fascination in the skilful handling of these, which the great poets and even prose-writers have not disdained to acknowledge and use to recommend their thought. What do you say to this line of Homer as a piece of poetical full-band music? I know you read the Greek characters with perfect ease, but permit me, just for my own satisfaction, to put it into English letters:

Aigle pamphanoosa di' aitheros ouranon ike!

as if he should have spoken in our poorer phrase of

Splendor far shining through ether to heaven ascending.

That Greek line, which I do not remember having heard mention of as remarkable, has nearly every consonantal and vowel sound in the language. Try it by the Greek and by the English alphabet; it is a curiosity. Tell me that old Homer did not roll his sightless eyeballs about with delight, as he thundered out these ringing syllables! It seems hard to think of his going round like a hand-organ man, with such music and such thought as his to earn his bread with. One can't help wishing that Mr. Pugh could have got at him for a single lecture, at least, of the "Star Course," or that he could have appeared in the Music Hall, "for this night only."

I know I have rambled, but I hope you see that this is a delicate way of letting you into the nature of the individual who is, officially, the principal personage at our table. It would hardly do to describe him directly, you know. But you must not think, because the lightning zigzags, it does not know where to strike.

I shall try to go through the rest of my description of our boarders with as little of digression as is consistent with my nature. I think we have a somewhat exceptional company. Since our Landlady has got up in the world, her board has been decidedly a favorite with persons a little above the average in point of intelligence and education. In fact, ever since a boarder of hers, not wholly unknown to the reading public, brought her establishment into notice, it has attracted a considerable number of literary and scientific people, and now and then a politician, like the Member of the House of Representatives, otherwise called the Great and General Court of the State of Massachusetts. The consequence is, that there is more individuality of character than in a good many similar boardinghouses, where all are business-men, engrossed in the same pursuit of money-making, or all are engaged in politics, and so deeply occupied with the welfare of the community that they can think and talk of little else.

At my left hand sits as singular-looking a human being as I remember seeing outside of a regular museum or tent-show. His black coat shines as if it had been polished; and it has been polished on the wearer's back, no doubt, for the arms and other points of maximum attrition are particularly smooth and bright. Round shoulders, stooping over some minute labor, I suppose. Very slender limbs, with bends like a grasshopper's; sits a great deal, I presume; looks as if he might straighten them out all of a sudden, and jump instead of walking. Wears goggles very commonly; says it rests his eyes, which he strains in looking at very small objects. Voice has a dry creak, as if made by some small piece of mechanism that wanted oiling. I don't think he is a botanist, for he does not smell of dried herbs, but carries a camphorated atmosphere about with him, as if to keep the moths from attacking him. I must find out what is his particular interest. One ought to know something about his immediate neighbors at the table. This is what I said to myself, before opening a conversation with him. Everybody in our ward of the city was in a great stir about a certain election, and I thought I might as well begin with that as anything.

How do you think the vote is likely to go tomorrow? I said.

It isn't to-morrow, he answered, it 's next month.

Next month! said I. Why, what election do you mean?

I mean the election to the Presidency of the Entomological Society, sir, he creaked, with an air of surprise, as if nobody could by any possibility have been thinking of any other. Great competition, sir, between the dipterists and the lepidopterists as to which shall get in their candidate. Several close ballotings already; adjourned for a fortnight. Poor concerns, both of 'em. Wait till our turn comes.

I suppose you are an entomologist? I said with a note of interrogation.

-Not quite so ambitious as that, sir. I should like to put my eyes on the individual entitled to that name! A society may call itself an Entomological Society, but the man who arrogates such a broad title as that to himself, in the present state of science, is a pretender, sir, a dilettante, an impostor! No man can be truly called an entomologist, sir; the subject is too vast for any single human intelligence to grasp.

May I venture to ask, I said, a little awed by his statement and manner, what is your special province of study?

I am often spoken of as a Coleopterist, he said, but I have no right to so comprehensive a name. The genus Scarabaeus is what I have chiefly confined myself to, and ought to have studied exclusively. The beetles proper are quite enough for the labor of one man's life. Call me a Scarabaeist if you will; if I can prove myself worthy of that name, my highest ambition will be more than satisfied.

I think, by way of compromise and convenience, I shall call him the Scarabee. He has come to look wonderfully like those creatures, the beetles, I mean, by being so much among them. His room is hung round with cases of them, each impaled on a pin driven through him, something as they used to bury suicides. These cases take the place for him of pictures and all other ornaments. That Boy steals into his room sometimes, and stares at them with great admiration, and has himself undertaken to form a rival cabinet, chiefly consisting of flies, so far, arranged in ranks superintended by an occasional spider.

The old Master, who is a bachelor, has a kindly feeling for this little monkey, and those of his kind.

I like children, he said to me one day at table, I like 'em, and I respect 'em. Pretty much all the honest truth-telling there is in the world is done by them. Do you know they play the part in the household which the king's jester, who very often had a mighty long head under his cap and bells, used to play for a monarch? There's no radical club like a nest of little folks in a nursery. Did you ever watch a baby's fingers? I have, often enough, though I never knew what it was to own one. The Master paused half a minute or so, sighed, perhaps at thinking what he had missed in life, looked up at me a little vacantly. I saw what was the matter; he had lost the thread of his talk.

Baby's fingers, I intercalated.

-Yes, yes; did you ever see how they will poke those wonderful little fingers of theirs into every fold and crack and crevice they can get at? That is their first education, feeling their way into the solid facts of the material world. When they begin to talk it is the same thing over again in another shape. If there is a crack or a flaw in your answer to their confounded shoulder-hitting questions, they will poke and poke until they have got it gaping just as the baby's fingers have made a rent out of that atom of a hole in his pinafore that your old eyes never took notice of. Then they make such fools of us by copying on a small scale what we do in the grand manner. I wonder if it ever occurs to our dried-up neighbor there to ask himself whether That Boy's collection of flies is n't about as significant in the Order of Things as his own Museum of Beetles?

I couldn't help thinking that perhaps That Boy's questions about the simpler mysteries of life might have a good deal of the same kind of significance as the Master's inquiries into the Order of Things.

On my left, beyond my next neighbor the Scarabee, at the end of the table, sits a person of whom we know little, except that he carries about him more palpable reminiscences of tobacco and the allied sources of comfort than a very sensitive organization might find acceptable. The Master does not seem to like him much, for some reason or other, perhaps he has a special aversion to the odor of tobacco. As his forefinger shows a little too distinctly that he uses a pen, I shall compliment him by calling him the Man of Letters, until I find out more about him.

The Young Girl who sits on my right, next beyond the Master, can hardly be more than nineteen or twenty years old. I wish I could paint her so as to interest others as much as she does me. But she has not a profusion of sunny tresses wreathing a neck of alabaster, and a cheek where the rose and the lily are trying to settle their old quarrel with alternating victory. Her hair is brown, her cheek is delicately pallid, her forehead is too ample for a ball-room beauty's. A single faint line between the eyebrows is the record of long, continued anxious efforts to please in the task she has chosen, or rather which has been forced upon her. It is the same line of anxious and conscientious effort which I saw not long since on the forehead of one of the sweetest and truest singers who has visited us; the same which is so striking on the masks of singing women painted upon the facade of our Great Organ, that Himalayan home of harmony which you are to see and then die, if you don't live where you can see and hear it often. Many deaths have happened in a neighboring large city from that well-known complaint, Icterus Invidiosorum, after returning from a visit to the Music Hall. The invariable symptom of a fatal attack is the Risus Sardonicus. But the Young Girl. She gets her living by writing stories for a newspaper. Every week she furnishes a new story. If her head aches or her heart is heavy, so that she does not come to time with her story, she falls behindhand and has to live on credit. It sounds well enough to say that "she supports herself by her pen," but her lot is a trying one; it repeats the doom of the Danaides. The "Weekly Bucket" has no bottom, and it is her business to help fill it. Imagine for one moment what it is to tell a tale that must flow on, flow ever, without pausing; the lover miserable and happy this week, to begin miserable again next week and end as before; the villain scowling, plotting, punished; to scowl, plot, and get punished again in our next; an endless series of woes and busses, into each paragraph of which the forlorn artist has to throw all the liveliness, all the emotion, all the graces of style she is mistress of, for the wages of a maid of all work, and no more recognition or thanks from anybody than the apprentice who sets the types for the paper that prints her ever-ending and ever-beginning stories. And yet she has a pretty talent, sensibility, a natural way of writing, an ear for the music of verse, in which she sometimes indulges to vary the dead monotony of everlasting narrative, and a sufficient amount of invention to make her stories readable. I have found my eyes dimmed over them oftener than once, more with thinking about her, perhaps, than about her heroes and heroines. Poor little body! Poor little mind! Poor little soul! She is one of that great company of delicate, intelligent, emotional young creatures, who are waiting, like that sail I spoke of, for some breath of heaven to fill their white bosoms, love, the right of every woman; religious emotion, sister of love, with the same passionate eyes, but cold, thin, bloodless hands, some enthusiasm of humanity or divinity; and find that life offers them, instead, a seat on a wooden bench, a chain to fasten them to it, and a heavy oar to pull day and night. We read the Arabian tales and pity the doomed lady who must amuse her lord and master from day to day or have her head cut off; how much better is a mouth without bread to fill it than no mouth at all to fill, because no head? We have all round us a weary-eyed company of Scheherezades! This is one of them, and I may call her by that name when it pleases me to do so.

The next boarder I have to mention is the one who sits between the Young Girl and the Landlady. In a little chamber into which a small thread of sunshine finds its way for half an hour or so every day during a month or six weeks of the spring or autumn, at all other times obliged to content itself with ungilded daylight, lives this boarder, whom, without wronging any others of our company, I may call, as she is very generally called in the household, The Lady. In giving her this name it is not meant that there are no other ladies at our table, or that the handmaids who serve us are not ladies, or to deny the general proposition that everybody who wears the unbifurcated garment is entitled to that appellation. Only this lady has a look and manner which there is no mistaking as belonging to a person always accustomed to refined and elegant society. Her style is perhaps a little more courtly and gracious than some would like. The language and manner which betray the habitual desire of pleasing, and which add a charm to intercourse in the higher social circles, are liable to be construed by sensitive beings unused to such amenities as an odious condescension when addressed to persons of less consideration than the accused, and as a still more odious, you know the word, when directed to those who are esteemed by the world as considerable person ages. But of all this the accused are fortunately wholly unconscious, for there is nothing so entirely natural and unaffected as the highest breeding.

From an aspect of dignified but undisguised economy which showed itself in her dress as well as in her limited quarters, I suspected a story of shipwrecked fortune, and determined to question our Landlady. That worthy woman was delighted to tell the history of her most distinguished boarder. She was, as I had supposed, a gentlewoman whom a change of circumstances had brought down from her high estate.

Did I know the Goldenrod family? Of course I did. Well, the Lady, was first cousin to Mrs. Midas Goldenrod. She had been here in her carriage to call upon her, not very often. Were her rich relations kind and helpful to her? Well, yes; at least they made her presents now and then. Three or four years ago they sent her a silver waiter, and every Christmas they sent her a boquet, it must cost as much as five dollars, the Landlady thought.

And how did the Lady receive these valuable and useful gifts?

Every Christmas she got out the silver waiter and borrowed a glass tumbler and filled it with water, and put the boquet in it and set it on the waiter. It smelt sweet enough and looked pretty for a day or two, but the Landlady thought it wouldn't have hurt 'em if they'd sent a piece of goods for a dress, or at least a pocket-handkercher or two, or something or other that she could 'a' made some kind of use of; but beggars must n't be choosers; not that she was a beggar, for she'd sooner die than do that if she was in want of a meal of victuals. There was a lady I remember, and she had a little boy and she was a widow, and after she'd buried her husband she was dreadful poor, and she was ashamed to let her little boy go out in his old shoes, and copper-toed shoes they was too, because his poor little ten toes was a coming out of 'em; and what do you think my husband's rich uncle, well, there now, it was me and my little Benjamin, as he was then, there's no use in hiding of it, and what do you think my husband's uncle sent me but a plaster of Paris image of a young woman, that was, well, her appearance wasn't respectable, and I had to take and wrap her up in a towel and poke her right into my closet, and there she stayed till she got her head broke and served her right, for she was n't fit to show folks. You need n't say anything about what I told you, but the fact is I was desperate poor before I began to support myself taking boarders, and a lone woman without her, her

The sentence plunged into the gulf of her great remembered sorrow, and was lost to the records of humanity.

Presently she continued in answer to my questions: The Lady was not very sociable; kept mostly to herself. The Young Girl (our Scheherezade) used to visit her sometimes, and they seemed to like each other, but the Young Girl had not many spare hours for visiting. The Lady never found fault, but she was very nice in her tastes, and kept everything about her looking as neat and pleasant as she could.

What did she do? Why, she read, and she drew pictures, and she did needlework patterns, and played on an old harp she had; the gilt was mostly off, but it sounded very sweet, and she sung to it sometimes, those old songs that used to be in fashion twenty or thirty years ago, with words to 'em that folks could understand.

Did she do anything to help support herself? The Landlady couldn't say she did, but she thought there was rich people enough that ought to buy the flowers and things she worked and painted.

All this points to the fact that she was bred to be an ornamental rather than what is called a useful member of society. This is all very well so long as fortune favors those who are chosen to be the ornamental personages; but if the golden tide recedes and leaves them stranded, they are more to be pitied than almost any other class. "I cannot dig, to beg I am ashamed."

I think it is unpopular in this country to talk much about gentlemen and gentlewomen. People are touchy about social distinctions, which no doubt are often invidious and quite arbitrary and accidental, but which it is impossible to avoid recognizing as facts of natural history. Society stratifies itself everywhere, and the stratum which is generally recognized as the uppermost will be apt to have the advantage in easy grace of manner and in unassuming confidence, and consequently be more agreeable in the superficial relations of life. To compare these advantages with the virtues and utilities would be foolish. Much of the noblest work in life is done by ill-dressed, awkward, ungainly persons; but that is no more reason for undervaluing good manners and what we call high-breeding, than the fact that the best part of the sturdy labor of the world is done by men with exceptionable hands is to be urged against the use of Brown Windsor as a preliminary to appearance in cultivated society.

I mean to stand up for this poor lady, whose usefulness in the world is apparently problematical. She seems to me like a picture which has fallen from its gilded frame and lies, face downward, on the dusty floor. The picture never was as needful as a window or a door, but it was pleasant to see it in its place, and it would be pleasant to see it there again, and I, for one, should be thankful to have the Lady restored by some turn of fortune to the position from which she has been so cruelly cast down.

I have asked the Landlady about the young man sitting near her, the same who attracted my attention the other day while I was talking, as I mentioned. He passes most of his time in a private observatory, it appears; a watcher of the stars. That I suppose gives the peculiar look to his lustrous eyes. The Master knows him and was pleased to tell me something about him.

You call yourself a Poet, he said, and we call you so, too, and so you are; I read your verses and like 'em. But that young man lives in a world beyond the imagination of poets, let me tell you. The daily home of his thought is in illimitable space, hovering between the two eternities. In his contemplations the divisions of time run together, as in the thought of his Maker. With him also, I say it not profanely, one day is as a thousand years and a thousand years as one day.

This account of his occupation increased the interest his look had excited in me, and I have observed him more particularly and found out more about him. Sometimes, after a long night's watching, he looks so pale and worn, that one would think the cold moonlight had stricken him with some malign effluence such as it is fabled to send upon those who sleep in it. At such times he seems more like one who has come from a planet farther away from the sun than our earth, than like one of us terrestrial creatures. His home is truly in the heavens, and he practises an asceticism in the cause of science almost comparable to that of Saint Simeon Stylites. Yet they tell me he might live in luxury if he spent on himself what he spends on science. His knowledge is of that strange, remote character, that it seems sometimes almost superhuman. He knows the ridges and chasms of the moon as a surveyor knows a garden-plot he has measured. He watches the snows that gather around the poles of Mars; he is on the lookout for the expected comet at the moment when its faint stain of diffused light first shows itself; he analyzes the ray that comes from the sun's photosphere; he measures the rings of Saturn; he counts his asteroids to see that none are missing, as the shepherd counts the sheep in his flock. A strange unearthly being; lonely, dwelling far apart from the thoughts and cares of the planet on which he lives, an enthusiast who gives his life to knowledge; a student of antiquity, to whom the records of the geologist are modern pages in the great volume of being, and the pyramids a memorandum of yesterday, as the eclipse or occultation that is to take place thousands of years hence is an event of to-morrow in the diary without beginning and without end where he enters the aspect of the passing moment as it is read on the celestial dial.

In very marked contrast with this young man is the something more than middle-aged Register of Deeds, a rusty, sallow, smoke-dried looking personage, who belongs to this earth as exclusively as the other belongs to the firmament. His movements are as mechanical as those of a pendulum, to the office, where he changes his coat and plunges into messuages and building-lots; then, after changing his coat again, back to our table, and so, day by day, the dust of years gradually gathering around him as it does on the old folios that fill the shelves all round the great cemetery of past transactions of which he is the sexton.

Of the Salesman who sits next him, nothing need be said except that he is good-looking, rosy, well-dressed, and of very polite manners, only a little more brisk than the approved style of carriage permits, as one in the habit of springing with a certain alacrity at the call of a customer.

You would like to see, I don't doubt, how we sit at the table, and I will help you by means of a diagram which shows the present arrangement of our seats.

```
4 3 2 1 14 13
---------------------------------
| O O O O O O |
| |
5 | O Breakfast-Table O |12
| |
| O O O O O O |
---------------------------------
6 7 8 9 10 11
```
1. The Poet.
2. The Master Of Arts.
3. The Young Girl (Scheherezade).
4. The Lady.
5. The Landlady.
6. Dr. B. Franklin.
7. That Boy.
8. The Astronomer.
9. The Member of the Haouse.
10. The Register of Deeds.
11. The Salesman.
12. The Capitalist.
13. The Man of Letters(?).
14. The Scarabee.

Our young Scheherezade varies her prose stories now and then, as I told you, with compositions in verse, one or two of which she has let me look over. Here is one of them, which she allowed me to copy. It is from a story of hers, "The Sun-Worshipper's Daughter," which you may find in the periodical before mentioned, to which she is a contributor, if your can lay your hand upon a file of it. I think our Scheherezade has never had a lover in human shape, or she would not play so lightly with the firebrands of the great passion.

FANTASIA.
Kiss mine eyelids, beauteous Morn,
Blushing into life new-born!
Lend me violets for my hair,
And thy russet robe to wear,
And thy ring of rosiest hue
Set in drops of diamond dew!

Kiss my cheek, thou noontide ray,
From my Love so far away!

Let thy splendor streaming down
Turn its pallid lilies brown,
Till its darkening shades reveal
Where his passion pressed its seal!

Kiss my lips, thou Lord of light,
Kiss my lips a soft good night!
Westward sinks thy golden car;
Leave me but the evening star,
And my solace that shall be,
Borrowing all its light from thee!

CHAPTER III

The old Master was talking about a concert he had been to hear. I don't like your chopped music anyway. That woman, she had more sense in her little finger than forty medical societies, Florence Nightingale, says that the music you pour out is good for sick folks, and the music you pound out isn't. Not that exactly, but something like it. I have been to hear some music-pounding. It was a young woman, with as many white muslin flounces round her as the planet Saturn has rings, that did it. She gave the music-stool a twirl or two and fluffed down on to it like a whirl of soap-suds in a hand-basin. Then she pushed up her cuffs as if she was going to fight for the champion's belt. Then she worked her wrists and her hands, to limber 'em, I suppose, and spread out her fingers till they looked as though they would pretty much cover the keyboard, from the growling end to the little squeaky one. Then those two hands of hers made a jump at the keys as if they were a couple of tigers coming down on a flock of black and white sheep, and the piano gave a great howl as if its tail had been trod on. Dead stop, so still you could hear your hair growing. Then another jump, and another howl, as if the piano had two tails and you had trod on both of 'em at once, and, then a grand clatter and scramble and string of jumps, up and down, back and forward, one hand over the other, like a stampede of rats and mice more than like anything I call music. I like to hear a woman sing, and I like to hear a fiddle sing, but these noises they hammer out of their wood and ivory anvils, don't talk to me, I know the difference between a bullfrog and a woodthrush and

Pop! went a small piece of artillery such as is made of a stick of elder and carries a pellet of very moderate consistency. That Boy was in his seat and looking demure enough, but there could be no question that he was the artillery-man who had discharged the missile. The aim was not a bad one, for it took the Master full in the forehead, and had the effect of checking the flow of his eloquence. How the little monkey had learned to time his interruptions I do not know, but I have observed more than once before this, that the popgun would go off just at the moment when some one of the company was getting too energetic or prolix. The Boy isn't old enough to judge for himself when to intervene to change the order of conversation; no, of course he isn't. Somebody must give him a hint. Somebody. Who is it? I suspect Dr. B. Franklin. He looks too knowing. There is certainly a trick somewhere. Why, a day or two ago I was myself discoursing, with considerable effect, as I thought, on some of the new aspects of humanity, when I was struck full on the cheek by one of these little pellets, and there was such a confounded laugh that I had to wind up and leave off with a preposition instead of a good mouthful of polysyllables. I have watched our young Doctor, however, and have been entirely unable to detect any signs of communication between him and this audacious child, who is like to become a power among us, for that popgun is fatal to any talker who is hit by its pellet. I have suspected a foot under the table as the prompter, but I have been unable to detect the slightest movement or look as if he were making one, on the part of Dr. Benjamin Franklin. I cannot help thinking of the flappers in Swift's Laputa, only they gave one a hint when to speak and another a hint to listen, whereas the popgun says unmistakably, "Shut up!"

I should be sorry to lose my confidence in Dr. B. Franklin, who seems very much devoted to his business, and whom I mean to consult about some small symptoms I have had lately. Perhaps it is coming to a new boarding-house. The young people who come into Paris from the provinces are very apt, so I have been told by one that knows, to have an attack of typhoid fever a few weeks or months after their arrival. I have not been long enough at this table to get well acclimated; perhaps that is it. Boarding-House Fever. Something like horse-ail, very likely, horses get it, you know, when they are brought to city stables. A little "off my feed," as Hiram Woodruff would say. A queer discoloration about my forehead. Query, a bump? Cannot remember any. Might have got it against bedpost or something while asleep. Very unpleasant to look so. I wonder how my portrait would look, if anybody should take it now! I hope not quite so badly as one I saw the other day, which I took for the end man of the Ethiopian Serenaders, or some traveller who had been exploring the sources of the Niger, until I read the name at the bottom and found it was a face I knew as well as my own.

I must consult somebody, and it is nothing more than fair to give our young Doctor a chance. Here goes for Dr. Benjamin Franklin.

The young Doctor has a very small office and a very large sign, with a transparency at night big enough for an oyster-shop. These young doctors are particularly strong, as I understand, on what they call diagnosis, an excellent branch of the healing art, full of satisfaction to the curious practitioner, who likes to give the right Latin name to one's complaint; not quite so satisfactory to the patient, as it is not so very much pleasanter to be bitten by a dog with a collar round his neck telling you that he is called Snap or Teaser, than by a dog without a collar. Sometimes, in fact, one would a little rather not know the exact name of his complaint, as if he does he is pretty sure to look it out in a medical dictionary, and then if he reads, This terrible disease is attended with vast suffering and is inevitably mortal, or any such statement, it is apt to affect him unpleasantly.

I confess to a little shakiness when I knocked at Dr. Benjamin's office door. "Come in!" exclaimed Dr. B. F. in tones that sounded ominous and sepulchral. And I went in.

I don't believe the chambers of the Inquisition ever presented a more alarming array of implements for extracting a confession, than our young Doctor's office did of instruments to make nature tell what was the matter with a poor body.

There were Ophthalmoscopes and Rhinoscopes and Otoscopes and Laryngoscopes and Stethoscopes; and Thermometers and Spirometers and Dynamometers and Sphygmometers and Pleximeters; and Probes and Probangs and all sorts of frightful inquisitive exploring contrivances; and scales to weigh you in, and tests and balances and pumps and electro-magnets and magneto-electric machines; in short, apparatus for doing everything but turn you inside out.

Dr. Benjamin set me down before his one window and began looking at me with such a superhuman air of sagacity, that I felt like one of those open-breasted clocks which make no secret of their inside arrangements, and almost thought he could see through me as one sees through a shrimp or a jelly-fish. First he looked at the place inculpated, which had a sort of greenish-brown color, with his naked eyes, with much corrugation of forehead and fearful concentration of attention; then through a pocket-glass which he carried. Then he drew back a space, for a perspective view. Then he made me put out my tongue and laid a slip of blue paper on it, which turned red and scared me a little. Next he took my wrist; but instead of counting my pulse in the old-fashioned way, he fastened a machine to it that marked all the beats on a sheet of paper, for all the world like a scale of the heights of mountains, say from Mount Tom up to Chimborazo and then down again, and up again, and so on. In the mean time he asked me all sorts of questions about myself and all my relatives, whether we had been subject to this and that malady, until I felt as if we must some of us have had more or less of them, and could not feel quite sure whether Elephantiasis and Beriberi and Progressive Locomotor Ataxy did not run in the family.

After all this overhauling of myself and my history, he paused and looked puzzled. Something was suggested about what he called an "exploratory puncture." This I at once declined, with thanks. Suddenly a thought struck him. He looked still more closely at the discoloration I have spoken of.

Looks like I declare it reminds me of very rare! very curious! It would be strange if my first case of this kind should be one of our boarders!

What kind of a case do you call it? I said, with a sort of feeling that he could inflict a severe or a light malady on me, as if he were a judge passing sentence.

The color reminds me, said Dr. B. Franklin, of what I have seen in a case of Addison's Disease, Morbus Addisonii.

But my habits are quite regular, I said; for I remembered that the distinguished essayist was too fond of his brandy and water, and I confess that the thought was not pleasant to me of following Dr. Johnson's advice, with the slight variation of giving my days and my nights to trying on the favorite maladies of Addison.

Temperance people are subject to it! exclaimed Dr. Benjamin, almost exultingly, I thought.

But I had the impression that the author of the Spectator was afflicted with a dropsy, or some such inflated malady, to which persons of sedentary and bibacious habits are liable. [A literary swell, I thought to myself, but I did not say it. I felt too serious.]

The author of the Spectator! cried out Dr. Benjamin, I mean the celebrated Dr. Addison, inventor, I would say discoverer, of the wonderful new disease called after him.

And what may this valuable invention or discovery consist in? I asked, for I was curious to know the nature of the gift which this benefactor of the race had bestowed upon us.

A most interesting affection, and rare, too. Allow me to look closely at that discoloration once more for a moment. Cutis cenea, bronze skin, they call it sometimes, extraordinary pigmentation, a little more to the light, if you please, ah! now I get the bronze coloring admirably, beautifully! Would you have any objection to showing your case to the Societies of Medical Improvement and Medical Observation?

[My case! O dear!] May I ask if any vital organ is commonly involved in this interesting complaint? I said, faintly.

Well, sir, the young Doctor replied, there is an organ which is sometimes a little touched, I may say; a very curious and ingenious little organ or pair of organs. Did you ever hear of the Capsulae, Suprarenales?

No, said I, is it a mortal complaint? I ought to have known better than to ask such a question, but I was getting nervous and thinking about all sorts of horrid maladies people are liable to, with horrid names to match.

It is n't a complaint, I mean they are not a complaint, they are two small organs, as I said, inside of you, and nobody knows what is the use of them. The most curious thing is that when anything is the matter with them you turn of the color of bronze. After all, I didn't mean to say I believed it was Morbus Addisonii; I only thought of that when I saw the discoloration.

So he gave me a recipe, which I took care to put where it could do no hurt to anybody, and I paid him his fee (which he took with the air of a man in the receipt of a great income) and said Good-morning.

What in the name of a thousand diablos is the reason these confounded doctors will mention their guesses about "a case," as they call it, and all its conceivable possibilities, out loud before their patients? I don't suppose there is anything in all this nonsense about "Addison's Disease," but I wish he hadn't spoken of that very interesting ailment, and I should feel a little easier if that discoloration would leave my forehead. I will ask the Landlady about it, these old women often know more than the young doctors just come home with long names for everything they don't know how to cure. But the name of this complaint sets me thinking. Bronzed skin! What an odd idea! Wonder if it spreads all over one. That would be picturesque and pleasant, now, wouldn't it? To be made a living statue of, nothing to do but strike an attitude. Arm up so, like the one in the Garden. John of Bologna's Mercury, thus on one foot. Needy knife-grinder in the Tribune at Florence. No, not "needy," come to think of it. Marcus Aurelius on horseback. Query. Are horses subject to the Morbus Addisonii? Advertise for a bronzed living horse, Lyceum invitations and engagements, bronze versus brass. What 's the use in being frightened? Bet it was a bump. Pretty certain I bumped my forehead against something. Never heard of a bronzed man before. Have seen white men, black men, red men, yellow men, two or three blue men, stained with doctor's stuff; some green ones, from the country; but never a bronzed man. Poh, poh! Sure it was a bump. Ask Landlady to look at it.

Landlady did look at it. Said it was a bump, and no mistake. Recommended a piece of brown paper dipped in vinegar. Made the house smell as if it were in quarantine for the plague from Smyrna, but discoloration soon disappeared, so I did not become a bronzed man after all, hope I never shall while I am alive. Should n't mind being done in bronze after I was dead. On second thoughts not so clear about it, remembering how some of them look that we have got stuck up in public; think I had rather go down to posterity in an Ethiopian Minstrel portrait, like our friend's the other day.

You were kind enough to say, I remarked to the Master, that you read my poems and liked them. Perhaps you would be good enough to tell me what it is you like about them?

The Master harpooned a breakfast-roll and held it up before me. Will you tell me, he said, why you like that breakfast-roll? I suppose he thought that would stop my mouth in two senses. But he was mistaken.

To be sure I will, said I. First, I like its mechanical consistency; brittle externally, that is for the teeth, which want resistance to be overcome; soft, spongy, well tempered and flavored internally, that is for the organ of taste; wholesome, nutritious, that is for the internal surfaces and the system generally.

Good, said the Master, and laughed a hearty terrestrial laugh.

I hope he will carry that faculty of an honest laugh with him wherever he goes, why shouldn't he? The "order of things," as he calls it, from which hilarity was excluded, would be crippled and one-sided enough. I don't believe the human gamut will be cheated of a single note after men have done breathing this fatal atmospheric mixture and die into the ether of immortality!

I did n't say all that; if I had said it, it would have brought a pellet from the popgun, I feel quite certain.

The Master went on after he had had out his laugh. There is one thing I am His Imperial Majesty about, and that is my likes and dislikes. What if I do like your verses, you can't help yourself. I don't doubt somebody or other hates 'em and hates you and everything you do, or ever did, or ever can do. He is all right; there is nothing you or I like that somebody does n't hate. Was there ever anything wholesome that was not poison to somebody? If you hate honey or cheese, or the products of the dairy, I know a family a good many of whose members can't touch milk, butter, cheese, and the like, why, say so, but don't find fault with the bees and the cows. Some are afraid of roses, and I have known those who thought a pond-lily a disagreeable neighbor. That Boy will give you the metaphysics of likes and dislikes. Look here, you young philosopher over there, do you like candy?

That Boy. You bet! Give me a stick and see if I don't.

And can you tell me why you like candy?

That Boy. Because I do.

There, now, that is the whole matter in a nutshell. Why do your teeth like crackling crust, and your organs of taste like spongy crumb, and your digestive contrivances take kindly to bread rather than toadstools

That Boy (thinking he was still being catechised). Because they do.

Whereupon the Landlady said, Sh! and the Young Girl laughed, and the Lady smiled; and Dr. Ben Franklin kicked him, moderately, under the table, and the Astronomer looked up at the ceiling to see what had happened, and the Member of the Haouse cried, Order! Order! and the Salesman said, Shut up, cash-boy! and the rest of the boarders kept on feeding; except the Master, who looked very hard but half approvingly at the small intruder, who had come about as nearly right as most professors would have done.

You poets, the Master said after this excitement had calmed down, you poets have one thing about you that is odd. You talk about everything as if you knew more about it than the people whose business it is to know all about it. I suppose you do a little of what we teachers used to call "cramming" now and then?

If you like your breakfast you must n't ask the cook too many questions, I answered.

Oh, come now, don't be afraid of letting out your secrets. I have a notion I can tell a poet that gets himself up just as I can tell a make-believe old man on the stage by the line where the gray skullcap joins the smooth forehead of the young fellow of seventy. You'll confess to a rhyming dictionary anyhow, won't you?

I would as lief use that as any other dictionary, but I don't want it. When a word comes up fit to end a line with I can feel all the rhymes in the language that are fit to go with it without naming them. I have tried them all so many times, I know all the polygamous words and all the monogamous ones, and all the unmarrying ones, the whole lot that have no mates, as soon as I hear their names called. Sometimes I run over a string of rhymes, but generally speaking it is strange what a short list it is of those that are good for anything. That is the pitiful side of all rhymed verse. Take two such words as home and world. What can you do with chrome or loam or gnome or tome? You have dome, foam, and roam, and not much more to use in your pome, as some of our fellow-countrymen call it. As for world, you know that in all human probability somebody or something will be hurled into it or out of it; its clouds may be furled or its grass impearled; possibly something may be whirled, or curled, or have swirled, one of Leigh Hunt's words, which with lush, one of Keats's, is an important part of the stock in trade of some dealers in rhyme.

And how much do you versifiers know of all those arts and sciences you refer to as if you were as familiar with them as a cobbler is with his wax and lapstone?

Enough not to make too many mistakes. The best way is to ask some expert before one risks himself very far in illustrations from a branch he does not know much about. Suppose, for instance, I wanted to use the double star to illustrate anything, say the relation of two human souls to each other, what would I do? Why, I would ask our young friend there to let me look at one of those loving celestial pairs through his telescope, and I don't doubt he'd let me do so, and tell me their names and all I wanted to know about them.

I should be most happy to show any of the double stars or whatever else there might be to see in the heavens to any of our friends at this table, the young man said, so cordially and kindly that it was a real invitation.

Show us the man in the moon, said That Boy. I should so like to see a double star! said Scheherezade, with a very pretty air of smiling modesty.

Will you go, if we make up a party? I asked the Master.

A cold in the head lasts me from three to five days, answered the Master. I am not so very fond of being out in the dew like Nebuchadnezzar: that will do for you young folks.

I suppose I must be one of the young folks, not so young as our Scheherezade, nor so old as the Capitalist, young enough at any rate to want to be of the party. So we agreed that on some fair night when the Astronomer should tell us that there was to be a fine show in the skies, we would make up a party and go to the Observatory. I asked the Scarabee whether he would not like to make one of us.

Out of the question, sir, out of the question. I am altogether too much occupied with an important scientific investigation to devote any considerable part of an evening to star-gazing.

Oh, indeed, said I, and may I venture to ask on what particular point you are engaged just at present?

Certainly, sir, you may. It is, I suppose, as difficult and important a matter to be investigated as often comes before a student of natural history. I wish to settle the point once for all whether the Pediculus Mellitae is or is not the larva of Meloe.

[Now is n't this the drollest world to live in that one could imagine, short of being in a fit of delirium tremens? Here is a fellow-creature of mine and yours who is asked to see all the glories of the firmament brought close to him, and he is too busy with a little unmentionable parasite that infests the bristly surface of a bee to spare an hour or two of a single evening for the splendors of the universe! I must get a peep through that microscope of his and see the pediculus which occupies a larger space in his mental vision than the midnight march of the solar systems. The creature, the human one, I mean, interests me.]

I am very curious, I said, about that pediculus melittae, (just as if I knew a good deal about the little wretch and wanted to know more, whereas I had never heard him spoken of before, to my knowledge,) could you let me have a sight of him in your microscope?

You ought to have seen the way in which the poor dried-up little Scarabee turned towards me. His eyes took on a really human look, and I almost thought those antennae-like arms of his would have stretched themselves out and embraced me. I don't believe any of the boarders had ever shown any interest in him, except the little monkey of a Boy, since he had been in the house. It is not strange; he had not seemed to me much like a human being, until all at once I touched the one point where his vitality had concentrated itself, and he stood revealed a man and a brother.

Come in, said he, come in, right after breakfast, and you shall see the animal that has convulsed the entomological world with questions as to his nature and origin.

So I went into the Scarabee's parlor, lodging-room, study, laboratory, and museum, a single apartment applied to these various uses, you understand.

I wish I had time to have you show me all your treasures, I said, but I am afraid I shall hardly be able to do more than look at the bee-parasite. But what a superb butterfly you have in that case!

Oh, yes, yes, well enough,came from South America with the beetle there; look at him! These Lepidoptera are for children to play with, pretty to look at, so some think. Give me the Coleoptera, and the kings of the Coleoptera are the beetles! Lepidoptera and Neuroptera for little folks; Coleopteras for men, sir!

The particular beetle he showed me in the case with the magnificent butterfly was an odious black wretch that one would say, Ugh! at, and kick out of his path, if he did not serve him worse than that. But he looked at it as a coin-collector would look at a Pescennius Niger, if the coins of that Emperor are as scarce as they used to be when I was collecting half-penny tokens and pine-tree shillings and battered bits of Roman brass with the head of Gallienus or some such old fellow on them.

A beauty! he exclaimed, and the only specimen of the kind in this country, to the best of my belief. A unique, sir, and there is a pleasure in exclusive possession. Not another beetle like that short of South America, sir.

I was glad to hear that there were no more like it in this neighborhood, the present supply of cockroaches answering every purpose, so far as I am concerned, that such an animal as this would be likely to serve.

Here are my bee-parasites, said the Scarabee, showing me a box full of glass slides, each with a specimen ready mounted for the microscope. I was most struck with one little beast flattened out like a turtle, semi-transparent, six-legged, as I remember him, and every leg terminated by a single claw hooked like a lion's and as formidable for the size of the creature as that of the royal beast.

Lives on a bumblebee, does he? I said. That's the way I call it. Bumblebee or bumblybee and huckleberry. Humblebee and whortleberry for people that say Woos-ses-ter and Nor-wich.

The Scarabee did not smile; he took no interest in trivial matters like this.

Lives on a bumblebee. When you come to think of it, he must lead a pleasant kind of life. Sails through the air without the trouble of flying. Free pass everywhere that the bee goes. No fear of being dislodged; look at those six grappling-hooks. Helps himself to such juices of the bee as he likes best; the bee feeds on the choicest vegetable nectars, and he feeds on the bee. Lives either in the air or in the perfumed pavilion of the fairest and sweetest flowers. Think what tents the hollyhocks and the great lilies spread for him! And wherever he travels a band of music goes with him, for this hum which wanders by us is doubtless to him a vast and inspiring strain of melody. I thought all this, while the Scarabee supposed I was studying the minute characters of the enigmatical specimen.

I know what I consider your pediculus melittae, I said at length.

Do you think it really the larva of meloe?

Oh, I don't know much about that, but I think he is the best cared for, on the whole, of any animal that I know of; and if I wasn't a man I believe I had rather be that little sybarite than anything that feasts at the board of nature.

The question is, whether he is the larva of meloe, the Scarabee said, as if he had not heard a word of what I had just been saying. If I live a few years longer it shall be settled, sir; and if my epitaph can say honestly that I settled it, I shall be willing to trust my posthumous fame to that achievement.

I said good morning to the specialist, and went off feeling not only kindly, but respectfully towards him. He is an enthusiast, at any rate, as "earnest" a man as any philanthropic reformer who, having passed his life in worrying people out of their misdoings into good behavior, comes at last to a state in which he is never contented except when he is making somebody uncomfortable. He does certainly know one thing well, very likely better than anybody in the world.

I find myself somewhat singularly placed at our table between a minute philosopher who has concentrated all his faculties on a single subject, and my friend who finds the present universe too restricted for his intelligence. I would not give much to hear what the Scarabee says about the old Master, for he does not pretend to form a judgment of anything but beetles, but I should like to hear what the Master has to say about the Scarabee. I waited after breakfast until he had gone, and then asked the Master what he could make of our dried-up friend.

Well, he said, I am hospitable enough in my feelings to him and all his tribe. These specialists are the coral-insects that build up a reef. By and by it will be an island, and for aught we know may grow into a continent. But I don't want to be a coral-insect myself. I had rather be a voyager that visits all the reefs and islands the creatures build, and sails over the seas where they have as yet built up nothing. I am a little afraid that science is breeding us down too fast into coral-insects. A man like Newton or Leibnitz or Haller used to paint a picture of outward or inward nature with a free hand, and stand back and look at it as a whole and feel like an archangel; but nowadays you have a Society, and they come together and make a great mosaic, each man bringing his little bit and sticking it in its place, but so taken up with his petty fragment that he never thinks of looking at the picture the little bits make when they are put together. You can't get any talk out of these specialists away from their own subjects, any more than you can get help from a policeman outside of his own beat.

Yes, said I, but why should n't we always set a man talking about the thing he knows best?

No doubt, no doubt, if you meet him once; but what are you going to do with him if you meet him every day? I travel with a man and we want to make change very often in paying bills. But every time I ask him to change a pistareen, or give me two fo'pencehappennies for a ninepence, or help me to make out two and thrippence (mark the old Master's archaisms about the currency), what does the fellow do but put his hand in his pocket and pull out an old Roman coin; I have no change, says he, but this assarion of Diocletian. Mighty deal of good that'll do me!

It isn't quite so handy as a few specimens of the modern currency would be, but you can pump him on numismatics.

To be sure, to be sure. I've pumped a thousand men of all they could teach me, or at least all I could learn from 'em; and if it comes to that, I never saw the man that couldn't teach me something. I can get along with everybody in his place, though I think the place of some of my friends is over there among the feeble-minded pupils, and I don't believe there's one of them, I couldn't go to school to for half an hour and be the wiser for it. But people you talk with every day have got to have feeders for their minds, as much as the stream that turns a millwheel has. It isn't one little rill that's going to keep the float-boards turning round. Take a dozen of the brightest men you can find in the brightest city, wherever that may be, perhaps you and I think we know, and let 'em come together once a month, and you'll find out in the course of a year or two the ones that have feeders from all the hillsides. Your common talkers, that exchange the gossip of the day, have no wheel in particular to turn, and the wash of the rain as it runs down the street is enough for them.

Do you mean you can always see the sources from which a man fills his mind, his feeders, as you call them?

I don't go quite so far as that, the Master said. I've seen men whose minds were always overflowing, and yet they did n't read much nor go much into the world. Sometimes you'll find a bit of a pond-hole in a pasture, and you'll plunge your walking-stick into it and think you are going to touch bottom. But you find you are mistaken. Some of these little stagnant pond-holes are a good deal deeper than you think; you may tie a stone to a bed-cord and not get soundings in some of 'em. The country boys will tell you they have no bottom, but that only means that they are mighty deep; and so a good many stagnant, stupid-seeming people are a great deal deeper than the length of your intellectual walking-stick, I can tell you. There are hidden springs that keep the little pond-holes full when the mountain brooks are all dried up. You poets ought to know that.

I can't help thinking you are more tolerant towards the specialists than I thought at first, by the way you seemed to look at our dried-up neighbor and his small pursuits.

I don't like the word tolerant, the Master said. As long as the Lord can tolerate me I think I can stand my fellow-creatures. Philosophically, I love 'em all; empirically, I don't think I am very fond of all of 'em. It depends on how you look at a man or a woman. Come here, Youngster, will you? he said to That Boy.

The Boy was trying to catch a blue-bottle to add to his collection, and was indisposed to give up the chase; but he presently saw that the Master had taken out a small coin and laid it on the table, and felt himself drawn in that direction.

Read that, said the Master.

U-n-i-ni United States of America 5 cents.

The Master turned the coin over. Now read that.

In God is our t-r-u-s-t - trust. 1869.

Is that the same piece of money as the other one?

There ain't any other one, said the Boy, there ain't but one, but it's got two sides to it with different reading.

That's it, that's it, said the Master, two sides to everybody, as there are to that piece of money. I've seen an old woman that wouldn't fetch five cents if you should put her up for sale at public auction; and yet come to read the other side of her, she had a trust in God Almighty that was like the bow anchor of a three-decker. It's faith in something and enthusiasm for something that makes a life worth looking at. I don't think your ant-eating specialist, with his sharp nose and pin-head eyes, is the best every-day companion; but any man who knows one thing well is worth listening to for once; and if you are of the large-brained variety of the race, and want to fill out your programme of the Order of Things in a systematic and exhaustive way, and get all the half-notes and flats and sharps of humanity into your scale, you'd a great deal better shut your front door and open your two side ones when you come across a fellow that has made a real business of doing anything.

That Boy stood all this time looking hard at the five-cent piece.

Take it, said the Master, with a good-natured smile.

The Boy made a snatch at it and was off for the purpose of investing it.

A child naturally snaps at a thing as a dog does at his meat, said the Master. If you think of it, we've all been quadrupeds. A child that can only crawl has all the instincts of a four-footed beast. It carries things in its mouth just as cats and dogs do. I've seen the little brutes do it over and over again. I suppose a good many children would stay quadrupeds all their lives, if they didn't learn the trick of walking on their hind legs from seeing all the grown people walking in that way.

Do you accept Mr. Darwin's notions about the origin of the race? said I.

The Master looked at me with that twinkle in his eye which means that he is going to parry a question.

Better stick to Blair's Chronology; that settles it. Adam and Eve, created Friday, October 28th, B. C. 4004. You've been in a ship for a good while, and here comes Mr. Darwin on deck with an armful of sticks and says, "Let's build a raft, and trust ourselves to that."

If your ship springs a leak, what would you do?

He looked me straight in the eyes for about half a minute. If I heard the pumps going, I'd look and see whether they were gaining on the leak or not. If they were gaining I'd stay where I was. Go and find out what's the matter with that young woman.

I had noticed that the Young Girl, the storywriter, our Scheherezade, as I called her, looked as if she had been crying or lying awake half the night. I found on asking her, for she is an honest little body and is disposed to be confidential with me for some reason or other, that she had been doing both.

And what was the matter now, I questioned her in a semi-paternal kind of way, as soon as I got a chance for a few quiet words with her.

She was engaged to write a serial story, it seems, and had only got as far as the second number, and some critic had been jumping upon it, she said, and grinding his heel into it, till she couldn't bear to look at it. He said she did not write half so well as half a dozen other young women. She did n't write half so well as she used to write herself. She hadn't any characters and she had n't any incidents. Then he went to work to show how her story was coming out, trying to anticipate everything she could make of it, so that her readers should have nothing to look forward to, and he should have credit for his sagacity in guessing, which was nothing so very wonderful, she seemed to think. Things she had merely hinted and left the reader to infer, he told right out in the bluntest and coarsest way. It had taken all the life out of her, she said. It was just as if at a dinner-party one of the guests should take a spoonful of soup and get up and say to the company, "Poor stuff, poor stuff; you won't get anything better; let's go somewhere else where things are fit to eat."

What do you read such things for, my dear? said I.

The film glistened in her eyes at the strange sound of those two soft words; she had not heard such very often, I am afraid.

I know I am a foolish creature to read them, she answered, but I can't help it; somebody always sends me everything that will make me wretched to read, and so I sit down and read it, and ache all over for my pains, and lie awake all night.

She smiled faintly as she said this, for she saw the sub-ridiculous side of it, but the film glittered still in her eyes. There are a good many real miseries in life that we cannot help smiling at, but they are the smiles that make wrinkles and not dimples. "Somebody always sends her everything that will make her wretched." Who can those creatures be who cut out the offensive paragraph and send it anonymously to us, who mail the newspaper which has the article we had much better not have seen, who take care that we shall know everything which can, by any possibility, help to make us discontented with ourselves and a little less light-hearted than we were before we had been fools enough to open their incendiary packages? I don't like to say it to myself, but I cannot help suspecting, in this instance, the doubtful-looking personage who sits on my left, beyond the Scarabee. I have some reason to think that he has made advances to the Young Girl which were not favorably received, to state the case in moderate terms, and it may be that he is taking his revenge in cutting up the poor girl's story. I know this very well, that some personal pique or favoritism is at the bottom of half the praise and dispraise which pretend to be so very ingenuous and discriminating. (Of course I have been thinking all this time and telling you what I thought.)

What you want is encouragement, my dear, said I, I know that as well, as you. I don't think the fellows that write such criticisms as you tell me of want to correct your faults. I don't mean to say that you can learn nothing from them, because they are not all fools by any means, and they will often pick out your weak points with a malignant sagacity, as a pettifogging lawyer will frequently find a real flaw in trying to get at everything he can quibble about. But is there nobody who will praise you generously when you do well, nobody that will lend you a hand now while you want it, or must they all wait until you have made yourself a name among strangers, and then all at once find out that you have something in you? Oh, said the girl, and the bright film gathered too fast for her young eyes to hold much longer, I ought not to be ungrateful! I have found the kindest friend in the world. Have you ever heard the Lady, the one that I sit next to at the table, say anything about me?

I have not really made her acquaintance, I said. She seems to me a little distant in her manners and I have respected her pretty evident liking for keeping mostly to herself.

Oh, but when you once do know her! I don't believe I could write stories all the time as I do, if she didn't ask me up to her chamber, and let me read them to her. Do you know, I can make her laugh and cry, reading my poor stories? And sometimes, when I feel as if I had written out all there is in me, and want to lie down and go to sleep and never wake up except in a world where there are no weekly papers, when everything goes wrong, like a car off the track, she takes hold and sets me on the rails again all right.

How does she go to work to help you?

Why, she listens to my stories, to begin with, as if she really liked to hear them. And then you know I am dreadfully troubled now and then with some of my characters, and can't think how to get rid of them. And she'll say, perhaps, Don't shoot your villain this time, you've shot three or four already in the last six weeks; let his mare stumble and throw him and break his neck. Or she'll give me a hint about some new way for my lover to make a declaration. She must have had a good many offers, it's my belief, for she has told me a dozen different ways for me to use in my stories. And whenever I read a story to her, she always laughs and cries in the right places; and that's such a comfort, for there are some people that think everything pitiable is so funny, and will burst out laughing when poor Rip Van Winkle, you've seen Mr. Jefferson, haven't you? is breaking your heart for you if you have one. Sometimes she takes a poem I have written and reads it to me so beautifully, that I fall in love with it, and sometimes she sets my verses to music and sings them to me.

You have a laugh together sometimes, do you?

Indeed we do. I write for what they call the "Comic Department" of the paper now and then. If I did not get so tired of story-telling, I suppose I should be gayer than I am; but as it is, we two get a little fun out of my comic pieces. I begin them half-crying sometimes, but after they are done they amuse me. I don't suppose my comic pieces are very laughable; at any rate the man who makes a business of writing me down says the last one I wrote is very melancholy reading, and that if it was only a little better perhaps some bereaved person might pick out a line or two that would do to put on a gravestone.

Well, that is hard, I must confess. Do let me see those lines which excite such sad emotions.

Will you read them very good-naturedly? If you will, I will get the paper that has "Aunt Tabitha." That is the one the fault-finder said produced such deep depression of feeling. It was written for the "Comic Department." Perhaps it will make you cry, but it was n't meant to.

I will finish my report this time with our Scheherezade's poem, hoping that any critic who deals with it will treat it with the courtesy due to all a young lady's literary efforts.

AUNT TABITHA.

Whatever I do, and whatever I say,
Aunt Tabitha tells me that isn't the way;
When she was a girl (forty summers ago)
Aunt Tabitha tells me they never did so.

Dear aunt! If I only would take her advice!
But I like my own way, and I find it so nice!
And besides, I forget half the things I am told;
But they all will come back to me when I am old.

If a youth passes by, it may happen, no doubt,
He may chance to look in as I chance to look out;
She would never endure an impertinent stare,
It is horrid, she says, and I mustn't sit there.

A walk in the moonlight has pleasures, I own,
But it is n't quite safe to be walking alone;

So I take a lad's arm, just for safety, you know,
But Aunt Tabitha tells me they didn't do so.

How wicked we are, and how good they were then!
They kept at arm's length those detestable men;
What an era of virtue she lived in! But stay
Were the men all such rogues in Aunt Tabitha's day?

If the men were so wicked, I'll ask my papa
How he dared to propose to my darling mamma;
Was he like the rest of them? Goodness! Who knows
And what shall I say if a wretch should propose?

I am thinking if aunt knew so little of sin,
What a wonder Aunt Tabitha's aunt must have been!
And her grand-aunt, it scares me, how shockingly sad.
That we girls of to-day are so frightfully bad!

A martyr will save us, and nothing else can;
Let me perish, to rescue some wretched young man!
Though when to the altar a victim I go,
Aunt Tabitha'll tell me she never did so!

CHAPTER IV

The old Master has developed one quality of late for which I am afraid I hardly gave him credit. He has turned out to be an excellent listener.

I love to talk, he said, as a goose loves to swim. Sometimes I think it is because I am a goose. For I never talked much at any one time in my life without saying something or other I was sorry for.

You too! said I. Now that is very odd, for it is an experience I have habitually. I thought you were rather too much of a philosopher to trouble yourself about such small matters as to whether you had said just what you meant to or not; especially as you know that the person you talk to does not remember a word of what you said the next morning, but is thinking, it is much more likely, of what she said, or how her new dress looked, or some other body's new dress which made hers look as if it had been patched together from the leaves of last November. That's what she's probably thinking about.

She! said the Master, with a look which it would take at least half a page to explain to the entire satisfaction of thoughtful readers of both sexes.

I paid the respect due to that most significant monosyllable, which, as the old Rabbi spoke it, with its targum of tone and expression, was not to be answered flippantly, but soberly, advisedly, and after a pause long enough for it to unfold its meaning in the listener's mind. For there are short single words (all the world remembers Rachel's Helas!) which are like those Japanese toys that look like nothing of any significance as you throw them on the water, but which after a little time open out into various strange and unexpected figures, and then you find that each little shred had a complicated story to tell of itself.

Yes, said I, at the close of this silent interval, during which the monosyllable had been opening out its meanings, She. When I think of talking, it is of course with a woman. For talking at its best being an inspiration, it wants a corresponding divine quality of receptiveness; and where will you find this but in woman?

The Master laughed a pleasant little laugh, not a harsh, sarcastic one, but playful, and tempered by so kind a look that it seemed as if every wrinkled line about his old eyes repeated, "God bless you," as the tracings on the walls of the Alhambra repeat a sentence of the Koran.

I said nothing, but looked the question, What are you laughing at?

Why, I laughed because I couldn't help saying to myself that a woman whose mind was taken up with thinking how she looked, and how her pretty neighbor looked, wouldn't have a great deal of thought to spare for all your fine discourse.

Come, now, said I, a man who contradicts himself in the course of two minutes must have a screw loose in his mental machinery. I never feel afraid that such a thing can happen to me, though it happens often enough when I turn a thought over suddenly, as you did that five-cent piece the other day, that it reads differently on its two sides. What I meant to say is something like this. A woman, notwithstanding she is the best of listeners, knows her business, and it is a woman's business to please. I don't say that it is not her business to vote, but I do say that a woman who does not please is a false note in the harmonies of nature. She may not have youth, or beauty, or even manner; but she must have something in her voice or expression, or both, which it makes you feel better disposed towards your race to look at or listen to. She knows that as well as we do; and her first question after you have been talking your soul into her consciousness is, Did I please? A woman never forgets her sex. She would rather talk with a man than an angel, any day.

This frightful speech of mine reached the ear of our Scheherezade, who said that it was perfectly shocking and that I deserved to be shown up as the outlaw in one of her bandit stories.

Hush, my dear, said the Lady, you will have to bring John Milton into your story with our friend there, if you punish everybody who says naughty things like that. Send the little boy up to my chamber for Paradise Lost, if you please. He will find it lying on my table. The little old volume, he can't mistake it.

So the girl called That Boy round and gave him the message; I don't know why she should give it, but she did, and the Lady helped her out with a word or two.

The little volume, its cover protected with soft white leather from a long kid glove, evidently suggesting the brilliant assemblies of the days when friends and fortune smiled-came presently and the Lady opened it. You may read that, if you like, she said, it may show you that our friend is to be pilloried in good company.

The Young Girl ran her eye along the passage the Lady pointed out, blushed, laughed, and slapped the book down as though she would have liked to box the ears of Mr. John Milton, if he had been a contemporary and fellow-contributor to the "Weekly Bucket." I won't touch the thing, she said. He was a horrid man to talk so: and he had as many wives as Blue-Beard.

Fair play, said the Master. Bring me the book, my little fractional superfluity, I mean you, my nursling, my boy, if that suits your small Highness better.

The Boy brought the book.

The old Master, not unfamiliar with the great epic opened pretty nearly to the place, and very soon found the passage: He read, aloud with grand scholastic intonation and in a deep voice that silenced the table as if a prophet had just uttered Thus saith the Lord:

"So spake our sire, and by his countenance seemed
Entering on studious thoughts abstruse; which Eve
Perceiving"

went to water her geraniums, to make a short story of it, and left the two "conversationists," to wit, the angel Raphael and the gentleman, there was but one gentleman in society then, you know, to talk it out.

"Yet went she not, as not with such discourse
Delighted, or not capable her ear
Of what was high; such pleasure she reserved,
Adam relating, she sole auditress;
Her husband the relater she preferred
Before the angel, and of him to ask
Chose rather; he she knew would intermix
Grateful digressions, and solve high dispute
With conjugal caresses: from his lips
Not words alone pleased her."

Everybody laughed, except the Capitalist, who was a little hard of hearing, and the Scarabee, whose life was too earnest for demonstrations of that kind. He had his eyes fixed on the volume, however, with eager interest.

The p'int 's carried, said the Member of the Haouse.

Will you let me look at that book a single minute? said the Scarabee. I passed it to him, wondering what in the world he wanted of Paradise Lost.

Dermestes lardarius, he said, pointing to a place where the edge of one side of the outer cover had been slightly tasted by some insect. Very fond of leather while they 're in the larva state.

Damage the goods as bad as mice, said the Salesman.

Eat half the binding off Folio 67, said the Register of Deeds. Something did, anyhow, and it was n't mice. Found the shelf covered with little hairy cases belonging to something or other that had no business there.

Skins of the Dermestes lardaraus, said the Scarabee, you can always tell them by those brown hairy coats. That 's the name to give them.

What good does it do to give 'em a name after they've eat the binding off my folios? asked the Register of Deeds.

The Scarabee had too much respect for science to answer such a question as that; and the book, having served its purposes, was passed back to the Lady.

I return to the previous question, said I, if our friend the Member of the House of Representatives will allow me to borrow the phrase. Womanly women are very kindly critics, except to themselves and now and then to their own sex. The less there is of sex about a woman, the more she is to be dreaded. But take a real woman at her best moment, well dressed enough to be pleased with herself, not so resplendent as to be a show and a sensation, with those varied outside influences which set vibrating the harmonic notes of her nature stirring in the air about her, and what has social life to compare with one of those vital interchanges of thought and feeling with her that make an hour memorable? What can equal her tact, her delicacy, her subtlety of apprehension, her quickness to feel the changes of temperature as the warm and cool currents of talk blow by turns? At one moment she is microscopically intellectual, critical, scrupulous in judgment as an analyst's balance, and the next as sympathetic as the open rose that sweetens the wind from whatever quarter it finds its way to her bosom. It is in the hospitable soul of a woman that a man forgets he is a stranger, and so becomes natural and truthful, at the same time that he is mesmerized by all those divine differences which make her a mystery and a bewilderment to

If you fire your popgun at me, you little chimpanzee, I will stick a pin right through the middle of you and put you into one of this gentleman's beetle-cases!

I caught the imp that time, but what started him was more than I could guess. It is rather hard that this spoiled child should spoil such a sentence as that was going to be; but the wind shifted all at once, and the talk had to come round on another tack, or at least fall off a point or two from its course.

I'll tell you who I think are the best talkers in all probability, said I to the Master, who, as I mentioned, was developing interesting talent as a listener, poets who never write verses. And there are a good many more of these than it would seem at first sight. I think you may say every young lover is a poet, to begin with. I don't mean either that all young lovers are good talkers, they have an eloquence all their own when they are with the beloved object, no doubt, emphasized after the fashion the solemn bard of Paradise refers to with such delicious humor in the passage we just heard, but a little talk goes a good way in most of these cooing matches, and it wouldn't do to report them too literally. What I mean is, that a man with the gift of musical and impassioned phrase (and love often deeds that to a young person for a while), who "wreaks" it, to borrow Byron's word, on conversation as the natural outlet of his sensibilities and spiritual activities, is likely to talk better than the poet, who plays on the instrument of verse. A great pianist or violinist is rarely a great singer. To write a poem is to expend the vital force which would have made one brilliant for an hour or two, and to expend it on an instrument with more pipes, reeds, keys, stops, and pedals than the Great Organ that shakes New England every time it is played in full blast.

Do you mean that it is hard work to write a poem? said the old Master. I had an idea that a poem wrote itself, as it were, very often; that it came by influx, without voluntary effort; indeed, you have spoken of it as an inspiration rather than a result of volition.

Did you ever see a great ballet-dancer? I asked him.

I have seen Taglioni, he answered. She used to take her steps rather prettily. I have seen the woman that danced the capstone on to Bunker Hill Monument, as Orpheus moved the rocks by music, the Elssler woman, Fanny Elssler. She would dance you a rigadoon or cut a pigeon's wing for you very respectably.

(Confound this old college book-worm, he has seen everything!)

Well, did these two ladies dance as if it was hard work to them?

Why no, I should say they danced as if they liked it and couldn't help dancing; they looked as if they felt so "corky" it was hard to keep them down.

And yet they had been through such work to get their limbs strong and flexible and obedient, that a cart-horse lives an easy life compared to theirs while they were in training.

The Master cut in just here. I had sprung the trap of a reminiscence.

When I was a boy, he said, some of the mothers in our small town, who meant that their children should know what was what as well as other people's children, laid their heads together and got a dancing-master to come out from the city and give instruction at a few dollars a quarter to the young folks of condition in the village. Some of their husbands were ministers and some were deacons, but the mothers knew what they were about, and they did n't see any reason why ministers' and deacons' wives' children shouldn't have as easy manners as the sons and daughters of Belial. So, as I tell you, they got a dancing-master to come out to our place, a man of good repute, a most respectable man, madam (to the Landlady), you must remember the worthy old citizen, in his advanced age, going about the streets, a most gentlemanly bundle of infirmities, only he always cocked his hat a little too much on one side, as they do here and there along the Connecticut River, and sometimes on our city sidewalks, when they've got a new beaver; they got him, I say, to give us boys and girls lessons in dancing and deportment. He was as gray and as lively as a squirrel, as I remember him, and used to spring up in the air and "cross his feet," as we called it, three times before he came down. Well, at the end of each term there was what they called an "exhibition ball," in which the scholars danced cotillons and country-dances; also something called a "gavotte," and I think one or more walked a minuet. But all this is not what I wanted to say. At this exhibition ball he used to bring out a number of hoops wreathed with roses, of the perennial kind, by the aid of which a number of amazingly complicated and startling evolutions were exhibited; and also his two daughters, who figured largely in these evolutions, and whose wonderful performances to us, who had not seen Miss Taglioni or Miss Elssler, were something quite bewildering, in fact, surpassing the natural possibilities of human beings. Their extraordinary powers were, however, accounted for by the following explanation, which was accepted in the school as entirely satisfactory. A certain little bone in the ankles of each of these young girls had been broken intentionally, secundum artem, at a very early age, and thus they had been fitted to accomplish these surprising feats which threw the achievements of the children who were left in the condition of the natural man into ignominious shadow.

Thank you, said I, you have helped out my illustration so as to make it better than I expected. Let me begin again. Every poem that is worthy of the name, no matter how easily it seems to be written, represents a great amount of vital force expended at some time or other. When you find a beach strewed with the shells and other spoils that belonged once to the deep sea, you know the tide has been there, and that the winds and waves have wrestled over its naked sands. And so, if I find a poem stranded in my soul and have nothing to do but seize it as a wrecker carries off the treasure he finds cast ashore, I know I have paid at some time for that poem with some inward commotion, were it only an excess of enjoyment, which has used up just so much of my vital capital. But besides all the impressions that furnished the stuff of the poem, there has been hard work to get the management of that wonderful instrument I spoke of, the great organ, language. An artist who works in marble or colors has them all to himself and his tribe, but the man who moulds his thought in verse has to employ the materials vulgarized by everybody's use, and glorify them by his handling. I don't know that you must break any bones in a poet's mechanism before his thought can dance in rhythm, but read your Milton and see what training, what patient labor, it took before he could shape our common speech into his majestic harmonies.

It is rather singular, but the same kind of thing has happened to me not very rarely before, as I suppose it has to most persons, that just when I happened to be thinking about poets and their conditions, this very morning, I saw a paragraph or two from a foreign paper which is apt to be sharp, if not cynical, relating to the same matter. I can't help it; I want to have my talk about it, and if I say the same things that writer did, somebody else can have the satisfaction of saying I stole them all.

[I thought the person whom I have called hypothetically the Man of Letters changed color a little and betrayed a certain awkward consciousness that some of us were looking at him or thinking of him; but I am a little suspicious about him and may do him wrong.]

That poets are treated as privileged persons by their admirers and the educated public can hardly be disputed. That they consider themselves so there is no doubt whatever. On the whole, I do not know so easy a way of shirking all the civic and social and domestic duties, as to settle it in one's mind that one is a poet. I have, therefore, taken great pains to advise other persons laboring under the impression that they were gifted beings, destined to soar in the atmosphere of song above the vulgar realities of earth, not to neglect any homely duty under the influence of that impression. The number of these persons is so great that if they were suffered to indulge their prejudice against every-day duties and labors, it would be a serious loss to the productive industry of the country. My skirts are clear (so far as other people are concerned) of countenancing that form of intellectual opium-eating in which rhyme takes the place of the narcotic. But what are you going to do when you find John Keats an apprentice to a surgeon or apothecary? Is n't it rather better to get another boy to sweep out the shop and shake out the powders and stir up the mixtures, and leave him undisturbed to write his Ode on a Grecian Urn or to a Nightingale? Oh yes, the critic I have referred to would say, if he is John Keats; but not if he is of a much lower grade, even though he be genuine, what there is of him. But the trouble is, the sensitive persons who belong to the lower grades of the poetical hierarchy do not know their own poetical limitations, while they do feel a natural unfitness and disinclination for many pursuits which young persons of the average balance of faculties take to pleasantly enough. What is forgotten is this, that every real poet, even of the humblest grade, is an artist. Now I venture to say that any painter or sculptor of real genius, though he may do nothing more than paint flowers and fruit, or carve cameos, is considered a privileged person. It is recognized perfectly that to get his best work he must be insured the freedom from disturbances which the creative power absolutely demands, more absolutely perhaps in these slighter artists than in the great masters. His nerves must be steady for him to finish a rose-leaf or the fold of a nymph's drapery in his best manner; and they will be unsteadied if he has to perform the honest drudgery which another can do for him quite as well. And it is just so with the poet, though he were only finishing an epigram; you must no more meddle roughly with him than you would shake a bottle of Chambertin and expect the "sunset glow" to redden your glass unclouded. On the other hand, it may be said that poetry is not an article of prime necessity, and potatoes are. There is a disposition in many persons just now to deny the poet his benefit of clergy, and to hold him no better than other people. Perhaps he is not, perhaps he is not so good, half the time; but he is a luxury, and if you want him you must pay for him, by not trying to make a drudge of him while he is all his lifetime struggling with the chills and heats of his artistic intermittent fever.

There may have been some lesser interruptions during the talk I have reported as if it was a set speech, but this was the drift of what I said and should have said if the other man, in the Review I referred to, had not seen fit to meddle with the subject, as some fellow always does, just about the time when I am going to say something about it. The old Master listened beautifully, except for cutting in once, as I told you he did. But now he had held in as long as it was in his nature to contain himself, and must have his say or go off in an apoplexy, or explode in some way. I think you're right about the poets, he said. They are to common folks what repeaters are to ordinary watches. They carry music in their inside arrangements, but they want to be handled carefully or you put them out of order. And perhaps you must n't expect them to be quite as good timekeepers as the professional chronometer watches that make a specialty of being exact within a few seconds a month. They think too much of themselves. So does everybody that considers himself as having a right to fall back on what he calls his idiosyncrasy. Yet a man has such a right, and it is no easy thing to adjust the private claim to the fair public demand on him. Suppose you are subject to tic douloureux, for instance. Every now and then a tiger that nobody can see catches one side of your face between his jaws and holds on till he is tired and lets go. Some concession must be made to you on that score, as everybody can see. It is fair to give you a seat that is not in the draught, and your friends ought not to find fault with you if you do not care to join a party that is going on a sleigh-ride. Now take a poet like Cowper. He had a mental neuralgia, a great deal worse in many respects than tic douloureux confined to the face. It was well that he was sheltered and relieved, by the cares of kind friends, especially those good women, from as many of the burdens of life as they could lift off from him. I am fair to the poets, don't you agree that I am?

Why, yes, I said, you have stated the case fairly enough, a good deal as I should have put it myself.

Now, then, the Master continued, I'll tell you what is necessary to all these artistic idiosyncrasies to bring them into good square human relations outside of the special province where their ways differ from those of other people. I am going to illustrate what I mean by a comparison. I don't know, by the way, but you would be disposed to think and perhaps call me a wine-bibber on the strength of the freedom with which I deal with that fluid for the purposes of illustration. But I make mighty little use of it, except as it furnishes me an image now and then, as it did, for that matter, to the Disciples and their Master. In my younger days they used to bring up the famous old wines, the White-top, the Juno, the Eclipse, the Essex Junior, and the rest, in their old cobwebbed, dusty bottles. The resurrection of one of these old sepulchred dignitaries had something of solemnity about it; it was like the disinterment of a king; the bringing to light of the Royal Martyr King Charles I., for instance, that Sir Henry Halford gave such an interesting account of. And the bottle seemed to inspire a personal respect; it was wrapped in a napkin and borne tenderly and reverently round to the guests, and sometimes a dead silence went before the first gush of its amber flood, and

"The boldest held his breath
For a time."

But nowadays the precious juice of a long-dead vintage is transferred carefully into a cut-glass decanter, and stands side by side with the sherry from a corner grocery, which looks just as bright and apparently thinks just as well of itself. The old historic Madeiras, which have warmed the periods of our famous rhetoricians of the past and burned in the impassioned eloquence of our earlier political demigods, have nothing to mark them externally but a bit of thread, it may be, round the neck of the decanter, or a slip of ribbon, pink on one of them and blue on another.

Go to a London club, perhaps I might find something nearer home that would serve my turn, but go to a London club, and there you will see the celebrities all looking alike modern, all decanted off from their historic antecedents and their costume of circumstance into the every-day aspect of the gentleman of common cultivated society. That is Sir Coeur de Lion Plantagenet in the mutton-chop whiskers and the plain gray suit; there is the Laureate in a frockcoat like your own, and the leader of the House of Commons in a necktie you do not envy. That is the kind of thing you want to take the nonsense out of you. If you are not decanted off from yourself every few days or weeks, you will think it sacrilege to brush a cobweb from your cork by and by. O little fool, that has published a little book full of little poems or other sputtering tokens of an uneasy condition, how I love you for the one soft nerve of special sensibility that runs through your exiguous organism, and the one phosphorescent particle in your unilluminated intelligence! But if you don't leave your spun-sugar confectionery business once in a while, and come out among lusty men, the bristly, pachydermatous fellows that hew out the highways for the material progress of society, and the broad-shouldered, out-of-door men that fight for the great prizes of life, you will come to think that the spun-sugar business is the chief end of man, and begin to feel and look as if you believed yourself as much above common people as that personage of whom Tourgueneff says that "he had the air of his own statue erected by national subscription."

The Master paused and fell into a deep thinking fit, as he does sometimes. He had had his own say, it is true, but he had established his character as a listener to my own perfect satisfaction, for I, too, was conscious of having preached with a certain prolixity.

I am always troubled when I think of my very limited mathematical capacities. It seems as if every well-organized mind should be able to handle numbers and quantities through their symbols to an indefinite extent; and yet, I am puzzled by what seems to a clever boy with a turn for calculation as plain as counting his fingers. I don't think any man feels well grounded in knowledge unless he has a good basis of mathematical certainties, and knows how to deal with them and apply them to every branch of knowledge where they can come in to advantage.

Our Young Astronomer is known for his mathematical ability, and I asked him what he thought was the difficulty in the minds that are weak in that particular direction, while they may be of remarkable force in other provinces of thought, as is notoriously the case with some men of great distinction in science.

The young man smiled and wrote a few letters and symbols on a piece of paper. Can you see through that at once? he said.

I puzzled over it for some minutes and gave it up.

He said, as I returned it to him, You have heard military men say that such a person had an eye for country, have n't you? One man will note all the landmarks, keep the points of compass in his head, observe how the streams run, in short, carry a map in his brain of any region that he has marched or galloped through. Another man takes no note of any of these things; always follows somebody else's lead when he can, and gets lost if he is left to himself; a mere owl in daylight. Just so some men have an eye for an equation, and would read at sight the one that puzzled you over. It is told of Sir Isaac Newton that he required no demonstration of the propositions in Euclid's Geometry, but as soon as he had read the enunciation the solution or answer was plain at once. The power may be cultivated, but I think it is to a great degree a natural gift, as is the eye for color, as is the ear for music.

I think I could read equations readily enough, I said, if I could only keep my attention fixed on them; and I think I could keep my attention on them if I were imprisoned in a thinking-cell, such as the Creative Intelligence shapes for its studio when at its divinest work.

The young man's lustrous eyes opened very widely as he asked me to explain what I meant.

What is the Creator's divinest work? I asked.

Is there anything more divine than the sun; than a sun with its planets revolving about it, warming them, lighting them, and giving conscious life to the beings that move on them?

You agree, then, that conscious life is the grand aim and end of all this vast mechanism. Without life that could feel and enjoy, the splendors and creative energy would all be thrown away. You know Harvey's saying, omnia animalia ex ovo, all animals come from an egg. You ought to know it, for the great controversy going on about spontaneous generation has brought it into special prominence lately. Well, then, the ovum, the egg, is, to speak in human phrase, the Creator's more private and sacred studio, for his magnum opus. Now, look at a hen's egg, which is a convenient one to study, because it is large enough and built solidly enough to look at and handle easily. That would be the form I would choose for my thinking-cell. Build me an oval with smooth, translucent walls, and put me in the centre of it with Newton's "Principia" or Kant's "Kritik," and I think I shall develop "an eye for an equation," as you call it, and a capacity for an abstraction.

But do tell me, said the Astronomer, a little incredulously, what there is in that particular form which is going to help you to be a mathematician or a metaphysician?

It is n't help I want, it is removing hindrances. I don't want to see anything to draw off my attention. I don't want a cornice, or an angle, or anything but a containing curve. I want diffused light and no single luminous centre to fix my eye, and so distract my mind from its one object of contemplation. The metaphysics of attention have hardly been sounded to their depths. The mere fixing the look on any single object for a long time may produce very strange effects. Gibbon's well-known story of the monks of Mount Athos and their contemplative practice is often laughed over, but it has a meaning. They were to shut the door of the cell, recline the beard and chin on the breast, and contemplate the abdominal centre.

"At first all will be dark and comfortless; but if you persevere day and night, you will feel an ineffable joy; and no sooner has the soul discovered the place of the heart, than it is involved in a mystic and ethereal light." And Mr. Braid produces absolute anaesthesia, so that surgical operations can be performed without suffering to the patient, only by making him fix his eyes and his mind on a single object; and Newton is said to have said, as you remember, "I keep the subject constantly before me, and wait till the first dawnings open slowly by little and little into a full and clear light." These are different, but certainly very wonderful, instances of what can be done by attention. But now suppose that your mind is in its nature discursive, erratic, subject to electric attractions and repulsions, volage; it may be impossible for you to compel your attention except by taking away all external disturbances. I think the poets have an advantage and a disadvantage as compared with the steadier-going people. Life is so vivid to the poet, that he is too eager to seize and exhaust its multitudinous impressions. Like Sindbad in the valley of precious stones, he wants to fill his pockets with diamonds, but, lo! there is a great ruby like a setting sun in its glory, and a sapphire that, like Bryant's blue gentian, seems to have dropped from the cerulean walls of heaven, and a nest of pearls that look as if they might be unhatched angel's eggs, and so he hardly knows what to seize, and tries for too many, and comes out of the enchanted valley with more gems than he can carry, and those that he lets fall by the wayside we call his poems. You may change the image a thousand ways to show you how hard it is to make a mathematician or a logician out of a poet. He carries the tropics with him wherever he goes; he is in the true sense felius naturae, and Nature tempts him, as she tempts a child walking through a garden where all the finest fruits are hanging over him and dropping round him, where

The luscious clusters of the vine
Upon (his) mouth do crush their wine,
The nectarine and curious peach,
Into (his) hands themselves do reach;

and he takes a bite out of the sunny side of this and the other, and, ever stimulated and never satisfied, is hurried through the garden, and, before he knows it, finds himself at an iron gate which opens outward, and leaves the place he knows and loves

For one he will perhaps soon learn to love and know better, said the Master. But I can help you out with another comparison, not quite so poetical as yours. Why did not you think of a railway-station, where the cars stop five minutes for refreshments? Is n't that a picture of the poet's hungry and hurried feast at the banquet of life? The traveller flings himself on the bewildering miscellany of delicacies spread before him, the various tempting forms of ambrosia and seducing draughts of nectar, with the same eager hurry and restless ardor that you describe in the poet. Dear me! If it wasn't for All aboard! that summons of the deaf conductor which tears one away from his half-finished sponge-cake and coffee, how I, who do not call myself a poet, but only a questioner, should have enjoyed a good long stop, say a couple of thousand years, at this way-station on the great railroad leading to the unknown terminus!

You say you are not a poet, I said, after a little pause, in which I suppose both of us were thinking where the great railroad would land us after carrying us into the dark tunnel, the farther end of which no man has seen and taken a return train to bring us news about it, you say you are not a poet, and yet it seems to me you have some of the elements which go to make one.

I don't think you mean to flatter me, the Master answered, and, what is more, for I am not afraid to be honest with you, I don't think you do flatter me. I have taken the inventory of my faculties as calmly as if I were an appraiser. I have some of the qualities, perhaps I may say many of the qualities, that make a man a poet, and yet I am not one. And in the course of a pretty wide experience of men and women (the Master sighed, I thought, but perhaps I was mistaken) I have met a good many poets who were not rhymesters and a good many rhymesters who were not poets. So I am only one of the Voiceless, that I remember one of you singers had some verses about. I think there is a little music in me, but it has not found a voice, and it never will. If I should confess the truth, there is no mere earthly immortality that I envy so much as the poet's. If your name is to live at all, it is so much more to have it live in people's hearts than only in their brains! I don't know that one's eyes fill with tears when he thinks of the famous inventor of logarithms, but song of Burns's or a hymn of Charles Wesley's goes straight to your heart, and you can't help loving both of them, the sinner as well as the saint. The works of other men live, but their personality dies out of their labors; the poet, who reproduces himself in his creation, as no other artist does or can, goes down to posterity with all his personality blended with whatever is imperishable in his song. We see nothing of the bees that built the honeycomb and stored it with its sweets, but we can trace the veining in the wings of insects that flitted through the forests which are now coal-beds, kept unchanging in the amber that holds them; and so the passion of Sappho, the tenderness of Simonides, the purity of holy George Herbert, the lofty contemplativeness of James Shirley, are before us to-day as if they were living, in a few tears of amber verse. It seems, when one reads,

"Sweet day! so cool, so calm, so bright,"

or,

"The glories of our birth and state,"

as if it were not a very difficult matter to gain immortality, such an immortality at least as a perishable language can give. A single lyric is enough, if one can only find in his soul and finish in his intellect one of those jewels fit to sparkle "on the stretched forefinger of all time." A coin, a ring, a string of verses. These last, and hardly anything else does. Every century is an overloaded ship that must sink at last with most of its cargo. The small portion of its crew that get on board the new vessel which takes them off don't pretend to save a great many of the bulky articles. But they must not and will not leave behind the hereditary jewels of the race; and if you have found and cut a diamond, were it only a spark with a single polished facet, it will stand a better chance of being saved from the wreck than anything, no matter what, that wants much room for stowage.

The pyramids last, it is true, but most of them have forgotten their builders' names. But the ring of Thothmes III., who reigned some fourteen hundred years before our era, before Homer sang, before the Argonauts sailed, before Troy was built, is in the possession of Lord Ashburnham, and proclaims the name of the monarch who wore it more than three thousand years ago. The gold coins with the head of Alexander the Great are some of them so fresh one might think they were newer than much of the silver currency we were lately handling. As we have been quoting from the poets this morning, I will follow the precedent, and give some lines from an epistle of Pope to Addison after the latter had written, but not yet published, his Dialogue on Medals. Some of these lines have been lingering in my memory for a great many years, but I looked at the original the other day and was so pleased with them that I got them by heart. I think you will say they are singularly pointed and elegant.

"Ambition sighed; she found it vain to trust
The faithless column and the crumbling bust;
Huge moles, whose shadows stretched from shore to shore,
Their ruins perished, and their place no more!
Convinced, she now contracts her vast design,
And all her triumphs shrink into a coin.
A narrow orb each crowded conquest keeps,
Beneath her palm here sad Judaea weeps;
Now scantier limits the proud arch confine,
And scarce are seen the prostrate Nile or Rhine;
A small Euphrates through the piece is rolled,
And little eagles wave their wings in gold."

It is the same thing in literature. Write half a dozen folios full of other people's ideas (as all folios are pretty sure to be), and you serve as ballast to the lower shelves of a library, about as like to be disturbed as the kentledge in the hold of a ship. Write a story, or a dozen stories, and your book will be in demand like an oyster while it is freshly opened, and after that the highways of literature are spread over with the shells of dead novels, each of which has been swallowed at a mouthful by the public, and is done with. But write a volume of poems. No matter if they are all bad but one, if that one is very good. It will carry your name down to posterity like the ring of Thothmes, like the coin of Alexander. I don't suppose one would care a great deal about it a hundred or a thousand years after he is dead, but I don't feel quite sure. It seems as if, even in heaven, King David might remember "The Lord is my Shepherd" with a certain twinge of earthly pleasure. But we don't know, we don't know.

What in the world can have become of That Boy and his popgun while all this somewhat extended sermonizing was going on? I don't wonder you ask, beloved Reader, and I suppose I must tell you how we got on so long without interruption. Well, the plain truth is, the youngster was contemplating his gastric centre, like the monks of Mount Athos, but in a less happy state of mind than those tranquil recluses, in consequence of indulgence in the heterogeneous assortment of luxuries procured with the five-cent piece given him by the kind-hearted old Master. But you need not think I am going to tell you every time his popgun goes off, making a Selah of him whenever I want to change the subject. Occasionally he was ill-timed in his artillery practice and ignominiously rebuked, sometimes he was harmlessly playful and nobody minded him, but every now and then he came in so apropos that I am morally certain he gets a hint from somebody who watches the course of the conversation, and means through him to have a hand in it and stop any of us when we are getting prosy. But in consequence of That Boy's indiscretion, we were without a check upon our expansiveness, and ran on in the way you have observed and may be disposed to find fault with.

One other thing the Master said before we left the table, after our long talk of that day.

I have been tempted sometimes, said he, to envy the immediate triumphs of the singer. He enjoys all that praise can do for him and at the very moment of exerting his talent. And the singing women! Once in a while, in the course of my life, I have found myself in the midst of a tulip-bed of full-dressed, handsome women in all their glory, and when some one among them has shaken her gauzy wings, and sat down before the piano, and then, only giving the keys a soft touch now and then to support her voice, has warbled some sweet, sad melody intertwined with the longings or regrets of some tender-hearted poet, it has seemed to me that so to hush the rustling of the silks and silence the babble of the buds, as they call the chicks of a new season, and light up the flame of romance in cold hearts, in desolate ones, in old burnt-out ones, like mine, I was going to say, but I won't, for it isn't so, and you may laugh to hear me say it isn't so, if you like, was perhaps better than to be remembered a few hundred years by a few perfect stanzas, when your gravestone is standing aslant, and your name is covered over with a lichen as big as a militia colonel's cockade, and nobody knows or cares enough about you to scrape it off and set the tipsy old slate-stone upright again.

I said nothing in reply to this, for I was thinking of a sweet singer to whose voice I had listened in its first freshness, and which is now only an echo in my memory. If any reader of the periodical in which these conversations are recorded can remember so far back as the first year of its publication, he will find among the papers contributed by a friend not yet wholly forgotten a few verses, lively enough in their way, headed "The Boys." The sweet singer was one of this company of college classmates, the constancy of whose friendship deserves a better tribute than the annual offerings, kindly meant, as they are, which for many years have not been wanting at their social gatherings. The small company counts many noted personages on its list, as is well known to those who are interested in such local matters, but it is not known that every fifth man of the whole number now living is more or less of a poet, using that word with a generous breadth of significance. But it should seem that the divine gift it implies is more freely dispensed than some others, for while there are (or were, for one has taken his Last Degree) eight musical quills, there was but one pair of lips which could claim any special consecration to vocal melody. Not that one that should undervalue the half-recitative of doubtful barytones, or the brilliant escapades of slightly unmanageable falsettos, or the concentrated efforts of the proprietors of two or three effective notes, who may be observed lying in wait for them, and coming down on them with all their might, and the look on their countenances of "I too am a singer." But the voice that led all, and that all loved to listen to, the voice that was at once full, rich, sweet, penetrating, expressive, whose ample overflow drowned all the imperfections and made up for all the shortcomings of the others, is silent henceforth forevermore for all earthly listeners.

And these were the lines that one of "The Boys," as they have always called themselves for ever so many years, read at the first meeting after the voice which had never failed them was hushed in the stillness of death.

J. A.

1871.

One memory trembles on our lips
It throbs in every breast;
In tear-dimmed eyes, in mirth's eclipse,
The shadow stands confessed.

O silent voice, that cheered so long
Our manhood's marching day,
Without thy breath of heavenly song,
How weary seems the way!

Vain every pictured phrase to tell
Our sorrowing hearts' desire;
The shattered harp, the broken shell,
The silent unstrung lyre;

For youth was round us while he sang;
It glowed in every tone;
With bridal chimes the echoes rang,
And made the past our own.

O blissful dream! Our nursery joys
We know must have an end,
But love and friendships broken toys
May God's good angels mend!

The cheering smile, the voice of mirth
And laughter's gay surprise
That please the children born of earth,
Why deem that Heaven denies?

Methinks in that refulgent sphere
That knows not sun or moon,
An earth-born saint might long to hear
One verse of "Bonny Doon";

Or walking through the streets of gold
In Heaven's unclouded light,
His lips recall the song of old
And hum "The sky is bright."

And can we smile when thou art dead?
Ah, brothers, even so!
The rose of summer will be red,
In spite of winter's snow.

Thou wouldst not leave us all in gloom
Because thy song is still,
Nor blight the banquet-garland's bloom
With grief's untimely chill.

The sighing wintry winds complain,
The singing bird has flown,
Hark! heard I not that ringing strain,
That clear celestial tone?

How poor these pallid phrases seem,
How weak this tinkling line,
As warbles through my waking dream
That angel voice of thine!

Thy requiem asks a sweeter lay;
It falters on my tongue;
For all we vainly strive to say,
Thou shouldst thyself have sung!

CHAPTER V

I fear that I have done injustice in my conversation and my report of it to a most worthy and promising young man whom I should be very sorry to injure in any way. Dr. Benjamin Franklin got hold of my account of my visit to him, and complained that I had made too much of the expression he used. He did not mean to say that he thought I was suffering from the rare disease he mentioned, but only that the color reminded him of it. It was true that he had shown me various instruments, among them one for exploring the state of a part by means of a puncture, but he did not propose to make use of it upon my person. In short, I had colored the story so as to make him look ridiculous.

I am afraid I did, I said, but was n't I colored myself so as to look ridiculous? I've heard it said that people with the jaundice see everything yellow; perhaps I saw things looking a little queerly, with that black and blue spot I could n't account for threatening to make a colored man and brother of me. But I am sorry if I have done you any wrong. I hope you won't lose any patients by my making a little fun of your meters and scopes and contrivances. They seem so odd to us outside people. Then the idea of being bronzed all over was such an alarming suggestion. But I did not mean to damage your business, which I trust is now considerable, and I shall certainly come to you again if I have need of the services of a physician. Only don't mention the names of any diseases in English or Latin before me next time. I dreamed about cutis oenea half the night after I came to see you.

Dr. Benjamin took my apology very pleasantly. He did not want to be touchy about it, he said, but he had his way to make in the world, and found it a little hard at first, as most young men did. People were afraid to trust them, no matter how much they knew. One of the old doctors asked him to come in and examine a patient's heart for him the other day. He went with him accordingly, and when they stood by the bedside, he offered his stethoscope to the old doctor. The old doctor took it and put the wrong end to his ear and the other to the patient's chest, and kept it there about two minutes, looking all the time as wise as an old owl. Then he, Dr. Benjamin, took it and applied it properly, and made out where the trouble was in no time at all. But what was the use of a young man's pretending to know anything in the presence of an old owl? I saw by their looks, he said, that they all thought I used the stethoscope wrong end up, and was nothing but a 'prentice hand to the old doctor.

I am much pleased to say that since Dr. Benjamin has had charge of a dispensary district, and been visiting forty or fifty patients a day, I have reason to think he has grown a great deal more practical than when I made my visit to his office. I think I was probably one of his first patients, and that he naturally made the most of me. But my second trial was much more satisfactory. I got an ugly cut from the carving-knife in an affair with a goose of iron constitution in which I came off second best. I at once adjourned with Dr. Benjamin to his small office, and put myself in his hands. It was astonishing to see what a little experience of miscellaneous practice had done for him. He did not ask me anymore questions about my hereditary predispositions on the paternal and maternal sides. He did not examine me with the stethoscope or the laryngoscope. He only strapped up my cut, and informed me that it would speedily get well by the "first intention," an odd phrase enough, but sounding much less formidable than cutis oenea.

I am afraid I have had something of the French prejudice which embodies itself in the maxim "young surgeon, old physician." But a young physician who has been taught by great masters of the profession, in ample hospitals, starts in his profession knowing more than some old doctors have learned in a lifetime. Give him a little time to get the use of his wits in emergencies, and to know the little arts that do so much for a patient's comfort, just as you give a young sailor time to get his sea-legs on and teach his stomach to behave itself, and he will do well enough.

The old Master knows ten times more about this matter and about all the professions, as he does about everything else, than I do. My opinion is that he has studied two, if not three, of these professions in a regular course. I don't know that he has ever preached, except as Charles Lamb said Coleridge always did, for when he gets the bit in his teeth he runs away with the conversation, and if he only took a text his talk would be a sermon; but if he has not preached, he has made a study of theology, as many laymen do. I know he has some shelves of medical books in his library, and has ideas on the subject of the healing art. He confesses to having attended law lectures and having had much intercourse with lawyers. So he has something to say on almost any subject that happens to come up. I told him my story about my visit to the young doctor, and asked him what he thought of youthful practitioners in general and of Dr. Benjamin in particular.

I 'll tell you what, the Master said, I know something about these young fellows that come home with their heads full of "science," as they call it, and stick up their signs to tell people they know how to cure their headaches and stomach-aches. Science is a first-rate piece of furniture for a man's upper chamber, if he has common sense on the ground-floor. But if a man has n't got plenty of good common sense, the more science he has the worse for his patient.

I don't know that I see exactly how it is worse for the patient, I said.

Well, I'll tell you, and you'll find it's a mighty simple matter. When a person is sick, there is always something to be done for him, and done at once. If it is only to open or shut a window, if it is only to tell him to keep on doing just what he is doing already, it wants a man to bring his mind right down to the fact of the present case and its immediate needs. Now the present case, as the doctor sees it, is just exactly such a collection of paltry individual facts as never was before, a snarl and tangle of special conditions which it is his business to wind as much thread out of as he can. It is a good deal as when a painter goes to take the portrait of any sitter who happens to send for him. He has seen just such noses and just such eyes and just such mouths, but he never saw exactly such a face before, and his business is with that and no other person's, with the features of the worthy father of a family before him, and not with the portraits he has seen in galleries or books, or Mr. Copley's grand pictures of the fine old Tories, or the Apollos and Jupiters of Greek sculpture. It is the same thing with the patient. His disease has features of its own; there never was and never will be another case in all respects exactly like it. If a doctor has science without common sense, he treats a fever, but not this man's fever. If he has common sense without science, he treats this man's fever without knowing the general laws that govern all fevers and all vital movements. I 'll tell you what saves these last fellows. They go for weakness whenever they see it, with stimulants and strengtheners, and they go for overaction, heat, and high pulse, and the rest, with cooling and reducing remedies. That is three quarters of medical practice. The other quarter wants science and common sense too. But the men that have science only, begin too far back, and, before they get as far as the case in hand, the patient has very likely gone to visit his deceased relatives. You remember Thomas Prince's "Chronological History of New England," I suppose? He begins, you recollect, with Adam, and has to work down five thousand six hundred and twenty-four years before he gets to the Pilgrim fathers and the Mayflower. It was all very well, only it did n't belong there, but got in the way of something else. So it is with "science" out of place. By far the larger part of the facts of structure and function you find in the books of anatomy and physiology have no immediate application to the daily duties of the practitioner. You must learn systematically, for all that; it is the easiest way and the only way that takes hold of the memory, except mere empirical repetition, like that of the handicraftsman. Did you ever see one of those Japanese figures with the points for acupuncture marked upon it?

I had to own that my schooling had left out that piece of information.

Well, I 'll tell you about it. You see they have a way of pushing long, slender needles into you for the cure of rheumatism and other complaints, and it seems there is a choice of spots for the operation, though it is very strange how little mischief it does in a good many places one would think unsafe to meddle with. So they had a doll made, and marked the spots where they had put in needles without doing any harm. They must have had accidents from sticking the needles into the wrong places now and then, but I suppose they did n't say a great deal about those. After a time, say a few centuries of experience, they had their doll all spotted over with safe places for sticking in the needles. That is their way of registering practical knowledge: We, on the other hand, study the structure of the body as a whole, systematically, and have no difficulty at all in remembering the track of the great vessels and nerves, and knowing just what tracks will be safe and what unsafe. It is just the same thing with the geologists. Here is a man close by us boring for water through one of our ledges, because somebody else got water somewhere else in that way; and a person who knows geology or ought to know it, because he has given his life to it, tells me he might as well bore there for lager-beer as for water.

I thought we had had enough of this particular matter, and that I should like to hear what the Master had to say about the three professions he knew something about, each compared with the others.

What is your general estimate of doctors, lawyers, and ministers? said I.

Wait a minute, till I have got through with your first question, said the Master. One thing at a time. You asked me about the young doctors, and about our young doctor. They come home tres biens chausses, as a Frenchman would say, mighty well shod with professional knowledge. But when they begin walking round among their poor patients, they don't commonly start with millionaires, they find that their new shoes of scientific acquirements have got to be broken in just like a pair of boots or brogans. I don't know that I have put it quite strong enough. Let me try again. You've seen those fellows at the circus that get up on horseback so big that you wonder how they could climb into the saddle. But pretty soon they throw off their outside coat, and the next minute another one, and then the one under that, and so they keep peeling off one garment after another till people begin to look queer and think they are going too far for strict propriety. Well, that is the way a fellow with a real practical turn serves a good many of his scientific wrappers, flings 'em off for other people to pick up, and goes right at the work of curing stomach-aches and all the other little mean unscientific complaints that make up the larger part of every doctor's business. I think our Dr. Benjamin is a worthy young man, and if you are in need of a doctor at any time I hope you will go to him; and if you come off without harm, I will recommend some other friend to try him.

I thought he was going to say he would try him in his own person, but the Master is not fond of committing himself.

Now, I will answer your other question, he said. The lawyers are the cleverest men, the ministers are the most learned, and the doctors are the most sensible.

The lawyers are a picked lot, "first scholars" and the like, but their business is as unsympathetic as Jack Ketch's. There is nothing humanizing in their relations with their fellow-creatures. They go for the side that retains them. They defend the man they know to be a rogue, and not very rarely throw suspicion on the man they know to be innocent. Mind you, I am not finding fault with them; every side of a case has a right to the best statement it admits of; but I say it does not tend to make them sympathetic. Suppose in a case of Fever vs. Patient, the doctor should side with either party according to whether the old miser or his expectant heir was his employer. Suppose the minister should side with the Lord or the Devil, according to the salary offered and other incidental advantages, where the soul of a sinner was in question. You can see what a piece of work it would make of their sympathies. But the lawyers are quicker witted than either of the other professions, and abler men generally. They are good-natured, or, if they quarrel, their quarrels are above-board. I don't think they are as accomplished as the ministers, but they have a way of cramming with special knowledge for a case which leaves a certain shallow sediment of intelligence in their memories about a good many things. They are apt to talk law in mixed company, and they have a way of looking round when they make a point, as if they were addressing a jury, that is mighty aggravating, as I once had occasion to see when one of 'em, and a pretty famous one, put me on the witness-stand at a dinner-party once.

The ministers come next in point of talent. They are far more curious and widely interested outside of their own calling than either of the other professions. I like to talk with 'em. They are interesting men, full of good feelings, hard workers, always foremost in good deeds, and on the whole the most efficient civilizing class, working downwards from knowledge to ignorance, that is, not so much upwards, perhaps, that we have. The trouble is, that so many of 'em work in harness, and it is pretty sure to chafe somewhere. They feed us on canned meats mostly. They cripple our instincts and reason, and give us a crutch of doctrine. I have talked with a great many of 'em of all sorts of belief, and I don't think they are quite so easy in their minds, the greater number of them; nor so clear in their convictions, as one would think to hear 'em lay down the law in the pulpit. They used to lead the intelligence of their parishes; now they do pretty well if they keep up with it, and they are very apt to lag behind it. Then they must have a colleague. The old minister thinks he can hold to his old course, sailing right into the wind's eye of human nature, as straight as that famous old skipper John Bunyan; the young minister falls off three or four points and catches the breeze that left the old man's sails all shivering. By and by the congregation will get ahead of him, and then it must, have another new skipper. The priest holds his own pretty well; the minister is coming down every generation nearer and nearer to the common level of the useful citizen, no oracle at all, but a man of more than average moral instincts, who, if he knows anything, knows how little he knows. The ministers are good talkers, only the struggle between nature and grace makes some of 'em a little awkward occasionally. The women do their best to spoil 'em, as they do the poets; you find it very pleasant to be spoiled, no doubt; so do they. Now and then one of 'em goes over the dam; no wonder, they're always in the rapids.

By this time our three ladies had their faces all turned toward the speaker, like the weathercocks in a northeaster, and I thought it best to switch off the talk on to another rail.

How about the doctors? I said.

Theirs is the least learned of the professions, in this country at least. They have not half the general culture of the lawyers, nor a quarter of that of the ministers. I rather think, though, they are more agreeable to the common run of people than the men with black coats or the men with green bags. People can swear before 'em if they want to, and they can't very well before ministers. I don't care whether they want to swear or not, they don't want to be on their good behavior. Besides, the minister has a little smack of the sexton about him; he comes when people are in extremis, but they don't send for him every time they make a slight moral slip, tell a lie for instance, or smuggle a silk dress through the customhouse; but they call in the doctor when a child is cutting a tooth or gets a splinter in its finger. So it does n't mean much to send for him, only a pleasant chat about the news of the day; for putting the baby to rights does n't take long. Besides, everybody does n't like to talk about the next world; people are modest in their desires, and find this world as good as they deserve; but everybody loves to talk physic. Everybody loves to hear of strange cases; people are eager to tell the doctor of the wonderful cures they have heard of; they want to know what is the matter with somebody or other who is said to be suffering from "a complication of diseases," and above all to get a hard name, Greek or Latin, for some complaint which sounds altogether too commonplace in plain English. If you will only call a headache a Cephalgia, it acquires dignity at once, and a patient becomes rather proud of it. So I think doctors are generally welcome in most companies.

In old times, when people were more afraid of the Devil and of witches than they are now, they liked to have a priest or a minister somewhere near to scare 'em off; but nowadays, if you could find an old woman that would ride round the room on a broomstick, Barnum would build an amphitheatre to exhibit her in; and if he could come across a young imp, with hoofs, tail, and budding horns, a lineal descendant of one of those "daemons" which the good people of Gloucester fired at, and were fired at by "for the best part of a month together" in the year 1692, the, great showman would have him at any cost for his museum or menagerie. Men are cowards, sir, and are driven by fear as the sovereign motive. Men are idolaters, and want something to look at and kiss and hug, or throw themselves down before; they always did, they always will; and if you don't make it of wood, you must make it of words, which are just as much used for idols as promissory notes are used for values. The ministers have a hard time of it without bell and book and holy water; they are dismounted men in armor since Luther cut their saddle-girths, and you can see they are quietly taking off one piece of iron after another until some of the best of 'em are fighting the devil (not the zoological Devil with the big D) with the sword of the Spirit, and precious little else in the way of weapons of offence or defence. But we couldn't get on without the spiritual brotherhood, whatever became of our special creeds. There is a genius for religion, just as there is for painting or sculpture. It is half-sister to the genius for music, and has some of the features which remind us of earthly love. But it lifts us all by its mere presence. To see a good man and hear his voice once a week would be reason enough for building churches and pulpits. The Master stopped all at once, and after about half a minute laughed his pleasant laugh.

What is it? I asked him.

I was thinking of the great coach and team that is carrying us fast enough, I don't know but too fast, somewhere or other. The D. D.'s used to be the leaders, but now they are the wheel-horses. It's pretty hard to tell how much they pull, but we know they can hold back like the

When we're going down hill, I said, as neatly as if I had been a High-Church curate trained to snap at the last word of the response, so that you couldn't wedge in the tail of a comma between the end of the congregation's closing syllable and the beginning of the next petition. They do it well, but it always spoils my devotion. To save my life, I can't help watching them, as I watch to see a duck dive at the flash of a gun, and that is not what I go to church for. It is a juggler's trick, and there is no more religion in it than in catching a ball on the fly.

I was looking at our Scheherezade the other day, and thinking what a pity it was that she had never had fair play in the world. I wish I knew more of her history. There is one way of learning it, making love to her. I wonder whether she would let me and like it. It is an absurd thing, and I ought not to confess, but I tell you and you only, Beloved, my heart gave a perceptible jump when it heard the whisper of that possibility overhead! Every day has its ebb and flow, but such a thought as that is like one of those tidal waves they talk about, that rolls in like a great wall and overtops and drowns out all your landmarks, and you, too, if you don't mind what you are about and stand ready to run or climb or swim. Not quite so bad as that, though, this time. I take an interest in our Scheherezade. I am glad she did n't smile on the pipe and the Bohemian-looking fellow that finds the best part of his life in sucking at it. A fine thing, isn't it; for a young woman to marry a man who will hold her

"Something better than his dog, a little dearer than his horse,"

but not quite so good as his meerschaum? It is n't for me to throw stones, though, who have been a Nicotian a good deal more than half my days. Cigar-stump out now, and consequently have become very bitter on more persevering sinners. I say I take an interest in our Scheherezade, but I rather think it is more paternal than anything else, though my heart did give that jump. It has jumped a good many times without anything very remarkable coming of it.

This visit to the Observatory is going to bring us all, or most of us, together in a new way, and it wouldn't be very odd if some of us should become better acquainted than we ever have been.

There is a chance for the elective affinities. What tremendous forces they are, if two subjects of them come within range! There lies a bit of iron. All the dynamic agencies of the universe are pledged to hold it just in that position, and there it will lie until it becomes a heap of red-brown rust. But see, I hold a magnet to it, it looks to you like just such a bit of iron as the other, and lo! it leaves them all, the tugging of the mighty earth; of the ghostly moon that walks in white, trailing the snaky waves of the ocean after her; of the awful sun, twice as large as a sphere that the whole orbit of the moon would but just girdle, it leaves the wrestling of all their forces, which are at a dead lock with each other, all fighting for it, and springs straight to the magnet. What a lucky thing it is for well-conducted persons that the maddening elective affinities don't come into play in full force very often!

I suppose I am making a good deal more of our prospective visit than it deserves. It must be because I have got it into my head that we are bound to have some kind of sentimental outbreak amongst us, and that this will give a chance for advances on the part of anybody disposed in that direction. A little change of circumstance often hastens on a movement that has been long in preparation. A chemist will show you a flask containing a clear liquid; he will give it a shake or two, and the whole contents of the flask will become solid in an instant. Or you may lay a little heap of iron-filings on a sheet of paper with a magnet beneath it, and they will be quiet enough as they are, but give the paper a slight jar and the specks of metal will suddenly find their way to the north or the south pole of the magnet and take a definite shape not unpleasing to contemplate, and curiously illustrating the laws of attraction, antagonism, and average, by which the worlds, conscious and unconscious, are alike governed. So with our little party, with any little party of persons who have got used to each other; leave them undisturbed and they might remain in a state of equilibrium forever; but let anything give them a shake or a jar, and the long-striving but hindered affinities come all at once into play and finish the work of a year in five minutes.

We were all a good deal excited by the anticipation of this visit. The Capitalist, who for the most part keeps entirely to himself, seemed to take an interest in it and joined the group in the parlor who were making arrangements as to the details of the eventful expedition, which was very soon to take place. The Young Girl was full of enthusiasm; she is one of those young persons, I think, who are impressible, and of necessity depressible when their nervous systems are overtasked, but elastic, recovering easily from mental worries and fatigues, and only wanting a little change of their conditions to get back their bloom and cheerfulness. I could not help being pleased to see how much of the child was left in her, after all the drudgery she had been through. What is there that youth will not endure and triumph over? Here she was; her story for the week was done in good season; she had got rid of her villain by a new and original catastrophe; she had received a sum of money for an extra string of verses, painfully small, it is true, but it would buy her a certain ribbon she wanted for the great excursion; and now her eyes sparkled so that I forgot how tired and hollow they sometimes looked when she had been sitting up half the night over her endless manuscript.

The morning of the day we had looked forward to promised as good an evening as we could wish. The Capitalist, whose courteous and bland demeanor would never have suggested the thought that he was a robber and an enemy of his race, who was to be trampled underfoot by the beneficent regenerators of the social order as preliminary to the universal reign of peace on earth and good-will to men, astonished us all with a proposal to escort the three ladies and procure a carriage for their conveyance. The Lady thanked him in a very cordial way, but said she thought nothing of the walk. The Landlady looked disappointed at this answer. For her part she was on her legs all day and should be glad enough to ride, if so be he was going to have a carriage at any rate. It would be a sight pleasanter than to trudge afoot, but she would n't have him go to the expense on her account. Don't mention it, madam, said the Capitalist, in a generous glow of enthusiasm. As for the Young Girl, she did not often get a chance for a drive, and liked the idea of it for its own sake, as children do, and she insisted that the Lady should go in the carriage with her. So it was settled that the Capitalist should take the three ladies in a carriage, and the rest of us go on foot.

The evening behaved as it was bound to do on so momentous an occasion. The Capitalist was dressed with almost suspicious nicety. We pedestrians could not help waiting to see them off, and I thought he handed the ladies into the carriage with the air of a French marquis.

I walked with Dr. Benjamin and That Boy, and we had to keep the little imp on the trot a good deal of the way in order not to be too long behind the carriage party. The Member of the Haouse walked with our two dummies, I beg their pardon, I mean the Register of Deeds and the Salesman.

The Man of Letters, hypothetically so called, walked by himself, smoking a short pipe which was very far from suggesting the spicy breezes that blow soft from Ceylon's isle.

I suppose everybody who reads this paper has visited one or more observatories, and of course knows all about them. But as it may hereafter be translated into some foreign tongue and circulated among barbarous, but rapidly improving people, people who have as yet no astronomers among them, it may be well to give a little notion of what kind of place an observatory is.

To begin then: a deep and solid stone foundation is laid in the earth, and a massive pier of masonry is built up on it. A heavy block of granite forms the summit of this pier, and on this block rests the equatorial telescope. Around this structure a circular tower is built, with two or more floors which come close up to the pier, but do not touch it at any point. It is crowned with a hemispherical dome, which, I may remark, half realizes the idea of my egg-shell studio. This dome is cleft from its base to its summit by a narrow, ribbon-like opening, through which is seen the naked sky. It revolves on cannon-balls, so easily that a single hand can move it, and thus the opening may be turned towards any point of the compass. As the telescope can be raised or depressed so as to be directed to any elevation from the horizon to the zenith, and turned around the entire circle with the dome, it can be pointed to any part of the heavens. But as the star or other celestial object is always apparently moving, in consequence of the real rotatory movement of the earth, the telescope is made to follow it automatically by an ingenious clock-work arrangement. No place, short of the temple of the living God, can be more solemn. The jars of the restless life around it do not disturb the serene intelligence of the half-reasoning apparatus. Nothing can stir the massive pier but the shocks that shake the solid earth itself. When an earthquake thrills the planet, the massive turret shudders with the shuddering rocks on which it rests, but it pays no heed to the wildest tempest, and while the heavens are convulsed and shut from the eye of the far-seeing instrument it waits without a tremor for the blue sky to come back. It is the type of the true and steadfast man of the Roman poet, whose soul remains unmoved while the firmament cracks and tumbles about him. It is the material image of the Christian; his heart resting on the Rock of Ages, his eye fixed on the brighter world above.

I did not say all this while we were looking round among these wonders, quite new to many of us. People don't talk in straight-off sentences like that. They stumble and stop, or get interrupted, change a word, begin again, miss connections of verbs and nouns, and so on, till they blunder out their meaning. But I did let fall a word or two, showing the impression the celestial laboratory produced upon me. I rather think I must own to the "Rock of Ages" comparison. Thereupon the "Man of Letters," so called, took his pipe from his mouth, and said that he did n't go in "for sentiment and that sort of thing. Gush was played out."

The Member of the Haouse, who, as I think, is not wanting in that homely good sense which one often finds in plain people from the huckleberry districts, but who evidently supposes the last speaker to be what he calls "a tahlented mahn," looked a little puzzled. My remark seemed natural and harmless enough to him, I suppose, but I had been distinctly snubbed, and the Member of the Haouse thought I must defend myself, as is customary in the deliberative body to which he belongs, when one gentleman accuses another gentleman of mental weakness or obliquity. I could not make up my mind to oblige him at that moment by showing fight. I suppose that would have pleased my assailant, as I don't think he has a great deal to lose, and might have made a little capital out of me if he could have got a laugh out of the Member or either of the dummies, I beg their pardon again, I mean the two undemonstrative boarders. But I will tell you, Beloved, just what I think about this matter.

We poets, you know, are much given to indulging in sentiment, which is a mode of consciousness at a discount just now with the new generation of analysts who are throwing everything into their crucibles. Now we must not claim too much for sentiment. It does not go a great way in deciding questions of arithmetic, or algebra, or geometry. Two and two will undoubtedly make four, irrespective of the emotions or other idiosyncrasies of the calculator; and the three angles of a triangle insist on being equal to two right angles, in the face of the most impassioned rhetoric or the most inspired verse. But inasmuch as religion and law and the whole social order of civilized society, to say nothing of literature and art, are so founded on and pervaded by sentiment that they would all go to pieces without it, it is a word not to be used too lightly in passing judgment, as if it were an element to be thrown out or treated with small consideration. Reason may be the lever, but sentiment gives you the fulcrum and the place to stand on if you want to move the world. Even "sentimentality," which is sentiment overdone, is better than that affectation of superiority to human weakness which is only tolerable as one of the stage properties of full-blown dandyism, and is, at best, but half-blown cynicism; which participle and noun you can translate, if you happen to remember the derivation of the last of them, by a single familiar word. There is a great deal of false sentiment in the world, as there is of bad logic and erroneous doctrine; but it is very much less disagreeable to hear a young poet overdo his emotions, or even deceive himself about them, than to hear a caustic-epithet flinger repeating such words as "sentimentality" and "entusymusy," one of the least admirable of Lord Byron's bequests to our language, for the purpose of ridiculing him into silence. An overdressed woman is not so pleasing as she might be, but at any rate she is better than the oil of vitriol squirter, whose profession it is to teach young ladies to avoid vanity by spoiling their showy silks and satins.

The Lady was the first of our party who was invited to look through the equatorial. Perhaps this world had proved so hard to her that she was pained to think that other worlds existed, to be homes of suffering and sorrow. Perhaps she was thinking it would be a happy change when she should leave this dark planet for one of those brighter spheres. She sighed, at any rate, but thanked the Young Astronomer for the beautiful sights he had shown her, and gave way to the next comer, who was That Boy, now in a state of irrepressible enthusiasm to see the Man in the Moon. He was greatly disappointed at not making out a colossal human figure moving round among the shining summits and shadowy ravines of the "spotty globe."

The Landlady came next and wished to see the moon also, in preference to any other object. She was astonished at the revelations of the powerful telescope. Was there any live creatures to be seen on the moon? she asked. The Young Astronomer shook his head, smiling a little at the question. Was there any meet'n'-houses? There was no evidence, he said, that the moon was inhabited. As there did not seem to be either air or water on its surface, the inhabitants would have a rather hard time of it, and if they went to meeting the sermons would be apt to be rather dry. If there were a building on it as big as York minster, as big as the Boston Coliseum, the great telescopes like Lord Rosse's would make it out. But it seemed to be a forlorn place; those who had studied it most agreed in considering it a "cold, crude, silent, and desolate" ruin of nature, without the possibility, if life were on it, of articulate speech, of music, even of sound. Sometimes a greenish tint was seen upon its surface, which might have been taken for vegetation, but it was thought not improbably to be a reflection from the vast forests of South America. The ancients had a fancy, some of them, that the face of the moon was a mirror in which the seas and shores of the earth were imaged. Now we know the geography of the side toward us about as well as that of Asia, better than that of Africa. The Astronomer showed them one of the common small photographs of the moon. He assured them that he had received letters inquiring in all seriousness if these alleged lunar photographs were not really taken from a peeled orange. People had got angry with him for laughing at them for asking such a question. Then he gave them an account of the famous moon-hoax which came out, he believed, in 1835. It was full of the most bare-faced absurdities, yet people swallowed it all, and even Arago is said to have treated it seriously as a thing that could not well be true, for Mr. Herschel would have certainly notified him of these marvellous discoveries. The writer of it had not troubled himself to invent probabilities, but had borrowed his scenery from the Arabian Nights and his lunar inhabitants from Peter Wilkins.

After this lecture the Capitalist stepped forward and applied his eye to the lens. I suspect it to have been shut most of the time, for I observe a good many elderly people adjust the organ of vision to any optical instrument in that way. I suppose it is from the instinct of protection to the eye, the same instinct as that which makes the raw militia-man close it when he pulls the trigger of his musket the first time. He expressed himself highly gratified, however, with what he saw, and retired from the instrument to make room for the Young Girl.

She threw her hair back and took her position at the instrument. Saint Simeon Stylites the Younger explained the wonders of the moon to her, Tycho and the grooves radiating from it, Kepler and Copernicus with their craters and ridges, and all the most brilliant shows of this wonderful little world. I thought he was more diffuse and more enthusiastic in his descriptions than he had been with the older members of the party. I don't doubt the old gentleman who lived so long on the top of his pillar would have kept a pretty sinner (if he could have had an elevator to hoist her up to him) longer than he would have kept her grandmother. These young people are so ignorant, you know. As for our Scheherezade, her delight was unbounded, and her curiosity insatiable. If there were any living creatures there, what odd things they must be. They could n't have any lungs, nor any hearts. What a pity! Did they ever die? How could they expire if they didn't breathe? Burn up? No air to burn in. Tumble into some of those horrid pits, perhaps, and break all to bits. She wondered how the young people there liked it, or whether there were any young people there; perhaps nobody was young and nobody was old, but they were like mummies all of them, what an idea, two mummies making love to each other! So she went on in a rattling, giddy kind of way, for she was excited by the strange scene in which she found herself, and quite astonished the Young Astronomer with her vivacity. All at once she turned to him.

Will you show me the double star you said I should see?

With the greatest pleasure, he said, and proceeded to wheel the ponderous dome, and then to adjust the instrument, I think to the one in Andromeda, or that in Cygnus, but I should not know one of them from the other.

How beautiful! she said as she looked at the wonderful object. One is orange red and one is emerald green.

The young man made an explanation in which he said something about complementary colors.

Goodness! exclaimed the Landlady. What! complimentary to our party?

Her wits must have been a good deal confused by the strange sights of the evening. She had seen tickets marked complimentary, she remembered, but she could not for the life of her understand why our party should be particularly favored at a celestial exhibition like this. On the whole, she questioned inwardly whether it might not be some subtle pleasantry, and smiled, experimentally, with a note of interrogation in the smile, but, finding no encouragement, allowed her features to subside gradually as if nothing had happened. I saw all this as plainly as if it had all been printed in great-primer type, instead of working itself out in her features. I like to see other people muddled now and then, because my own occasional dulness is relieved by a good solid background of stupidity in my neighbors.

And the two revolve round each other? said the Young Girl.

Yes, he answered, two suns, a greater and a less, each shining, but with a different light, for the other.

How charming! It must be so much pleasanter than to be alone in such a great empty space! I should think one would hardly care to shine if its light wasted itself in the monstrous solitude of the sky. Does not a single star seem very lonely to you up there?

Not more lonely than I am myself, answered the Young Astronomer.

I don't know what there was in those few words, but I noticed that for a minute or two after they, were uttered I heard the ticking of the clock-work that moved the telescope as clearly as if we had all been holding our breath, and listening for the music of the spheres.

The Young Girl kept her eye closely applied to the eye-piece of the telescope a very long time, it seemed to me. Those double stars interested her a good deal, no doubt. When she looked off from the glass I thought both her eyes appeared very much as if they had been a little strained, for they were suffused and glistening. It may be that she pitied the lonely young man.

I know nothing in the world tenderer than the pity that a kind-hearted young girl has for a young man who feels lonely. It is true that these dear creatures are all compassion for every form of human woe, and anxious to alleviate all human misfortunes. They will go to Sunday-schools through storms their brothers are afraid of, to teach the most unpleasant and intractable classes of little children the age of Methuselah and the dimensions of Og the King of Bashan's bedstead. They will stand behind a table at a fair all day until they are ready to drop, dressed in their prettiest clothes and their sweetest smiles, and lay hands upon you, like so many Lady Potiphars, perfectly correct ones, of course, to make you buy what you do not want, at prices which you cannot afford; all this as cheerfully as if it were not martyrdom to them as well as to you. Such is their love for all good objects, such their eagerness to sympathize with all their suffering fellow-creatures! But there is nothing they pity as they pity a lonely young man.

I am sure, I sympathize with her in this instance. To see a pale student burning away, like his own midnight lamp, with only dead men's hands to hold, stretched out to him from the sepulchres of books, and dead men's souls imploring him from their tablets to warm them over again just for a little while in a human consciousness, when all this time there are soft, warm, living hands that would ask nothing better than to bring the blood back into those cold thin fingers, and gently caressing natures that would wind all their tendrils about the unawakened heart which knows so little of itself, is pitiable enough and would be sadder still if we did not have the feeling that sooner or later the pale student will be pretty sure to feel the breath of a young girl against his cheek as she looks over his shoulder; and that he will come all at once to an illuminated page in his book that never writer traced in characters, and never printer set up in type, and never binder enclosed within his covers! But our young man seems farther away from life than any student whose head is bent downwards over his books. His eyes are turned away from all human things. How cold the moonlight is that falls upon his forehead, and how white he looks in it! Will not the rays strike through to his brain at last, and send him to a narrower cell than this egg-shell dome which is his workshop and his prison?

I cannot say that the Young Astronomer seemed particularly impressed with a sense of his miserable condition. He said he was lonely, it is true, but he said it in a manly tone, and not as if he were repining at the inevitable condition of his devoting himself to that particular branch of science. Of course, he is lonely, the most lonely being that lives in the midst of our breathing world. If he would only stay a little longer with us when we get talking; but he is busy almost always either in observation or with his calculations and studies, and when the nights are fair loses so much sleep that he must make it up by day. He wants contact with human beings. I wish he would change his seat and come round and sit by our Scheherezade!

The rest of the visit went off well enough, except that the "Man of Letters," so called, rather snubbed some of the heavenly bodies as not quite up to his standard of brilliancy. I thought myself that the double-star episode was the best part of it.

I have an unexpected revelation to make to the reader. Not long after our visit to the Observatory, the Young Astronomer put a package into my hands, a manuscript, evidently, which he said he would like to have me glance over. I found something in it which interested me, and told him the next day that I should like to read it with some care. He seemed rather pleased at this, and said that he wished I would criticise it as roughly as I liked, and if I saw anything in it which might be dressed to better advantage to treat it freely, just as if it were my own production. It had often happened to him, he went on to say, to be interrupted in his observations by clouds covering the objects he was examining for a longer or shorter time. In these idle moments he had put down many thoughts, unskilfully he feared, but just as they came into his mind. His blank verse he suspected was often faulty. His thoughts he knew must be crude, many of them. It would please him to have me amuse myself by putting them into shape. He was kind enough to say that I was an artist in words, but he held himself as an unskilled apprentice.

I confess I was appalled when I cast my eye upon the title of the manuscript, "Cirri and Nebulae."

Oh! oh! I said, that will never do. People don't know what Cirri are, at least not one out of fifty readers. "Wind-Clouds and Star-Drifts" will do better than that.

Anything you like, he answered, what difference does it make how you christen a foundling? These are not my legitimate scientific offspring, and you may consider them left on your doorstep.

I will not attempt to say just how much of the diction of these lines belongs to him, and how much to me. He said he would never claim them, after I read them to him in my version. I, on my part, do not wish to be held responsible for some of his more daring thoughts, if I should see fit to reproduce them hereafter. At this time I shall give only the first part of the series of poetical outbreaks for which the young devotee of science must claim his share of the responsibility. I may put some more passages into shape by and by.

WIND-CLOUDS AND STAR-DRIFTS.

I
Another clouded night; the stars are hid,
The orb that waits my search is hid with them.
Patience! Why grudge an hour, a month, a year,
To plant my ladder and to gain the round
That leads my footsteps to the heaven of fame,
Where waits the wreath my sleepless midnights won?
Not the stained laurel such as heroes wear
That withers when some stronger conqueror's heel

Treads down their shrivelling trophies in the dust;
But the fair garland whose undying green
Not time can change, nor wrath of gods or men!

With quickened heart-beats I shall hear the tongues
That speak my praise; but better far the sense
That in the unshaped ages, buried deep
In the dark mines of unaccomplished time
Yet to be stamped with morning's royal die
And coined in golden days, in those dim years
I shall be reckoned with the undying dead,
My name emblazoned on the fiery arch,
Unfading till the stars themselves shall fade.
Then, as they call the roll of shining worlds,
Sages of race unborn in accents new
Shall count me with the Olympian ones of old,
Whose glories kindle through the midnight sky
Here glows the God of Battles; this recalls
The Lord of Ocean, and yon far-off sphere
The Sire of Him who gave his ancient name
To the dim planet with the wondrous rings;
Here flames the Queen of Beauty's silver lamp,
And there the moon-girt orb of mighty Jove;
But this, unseen through all earth's aeons past,
A youth who watched beneath the western star
Sought in the darkness, found, and showed to men;
Linked with his name thenceforth and evermore!
So shall that name be syllabled anew
In all the tongues of all the tribes of men:
I that have been through immemorial years
Dust in the dust of my forgotten time
Shall live in accents shaped of blood-warm breath,
Yea, rise in mortal semblance, newly born
In shining stone, in undecaying bronze,
And stand on high, and look serenely down
On the new race that calls the earth its own.

Is this a cloud, that, blown athwart my soul,
Wears a false seeming of the pearly stain
Where worlds beyond the world their mingling rays
Blend in soft white, a cloud that, born of earth,
Would cheat the soul that looks for light from heaven?
Must every coral-insect leave his sign
On each poor grain he lent to build the reef,
As Babel's builders stamped their sunburnt clay,
Or deem his patient service all in vain?
What if another sit beneath the shade
Of the broad elm I planted by the way,
What if another heed the beacon light
I set upon the rock that wrecked my keel,
Have I not done my task and served my kind?
Nay, rather act thy part, unnamed, unknown,
And let Fame blow her trumpet through the world
With noisy wind to swell a fool's renown,

Joined with some truth be stumbled blindly o'er,
Or coupled with some single shining deed
That in the great account of all his days
Will stand alone upon the bankrupt sheet
His pitying angel shows the clerk of Heaven.
The noblest service comes from nameless hands,
And the best servant does his work unseen.
Who found the seeds of fire and made them shoot,
Fed by his breath, in buds and flowers of flame?
Who forged in roaring flames the ponderous stone,
And shaped the moulded metal to his need?
Who gave the dragging car its rolling wheel,
And tamed the steed that whirls its circling round?
All these have left their work and not their names,
Why should I murmur at a fate like theirs?
This is the heavenly light; the pearly stain
Was but a wind-cloud drifting oer the stars!

CHAPTER VI

I find I have so many things in common with the old Master of Arts, that I do not always know whether a thought was originally his or mine. That is what always happens where two persons of a similar cast of mind talk much together. And both of them often gain by the interchange. Many ideas grow better when transplanted into another mind than in the one where they sprang up. That which was a weed in one intelligence becomes a flower in the other. A flower, on the other hand, may dwindle down to a mere weed by the same change. Healthy growths may become poisonous by falling upon the wrong mental soil, and what seemed a night-shade in one mind unfold as a morning-glory in the other.

I thank God, the Master said, that a great many people believe a great deal more than I do. I think, when it comes to serious matters, I like those who believe more than I do better than those who believe less.

Why, said I, you have got hold of one of my own working axioms. I should like to hear you develop it.

The Member of the Haouse said he should be glad to listen to the debate. The gentleman had the floor. The Scarabee rose from his chair and departed; I thought his joints creaked as he straightened himself.

The Young Girl made a slight movement; it was a purely accidental coincidence, no doubt, but I saw That Boy put his hand in his pocket and pull out his popgun, and begin loading it. It cannot be that our Scheherezade, who looks so quiet and proper at the table, can make use of That Boy and his catapult to control the course of conversation and change it to suit herself! She certainly looks innocent enough; but what does a blush prove, and what does its absence prove, on one of these innocent faces? There is nothing in all this world that can lie and cheat like the face and the tongue of a young girl. Just give her a little touch of hysteria, I don't mean enough of it to make her friends call the doctor in, but a slight hint of it in the nervous system, and "Machiavel the waiting-maid" might take lessons of her. But I cannot think our Scheherezade is one of that kind, and I am ashamed of myself for noting such a trifling coincidence as that which excited my suspicion.

I say, the Master continued, that I had rather be in the company of those who believe more than I do, in spiritual matters at least, than of those who doubt what I accept as a part of my belief.

To tell the truth, said I, I find that difficulty sometimes in talking with you. You have not quite so many hesitations as I have in following out your logical conclusions. I suppose you would bring some things out into daylight questioning that I had rather leave in that twilight of half-belief peopled with shadows, if they are only shadows, more sacred to me than many realities.

There is nothing I do not question, said the Master; I not only begin with the precept of Descartes, but I hold all my opinions involving any chain of reasoning always open to revision.

I confess that I smiled internally to hear him say that. The old Master thinks he is open to conviction on all subjects; but if you meddle with some of his notions and don't get tossed on his horns as if a bull had hold of you, I should call you lucky.

You don't mean you doubt everything? I said.

What do you think I question everything for, the Master replied, if I never get any answers? You've seen a blind man with a stick, feeling his way along? Well, I am a blind man with a stick, and I find the world pretty full of men just as blind as I am, but without any stick. I try the ground to find out whether it is firm or not before I rest my weight on it; but after it has borne my weight, that question at least is answered. It very certainly was strong enough once; the presumption is that it is strong enough now. Still the soil may have been undermined, or I may have grown heavier. Make as much of that as you will. I say I question everything; but if I find Bunker Hill Monument standing as straight as when I leaned against it a year or ten years ago, I am not very much afraid that Bunker Hill will cave in if I trust myself again on the soil of it.

I glanced off, as one often does in talk.

The Monument is an awful place to visit, I said. The waves of time are like the waves of the ocean; the only thing they beat against without destroying it is a rock; and they destroy that at last. But it takes a good while. There is a stone now standing in very good order that was as old as a monument of Louis XIV. and Queen Anne's day is now when Joseph went down into Egypt. Think of the shaft on Bunker Hill standing in the sunshine on the morning of January 1st in the year 5872!

It won't be standing, the Master said. We are poor bunglers compared to those old Egyptians. There are no joints in one of their obelisks. They are our masters in more ways than we know of, and in more ways than some of us are willing to know. That old Lawgiver wasn't learned in all the wisdom of the Egyptians for nothing. It scared people well a couple of hundred years ago when Sir John Marsham and Dr. John Spencer ventured to tell their stories about the sacred ceremonies of the Egyptian priesthood. People are beginning to find out now that you can't study any religion by itself to any good purpose. You must have comparative theology as you have comparative anatomy. What would you make of a cat's foolish little good-for-nothing collar-bone, if you did not know how the same bone means a good deal in other creatures, in yourself, for instance, as you 'll find out if you break it? You can't know too much of your race and its beliefs, if you want to know anything about your Maker. I never found but one sect large enough to hold the whole of me.

And may I ask what that was? I said.

The Human sect, the Master answered. That has about room enough for me, at present, I mean to say.

Including cannibals and all? said I.

Oh, as to that, the eating of one's kind is a matter of taste, but the roasting of them has been rather more a specialty of our own particular belief than of any other I am acquainted with. If you broil a saint, I don't see why, if you have a mind, you shouldn't serve him up at your

Pop! went the little piece of artillery. Don't tell me it was accident. I know better. You can't suppose for one minute that a boy like that one would time his interruptions so cleverly. Now it so happened that at that particular moment Dr. B. Franklin was not at the table. You may draw your own conclusions. I say nothing, but I think a good deal.

I came back to the Bunker Hill Monument. I often think I said of the dynasty which is to reign in its shadow for some thousands of years, it may be.

The "Man of Letters," so called, asked me, in a tone I did not exactly like, whether I expected to live long enough to see a monarchy take the place of a republic in this country.

No, said I, I was thinking of something very different. I was indulging a fancy of mine about the Man who is to sit at the foot of the monument for one, or it may be two or three thousand years. As long as the monument stands and there is a city near it, there will always be a man to take the names of visitors and extract some small tribute from their pockets, I suppose. I sometimes get thinking of the long, unbroken succession of these men, until they come to look like one Man; continuous in being, unchanging as the stone he watches, looking upon the successive generations of human beings as they come and go, and outliving all the dynasties of the world in all probability. It has come to such a pass that I never speak to the Man of the Monument without wanting to take my hat off and feeling as if I were looking down a vista of twenty or thirty centuries.

The "Man of Letters," so called, said, in a rather contemptuous way, I thought, that he had n't got so far as that. He was n't quite up to moral reflections on toll-men and ticket-takers. Sentiment was n't his tap.

He looked round triumphantly for a response: but the Capitalist was a little hard of hearing just then; the Register of Deeds was browsing on his food in the calm bovine abstraction of a quadruped, and paid no attention; the Salesman had bolted his breakfast, and whisked himself away with that peculiar alacrity which belongs to the retail dealer's assistant; and the Member of the Haouse, who had sometimes seemed to be impressed with his "tahlented mahn's" air of superiority to the rest of us, looked as if he thought the speaker was not exactly parliamentary. So he failed to make his point, and reddened a little, and was not in the best humor, I thought, when he left the table. I hope he will not let off any of his irritation on our poor little Scheherezade; but the truth is, the first person a man of this sort (if he is what I think him) meets, when he is out of humor, has to be made a victim of, and I only hope our Young Girl will not have to play Jephthah's daughter.

And that leads me to say, I cannot help thinking that the kind of criticism to which this Young Girl has been subjected from some person or other, who is willing to be smart at her expense, is hurtful and not wholesome. The question is a delicate one. So many foolish persons are rushing into print, that it requires a kind of literary police to hold them back and keep them in order. Where there are mice there must be cats, and where there are rats we may think it worth our while to keep a terrier, who will give them a shake and let them drop, with all the mischief taken out of them. But the process is a rude and cruel one at best, and it too often breeds a love of destructiveness for its own sake in those who get their living by it. A poor poem or essay does not do much harm after all; nobody reads it who is like to be seriously hurt by it. But a sharp criticism with a drop of witty venom in it stings a young author almost to death, and makes an old one uncomfortable to no purpose. If it were my business to sit in judgment on my neighbors, I would try to be courteous, at least, to those who had done any good service, but, above all, I would handle tenderly those young authors who are coming before the public in the flutter of their first or early appearance, and are in the trembling delirium of stage-fright already. Before you write that brilliant notice of some alliterative Angelina's book of verses, I wish you would try this experiment.

Take half a sheet of paper and copy upon it any of Angelina's stanzas, the ones you were going to make fun of, if you will. Now go to your window, if it is a still day, open it, and let the half-sheet of paper drop on the outside. How gently it falls through the soft air, always tending downwards, but sliding softly, from side to side, wavering, hesitating, balancing, until it settles as noiselessly as a snow-flake upon the all-receiving bosom of the earth! Just such would have been the fate of poor Angelina's fluttering effort, if you had left it to itself. It would have slanted downward into oblivion so sweetly and softly that she would have never known when it reached that harmless consummation.

Our epizoic literature is becoming so extensive that nobody is safe from its ad infinitum progeny. A man writes a book of criticisms. A Quarterly Review criticises the critic. A Monthly Magazine takes up the critic's critic. A Weekly Journal criticises the critic of the critic's critic, and a daily paper favors us with some critical remarks on the performance of the writer in the Weekly, who has criticised the critical notice in the Monthly of the critical essay in the Quarterly on the critical work we started with. And thus we see that as each flea "has smaller fleas that on him prey," even the critic himself cannot escape the common lot of being bitten. Whether all this is a blessing or a curse, like that one which made Pharaoh and all his household run to their toilet-tables, is a question about which opinions might differ. The physiologists of the time of Moses, if there were vivisectors other than priests in those days, would probably have considered that other plague, of the frogs, as a fortunate opportunity for science, as this poor little beast has been the souffre-douleur of experimenters and schoolboys from time immemorial.

But there is a form of criticism to which none will object. It is impossible to come before a public so alive with sensibilities as this we live in, with the smallest evidence of a sympathetic disposition, without making friends in a very unexpected way. Everywhere there are minds tossing on the unquiet waves of doubt. If you confess to the same perplexities and uncertainties that torture them, they are grateful for your companionship. If you have groped your way out of the wilderness in which you were once wandering with them, they will follow your footsteps, it may be, and bless you as their deliverer. So, all at once, a writer finds he has a parish of devout listeners, scattered, it is true, beyond the reach of any summons but that of a trumpet like the archangel's, to whom his slight discourse may be of more value than the exhortations they hear from the pulpit, if these last do not happen to suit their special needs. Young men with more ambition and intelligence than force of character, who have missed their first steps in life and are stumbling irresolute amidst vague aims and changing purposes, hold out their hands, imploring to be led into, or at least pointed towards, some path where they can find a firm foothold. Young women born into a chilling atmosphere of circumstance which keeps all the buds of their nature unopened and always striving to get to a ray of sunshine, if one finds its way to their neighborhood, tell their stories, sometimes simply and touchingly, sometimes in a more or less affected and rhetorical way, but still stories of defeated and disappointed instincts which ought to make any moderately impressible person feel very tenderly toward them.

In speaking privately to these young persons, many of whom have literary aspirations, one should be very considerate of their human feelings. But addressing them collectively a few plain truths will not give any one of them much pain. Indeed, almost every individual among them will feel sure that he or she is an exception to those generalities which apply so well to the rest.

If I were a literary Pope sending out an Encyclical, I would tell these inexperienced persons that nothing is so frequent as to mistake an ordinary human gift for a special and extraordinary endowment. The mechanism of breathing and that of swallowing are very wonderful, and if one had seen and studied them in his own person only, he might well think himself a prodigy. Everybody knows these and other bodily faculties are common gifts; but nobody except editors and school-teachers and here and there a literary than knows how common is the capacity of rhyming and prattling in readable prose, especially among young women of a certain degree of education. In my character of Pontiff, I should tell these young persons that most of them labored under a delusion. It is very hard to believe it; one feels so full of intelligence and so decidedly superior to one's dull relations and schoolmates; one writes so easily and the lines sound so prettily to one's self; there are such felicities of expression, just like those we hear quoted from the great poets; and besides one has been told by so many friends that all one had to do was to print and be famous! Delusion, my poor dear, delusion at least nineteen times out of twenty, yes, ninety-nine times in a hundred.

But as private father confessor, I always allow as much as I can for the one chance in the hundred. I try not to take away all hope, unless the case is clearly desperate, and then to direct the activities into some other channel.

Using kind language, I can talk pretty freely. I have counselled more than one aspirant after literary fame to go back to his tailor's board or his lapstone. I have advised the dilettanti, whose foolish friends praised their verses or their stories, to give up all their deceptive dreams of making a name by their genius, and go to work in the study of a profession which asked only for the diligent use of average; ordinary talents. It is a very grave responsibility which these unknown correspondents throw upon their chosen counsellors. One whom you have never seen, who lives in a community of which you know nothing, sends you specimens more or less painfully voluminous of his writings, which he asks you to read over, think over, and pray over, and send back an answer informing him whether fame and fortune are awaiting him as the possessor of the wonderful gifts his writings manifest, and whether you advise him to leave all, the shop he sweeps out every morning, the ledger he posts, the mortar in which he pounds, the bench at which he urges the reluctant plane, and follow his genius whithersoever it may lead him. The next correspondent wants you to mark out a whole course of life for him, and the means of judgment he gives you are about as adequate as the brick which the simpleton of old carried round as an advertisement of the house he had to sell. My advice to all the young men that write to me depends somewhat on the handwriting and spelling. If these are of a certain character, and they have reached a mature age, I recommend some honest manual calling, such as they have very probably been bred to, and which will, at least, give them a chance of becoming President of the United States by and by, if that is any object to them. What would you have done with the young person who called on me a good many years ago, so many that he has probably forgotten his literary effort, and read as specimens of his literary workmanship lines like those which I will favor you with presently? He was an able-bodied, grown-up young person, whose ingenuousness interested me; and I am sure if I thought he would ever be pained to see his maiden effort in print, I would deny myself the pleasure of submitting it to the reader. The following is an exact transcript of the lines he showed me, and which I took down on the spot:

"Are you in the vein for cider?
Are you in the tune for pork?
Hist! for Betty's cleared the larder
And turned the pork to soap."

Do not judge too hastily this sincere effort of a maiden muse. Here was a sense of rhythm, and an effort in the direction of rhyme; here was an honest transcript of an occurrence of daily life, told with a certain idealizing expression, recognizing the existence of impulses, mysterious instincts, impelling us even in the selection of our bodily sustenance. But I had to tell him that it wanted dignity of incident and grace of narrative, that there was no atmosphere to it, nothing of the light that never was and so forth. I did not say this in these very words, but I gave him to understand, without being too hard upon him, that he had better not desert his honest toil in pursuit of the poet's bays. This, it must be confessed, was a rather discouraging case. A young person like this may pierce, as the Frenchmen say, by and by, but the chances are all the other way.

I advise aimless young men to choose some profession without needless delay, and so get into a good strong current of human affairs, and find themselves bound up in interests with a compact body of their fellow-men.

I advise young women who write to me for counsel, perhaps I do not advise them at all, only sympathize a little with them, and listen to what they have to say (eight closely written pages on the average, which I always read from beginning to end, thinking of the widow's cruse and myself in the character of Elijah) and, and come now, I don't believe Methuselah would tell you what he said in his letters to young ladies, written when he was in his nine hundred and sixty-ninth year.

But, dear me! how much work all this private criticism involves! An editor has only to say "respectfully declined," and there is the end of it. But the confidential adviser is expected to give the reasons of his likes and dislikes in detail, and sometimes to enter into an argument for their support. That is more than any martyr can stand, but what trials he must go through, as it is! Great bundles of manuscripts, verse or prose, which the recipient is expected to read, perhaps to recommend to a publisher, at any rate to express a well-digested and agreeably flavored opinion about; which opinion, nine times out of ten, disguise it as we may, has to be a bitter draught; every form of egotism, conceit, false sentiment, hunger for notoriety, and eagerness for display of anserine plumage before the admiring public; all these come in by mail or express, covered with postage-stamps of so much more cost than the value of the waste words they overlie, that one comes at last to groan and change color at the very sight of a package, and to dread the postman's knock as if it were that of the other visitor whose naked knuckles rap at every door.

Still there are experiences which go far towards repaying all these inflictions. My last young man's case looked desperate enough; some of his sails had blown from the rigging, some were backing in the wind, and some were flapping and shivering, but I told him which way to head, and to my surprise he promised to do just as I directed, and I do not doubt is under full sail at this moment.

What if I should tell my last, my very recent experience with the other sex? I received a paper containing the inner history of a young woman's life, the evolution of her consciousness from its earliest record of itself, written so thoughtfully, so sincerely, with so much firmness and yet so much delicacy, with such truth of detail and such grace in the manner of telling, that I finished the long manuscript almost at a sitting, with a pleasure rarely, almost never experienced in voluminous communications which one has to spell out of handwriting. This was from a correspondent who made my acquaintance by letter when she was little more than a child, some years ago. How easy at that early period to have silenced her by indifference, to have wounded her by a careless epithet, perhaps even to have crushed her as one puts his heel on a weed! A very little encouragement kept her from despondency, and brought back one of those overflows of gratitude which make one more ashamed of himself for being so overpaid than he would be for having committed any of the lesser sins. But what pleased me most in the paper lately received was to see how far the writer had outgrown the need of any encouragement of mine; that she had strengthened out of her tremulous questionings into a self-reliance and self-poise which I had hardly dared to anticipate for her. Some of my readers who are also writers have very probably had more numerous experiences of this kind than I can lay claim to; self-revelations from unknown and sometimes nameless friends, who write from strange corners where the winds have wafted some stray words of theirs which have lighted in the minds and reached the hearts of those to whom they were as the angel that stirred the pool of Bethesda. Perhaps this is the best reward authorship brings; it may not imply much talent or literary excellence, but it means that your way of thinking and feeling is just what some one of your fellow-creatures needed.

I have been putting into shape, according to his request, some further passages from the Young Astronomer's manuscript, some of which the reader will have a chance to read if he is so disposed. The conflict in the young man's mind between the desire for fame and the sense of its emptiness as compared with nobler aims has set me thinking about the subject from a somewhat humbler point of view. As I am in the habit of telling you, Beloved, many of my thoughts, as well as of repeating what was said at our table, you may read what follows as if it were addressed to you in the course of an ordinary conversation, where I claimed rather more than my share, as I am afraid I am a little in the habit of doing.

I suppose we all, those of us who write in verse or prose, have the habitual feeling that we should like to be remembered. It is to be awake when all of those who were round us have been long wrapped in slumber. It is a pleasant thought enough that the name by which we have been called shall be familiar on the lips of those who come after us, and the thoughts that wrought themselves out in our intelligence, the emotions that trembled through our frames, shall live themselves over again in the minds and hearts of others.

But is there not something of rest, of calm, in the thought of gently and gradually fading away out of human remembrance? What line have we written that was on a level with our conceptions? What page of ours that does not betray some weakness we would fain have left unrecorded? To become a classic and share the life of a language is to be ever open to criticisms, to comparisons, to the caprices of successive generations, to be called into court and stand a trial before a new jury, once or more than once in every century. To be forgotten is to sleep in peace with the undisturbed myriads, no longer subject to the chills and heats, the blasts, the sleet, the dust, which assail in endless succession that shadow of a man which we call his reputation. The line which dying we could wish to blot has been blotted out for us by a hand so tender, so patient, so used to its kindly task, that the page looks as fair as if it had never borne the record of our infirmity or our transgression. And then so few would be wholly content with their legacy of fame. You remember poor Monsieur Jacques's complaint of the favoritism shown to Monsieur Berthier, it is in that exquisite "Week in a French Country-House." "Have you seen his room? Have you seen how large it is? Twice as large as mine! He has two jugs, a large one and a little one. I have only one small one. And a tea-service and a gilt Cupid on the top of his looking-glass." The famous survivor of himself has had his features preserved in a medallion, and the slice of his countenance seems clouded with the thought that it does not belong to a bust; the bust ought to look happy in its niche, but the statue opposite makes it feel as if it had been cheated out of half its personality, and the statue looks uneasy because another stands on a loftier pedestal. But "Ignotus" and "Miserrimus" are of the great majority in that vast assembly, that House of Commons whose members are all peers, where to be forgotten is the standing rule. The dignity of a silent memory is not to be undervalued. Fame is after all a kind of rude handling, and a name that is often on vulgar lips seems to borrow something not to be desired, as the paper money that passes from hand to hand gains somewhat which is a loss thereby. O sweet, tranquil refuge of oblivion, so far as earth is concerned, for us poor blundering, stammering, misbehaving creatures who cannot turn over a leaf of our life's diary without feeling thankful that its failure can no longer stare us in the face! Not unwelcome shall be the baptism of dust which hides forever the name that was given in the baptism of water! We shall have good company whose names are left unspoken by posterity. "Who knows whether the best of men be known, or whether there be not more remarkable persons forgot than any that stand remembered in the known account of time? The greater part must be content to be as though they had not been; to be found in the register of God, not in the record of man. Twenty-seven names make up the first story before the flood, and the recorded names ever since contain not one living century."

I have my moods about such things as the Young Astronomer has, as we all have. There are times when the thought of becoming utterly nothing to the world we knew so well and loved so much is painful and oppressive; we gasp as if in a vacuum, missing the atmosphere of life we have so long been in the habit of breathing. Not the less are there moments when the aching need of repose comes over us and the requiescat in pace, heathen benediction as it is, sounds more sweetly in our ears than all the promises that Fame can hold out to us.

I wonder whether it ever occurred to you to reflect upon another horror there must be in leaving a name behind you. Think what a horrid piece of work the biographers make of a man's private history! Just imagine the subject of one of those extraordinary fictions called biographies coming back and reading the life of himself, written very probably by somebody or other who thought he could turn a penny by doing it, and having the pleasure of seeing

"His little bark attendant sail,
Pursue the triumph and partake the gale."

The ghost of the person condemned to walk the earth in a biography glides into a public library, and goes to the shelf where his mummied life lies in its paper cerements. I can see the pale shadow glancing through the pages and hear the comments that shape themselves in the bodiless intelligence as if they were made vocal by living lips.

"Born in July, 1776!" And my honored father killed at the battle of Bunker Hill! Atrocious libeller! to slander one's family at the start after such a fashion!

"The death of his parents left him in charge of his Aunt Nancy, whose tender care took the place of those parental attentions which should have guided and protected his infant years, and consoled him for the severity of another relative."

Aunt Nancy! It was Aunt Betsey, you fool! Aunt Nancy used to, she has been dead these eighty years, so there is no use in mincing matters, she used to keep a bottle and a stick, and when she had been tasting a drop out of the bottle the stick used to come off the shelf and I had to taste that. And here she is made a saint of, and poor Aunt Betsey, that did everything for me, is slandered by implication as a horrid tyrant.

"The subject of this commemorative history was remarkable for a precocious development of intelligence. An old nurse who saw him at the very earliest period of his existence is said to have spoken of him as one of the most promising infants she had seen in her long experience. At school he was equally remarkable, and at a tender age he received a paper adorned with a cut, inscribed REWARD OF MERIT."

I don't doubt the nurse said that, there were several promising children born about that time. As for cuts, I got more from the schoolmaster's rattan than in any other shape. Didn't one of my teachers split a Gunter's scale into three pieces over the palm of my hand? And didn't I grin when I saw the pieces fly? No humbug, now, about my boyhood!

"His personal appearance was not singularly prepossessing. Inconspicuous in stature and unattractive in features."

You misbegotten son of an ourang and grandson of an ascidian (ghosts keep up with science, you observe), what business have you to be holding up my person to the contempt of my posterity? Haven't I been sleeping for this many a year in quiet, and don't the dandelions and buttercups look as yellow over me as over the best-looking neighbor I have in the dormitory? Why do you want to people the minds of everybody that reads your good-for-nothing libel which you call a "biography" with your impudent caricatures of a man who was a better-looking fellow than yourself, I'll bet you ten to one, a man whom his Latin tutor called fommosus puer when he was only a freshman? If that's what it means to make a reputation, to leave your character and your person, and the good name of your sainted relatives, and all you were, and all you had and thought and felt, so far as can be gathered by digging you out of your most private records, to be manipulated and bandied about and cheapened in the literary market as a chicken or a turkey or a goose is handled and bargained over at a provision stall, is n't it better to be content with the honest blue slate-stone and its inscription informing posterity that you were a worthy citizen and a respected father of a family?

I should like to see any man's biography with corrections and emendations by his ghost. We don't know each other's secrets quite so well as we flatter ourselves we do. We don't always know our own secrets as well as we might. You have seen a tree with different grafts upon it, an apple or a pear tree we will say. In the late summer months the fruit on one bough will ripen; I remember just such a tree, and the early ripening fruit was the Jargonelle. By and by the fruit of another bough will begin to come into condition; the lovely Saint Michael, as I remember, grew on the same stock as the Jargonelle in the tree I am thinking of; and then, when these have all fallen or been gathered, another, we will say the Winter Nelis, has its turn, and so out of the same juices have come in succession fruits of the most varied aspects and flavors. It is the same thing with ourselves, but it takes us a long while to find it out. The various inherited instincts ripen in succession. You may be nine tenths paternal at one period of your life, and nine tenths maternal at another. All at once the traits of some immediate ancestor may come to maturity unexpectedly on one of the branches of your character, just as your features at different periods of your life betray different resemblances to your nearer or more remote relatives.

But I want you to let me go back to the Bunker Hill Monument and the dynasty of twenty or thirty centuries whose successive representatives are to sit in the gate, like the Jewish monarchs, while the people shall come by hundreds and by thousands to visit the memorial shaft until the story of Bunker's Hill is as old as that of Marathon.

Would not one like to attend twenty consecutive soirees, at each one of which the lion of the party should be the Man of the Monument, at the beginning of each century, all the way, we will say, from Anno Domini 2000 to Ann. Dom. 4000, or, if you think the style of dating will be changed, say to Ann. Darwinii (we can keep A. D. you see) 1872? Will the Man be of the Indian type, as President Samuel Stanhope Smith and others have supposed the transplanted European will become by and by? Will he have shortened down to four feet and a little more, like the Esquimaux, or will he have been bred up to seven feet by the use of new chemical diets, ozonized and otherwise improved atmospheres, and animal fertilizers? Let us summon him in imagination and ask him a few questions.

Is n't it like splitting a toad out of a rock to think of this man of nineteen or twenty centuries hence coming out from his stony dwelling-place and speaking with us? What are the questions we should ask him? He has but a few minutes to stay. Make out your own list; I will set down a few that come up to me as I write.

What is the prevalent religious creed of civilization?

Has the planet met with any accident of importance?

How general is the republican form of government?

Do men fly yet?

Has the universal language come into use?

Is there a new fuel since the English coal-mines have given out?

Is the euthanasia a recognized branch of medical science?

Is the oldest inhabitant still living?

Is the Daily Advertiser still published?

And the Evening Transcript?

Is there much inquiry for the works of a writer of the nineteenth century (Old Style) by the name of, of

My tongue cleaves to the roof of my mouth. I cannot imagine the putting of that question without feeling the tremors which shake a wooer as he falters out the words the answer to which will make him happy or wretched.

Whose works was I going to question him about, do you ask me? Oh, the writings of a friend of mine, much esteemed by his relatives and others. But it's of no consequence, after all; I think he says he does not care much for posthumous reputation.

I find something of the same interest in thinking about one of the boarders at our table that I find in my waking dreams concerning the Man of the Monument. This personage is the Register of Deeds. He is an unemotional character, living in his business almost as exclusively as the Scarabee, but without any of that eagerness and enthusiasm which belong to our scientific specialist. His work is largely, principally, I may say, mechanical. He has developed, however, a certain amount of taste for the antiquities of his department, and once in a while brings out some curious result of his investigations into ancient documents. He too belongs to a dynasty which will last as long as there is such a thing as property in land and dwellings. When that is done away with, and we return to the state of villanage, holding our tenement-houses, all to be of the same pattern, of the State, that is to say, of the Tammany Ring which is to take the place of the feudal lord, the office of Register of Deeds will, I presume, become useless, and the dynasty will be deposed.

As we grow older we think more and more of old persons and of old things and places. As to old persons, it seems as if we never know how much they have to tell until we are old ourselves and they have been gone twenty or thirty years. Once in a while we come upon some survivor of his or her generation that we have overlooked, and feel as if we had recovered one of the lost books of Livy or fished up the golden candlestick from the ooze of the Tiber. So it was the other day after my reminiscences of the old gambrel-roofed house and its visitors. They found an echo in the recollections of one of the brightest and liveliest of my suburban friends, whose memory is exact about everything except her own age, which, there can be no doubt, she makes out a score or two of years more than it really is. Still she was old enough to touch some lights, and a shadow or two, into the portraits I had drawn, which made me wish that she and not I had been the artist who sketched the pictures. Among the lesser regrets that mingle with graver sorrows for the friends of an earlier generation we have lost, are our omissions to ask them so many questions they could have answered easily enough, and would have been pleased to be asked. There! I say to myself sometimes, in an absent mood, I must ask her about that. But she of whom I am now thinking has long been beyond the reach of any earthly questioning, and I sigh to think how easily I could have learned some fact which I should have been happy to have transmitted with pious care to those who are to come after me. How many times I have heard her quote the line about blessings brightening as they take their flight, and how true it proves in many little ways that one never thinks of until it is too late.

The Register of Deeds is not himself advanced in years. But he borrows an air of antiquity from the ancient records which are stored in his sepulchral archives. I love to go to his ossuary of dead transactions, as I would visit the catacombs of Rome or Paris. It is like wandering up the Nile to stray among the shelves of his monumental folios. Here stands a series of volumes, extending over a considerable number of years, all of which volumes are in his handwriting. But as you go backward there is a break, and you come upon the writing of another person, who was getting old apparently, for it is beginning to be a little shaky, and then you know that you have gone back as far as the last days of his predecessor. Thirty or forty years more carry you to the time when this incumbent began the duties of his office; his hand was steady then; and the next volume beyond it in date betrays the work of a still different writer. All this interests me, but I do not see how it is going to interest my reader. I do not feel very happy about the Register of Deeds. What can I do with him? Of what use is he going to be in my record of what I have seen and heard at the breakfast-table? The fact of his being one of the boarders was not so important that I was obliged to speak of him, and I might just as well have drawn on my imagination and not allowed this dummy to take up the room which another guest might have profitably filled at our breakfast-table.

I suppose he will prove a superfluity, but I have got him on my hands, and I mean that he shall be as little in the way as possible. One always comes across people in actual life who have no particular business to be where we find them, and whose right to be at all is somewhat questionable.

I am not going to get rid of the Register of Deeds by putting him out of the way; but I confess I do not see of what service he is going to be to me in my record. I have often found, however, that the Disposer of men and things understands much better than we do how to place his pawns and other pieces on the chess-board of life. A fish more or less in the ocean does not seem to amount to much. It is not extravagant to say that any one fish may be considered a supernumerary. But when Captain Coram's ship sprung a leak and the carpenter could not stop it, and the passengers had made up their minds that it was all over with them, all at once, without any apparent reason, the pumps began gaining on the leak, and the sinking ship to lift herself out of the abyss which was swallowing her up. And what do you think it was that saved the ship, and Captain Coram, and so in due time gave to London that Foundling Hospital which he endowed, and under the floor of which he lies buried? Why, it was that very supernumerary fish, which we held of so little account, but which had wedged itself into the rent of the yawning planks, and served to keep out the water until the leak was finally stopped.

I am very sure it was Captain Coram, but I almost hope it was somebody else, in order to give some poor fellow who is lying in wait for the periodicals a chance to correct me. That will make him happy for a month, and besides, he will not want to pick a quarrel about anything else if he has that splendid triumph. You remember Alcibiades and his dog's tail.

Here you have the extracts I spoke of from the manuscript placed in my hands for revision and emendation. I can understand these alternations of feeling in a young person who has been long absorbed in a single pursuit, and in whom the human instincts which have been long silent are now beginning to find expression. I know well what he wants; a great deal better, I think, than he knows himself.

WIND-CLOUDS AND STAR-DRIFTS.

II

Brief glimpses of the bright celestial spheres,
False lights, false shadows, vague, uncertain gleams,
Pale vaporous mists, wan streaks of lurid flame,
The climbing of the upward-sailing cloud,
The sinking of the downward-falling star,
All these are pictures of the changing moods
Borne through the midnight stillness of my soul.

Here am I, bound upon this pillared rock,
Prey to the vulture of a vast desire
That feeds upon my life. I burst my bands
And steal a moment's freedom from the beak,
The clinging talons and the shadowing plumes;
Then comes the false enchantress, with her song;
"Thou wouldst not lay thy forehead in the dust
Like the base herd that feeds and breeds and dies!
Lo, the fair garlands that I weave for thee,
Unchanging as the belt Orion wears,
Bright as the jewels of the seven-starred Crown,
The spangled stream of Berenice's hair!"
And so she twines the fetters with the flowers
Around my yielding limbs, and the fierce bird
Stoops to his quarry, then to feed his rage
Of ravening hunger I must drain my blood
And let the dew-drenched, poison-breeding night
Steal all the freshness from my fading cheek,
And leave its shadows round my caverned eyes.
All for a line in some unheeded scroll;
All for a stone that tells to gaping clowns,
"Here lies a restless wretch beneath a clod
Where squats the jealous nightmare men call Fame!"

I marvel not at him who scorns his kind
And thinks not sadly of the time foretold
When the old hulk we tread shall be a wreck,
A slag, a cinder drifting through the sky
Without its crew of fools! We live too long
And even so are not content to die,
But load the mould that covers up our bones
With stones that stand like beggars by the road
And show death's grievous wound and ask for tears;
Write our great books to teach men who we are,
Sing our fine songs that tell in artful phrase
The secrets of our lives, and plead and pray
For alms of memory with the after time,
Those few swift seasons while the earth shall wear
Its leafy summers, ere its core grows cold
And the moist life of all that breathes shall die;
Or as the new-born seer, perchance more wise,
Would have us deem, before its growing mass,
Pelted with stardust, atoned with meteor-balls,
Heats like a hammered anvil, till at last Man
and his works and all that stirred itself

Of its own motion, in the fiery glow
Turns to a flaming vapor, and our orb
Shines a new sun for earths that shall be born.

I am as old as Egypt to myself,
Brother to them that squared the pyramids
By the same stars I watch. I read the page
Where every letter is a glittering world,
With them who looked from Shinar's clay-built towers,
Ere yet the wanderer of the Midland sea
Had missed the fallen sister of the seven.
I dwell in spaces vague, remote, unknown,
Save to the silent few, who, leaving earth,
Quit all communion with their living time.
I lose myself in that ethereal void,
Till I have tired my wings and long to fill
My breast with denser air, to stand, to walk
With eyes not raised above my fellow-men.
Sick of my unwalled, solitary realm,
I ask to change the myriad lifeless worlds
I visit as mine own for one poor patch
Of this dull spheroid and a little breath
To shape in word or deed to serve my kind.

Was ever giant's dungeon dug so deep,
Was ever tyrant's fetter forged so strong,
Was e'er such deadly poison in the draught
The false wife mingles for the trusting fool,
As he whose willing victim is himself,
Digs, forges, mingles, for his captive soul?

CHAPTER VII

I was very sure that the old Master was hard at work about something, he is always very busy with something, but I mean something particular.

Whether it was a question of history or of cosmogony, or whether he was handling a test-tube or a blow-pipe; what he was about I did not feel sure; but I took it for granted that it was some crucial question or other he was at work on, some point bearing on the thought of the time. For the Master, I have observed, is pretty sagacious in striking for the points where his work will be like to tell. We all know that class of scientific laborers to whom all facts are alike nourishing mental food, and who seem to exercise no choice whatever, provided only they can get hold of these same indiscriminate facts in quantity sufficient. They browse on them, as the animal to which they would not like to be compared browses on his thistles. But the Master knows the movement of the age he belongs to; and if he seems to be busy with what looks like a small piece of trivial experimenting, one may feel pretty sure that he knows what he is about, and that his minute operations are looking to a result that will help him towards attaining his great end in life, an insight, so far as his faculties and opportunities will allow, into that order of things which he believes he can study with some prospect of taking in its significance.

I became so anxious to know what particular matter he was busy with, that I had to call upon him to satisfy my curiosity. It was with a little trepidation that I knocked at his door. I felt a good deal as one might have felt on disturbing an alchemist at his work, at the very moment, it might be, when he was about to make projection.

Come in! said the Master in his grave, massive tones.

I passed through the library with him into a little room evidently devoted to his experiments.

You have come just at the right moment, he said. Your eyes are better than mine. I have been looking at this flask, and I should like to have you look at it.

It was a small matrass, as one of the elder chemists would have called it, containing a fluid, and hermetically sealed. He held it up at the window; perhaps you remember the physician holding a flask to the light in Gerard Douw's "Femme hydropique"; I thought of that fine figure as I looked at him. Look! said he, is it clear or cloudy?

You need not ask me that, I answered. It is very plainly turbid. I should think that some sediment had been shaken up in it. What is it, Elixir Vitae or Aurum potabile?

Something that means more than alchemy ever did! Boiled just three hours, and as clear as a bell until within the last few days; since then has been clouding up.

I began to form a pretty shrewd guess at the meaning of all this, and to think I knew very nearly what was coming next. I was right in my conjecture. The Master broke off the sealed end of his little flask, took out a small portion of the fluid on a glass rod, and placed it on a slip of glass in the usual way for a microscopic examination.

One thousand diameters, he said, as he placed it on the stage of the microscope. We shall find signs of life, of course. He bent over the instrument and looked but an instant.

There they are! he exclaimed, look in.

I looked in and saw some objects:

The straight linear bodies were darting backward and forward in every direction. The wavy ones were wriggling about like eels or water-snakes. The round ones were spinning on their axes and rolling in every direction. All of them were in a state of incessant activity, as if perpetually seeking something and never finding it.

They are tough, the germs of these little bodies, said the Master. Three hours' boiling has n't killed 'em. Now, then, let us see what has been the effect of six hours' boiling.

He took up another flask just like the first, containing fluid and hermetically sealed in the same way.

Boiled just three hours longer than the other, he said, six hours in all. This is the experimentum crucis. Do you see any cloudiness in it?

Not a sign of it; it is as clear as crystal, except that there may be a little sediment at the bottom.

That is nothing. The liquid is clear. We shall find no signs of life. He put a minute drop of the liquid under the microscope as before. Nothing stirred. Nothing to be seen but a clear circle of light. We looked at it again and again, but with the same result.

Six hours kill 'em all, according to this experiment, said the Master. Good as far as it goes. One more negative result. Do you know what would have happened if that liquid had been clouded, and we had found life in the sealed flask? Sir, if that liquid had held life in it the Vatican would have trembled to hear it, and there would have been anxious questionings and ominous whisperings in the halls of Lambeth palace! The accepted cosmogonies on trial, sir!

Traditions, sanctities, creeds, ecclesiastical establishments, all shaking to know whether my little sixpenny flask of fluid looks muddy or not! I don't know whether to laugh or shudder. The thought of an oecumenical council having its leading feature dislocated by my trifling experiment! The thought, again, of the mighty revolution in human beliefs and affairs that might grow out of the same insignificant little phenomenon. A wine-glassful of clear liquid growing muddy. If we had found a wriggle, or a zigzag, or a shoot from one side to the other, in this last flask, what a scare there would have been, to be sure, in the schools of the prophets! Talk about your megatherium and your megalosaurus, what are these to the bacterium and the vibrio? These are the dreadful monsters of today. If they show themselves where they have no business, the little rascals frighten honest folks worse than ever people were frightened by the Dragon of Rhodes!

The Master gets going sometimes, there is no denying it, until his imagination runs away with him. He had been trying, as the reader sees, one of those curious experiments in spontaneous generation, as it is called, which have been so often instituted of late years, and by none more thoroughly than by that eminent American student of nature (Professor Jeffries Wyman) whose process he had imitated with a result like his.

We got talking over these matters among us the next morning at the breakfast-table.

We must agree they couldn't stand six hours' boiling, I said.

Good for the Pope of Rome! exclaimed the Master.

The Landlady drew back with a certain expression of dismay in her countenance. She hoped he did n't want the Pope to make any more converts in this country. She had heard a sermon only last Sabbath, and the minister had made it out, she thought, as plain as could be, that the Pope was the Man of Sin and that the Church of Rome was, well, there was very strong names applied to her in Scripture.

What was good for the Pope was good for your minister, too, my dear madam, said the Master. Good for everybody that is afraid of what people call "science." If it should prove that dead things come to life of themselves, it would be awkward, you know, because then somebody will get up and say if one dead thing made itself alive another might, and so perhaps the earth peopled itself without any help. Possibly the difficulty wouldn't be so great as many people suppose. We might perhaps find room for a Creator after all, as we do now, though we see a little brown seed grow till it sucks up the juices of half an acre of ground, apparently all by its own inherent power. That does not stagger us; I am not sure that it would if Mr. Crosses or Mr. Weekes's acarus should show himself all of a sudden, as they said he did, in certain mineral mixtures acted on by electricity.

The Landlady was off soundings, and looking vacant enough by this time.

The Master turned to me. Don't think too much of the result of our one experiment. It means something, because it confirms those other experiments of which it was a copy; but we must remember that a hundred negatives don't settle such a question. Life does get into the world somehow. You don't suppose Adam had the cutaneous unpleasantness politely called psora, do you?

Hardly, I answered. He must have been a walking hospital if he carried all the maladies about him which have plagued his descendants.

Well, then, how did the little beast which is peculiar to that special complaint intrude himself into the Order of Things? You don't suppose there was a special act of creation for the express purpose of bestowing that little wretch on humanity, do you?

I thought, on the whole, I would n't answer that question.

You and I are at work on the same problem, said the Young Astronomer to the Master. I have looked into a microscope now and then, and I have seen that perpetual dancing about of minute atoms in a fluid, which you call molecular motion. Just so, when I look through my telescope I see the star-dust whirling about in the infinite expanse of ether; or if I do not see its motion, I know that it is only on account of its immeasurable distance. Matter and motion everywhere; void and rest nowhere. You ask why your restless microscopic atoms may not come together and become self-conscious and self-moving organisms. I ask why my telescopic star-dust may not come together and grow and organize into habitable worlds, the ripened fruit on the branches of the tree Yggdrasil, if I may borrow from our friend the Poet's province. It frightens people, though, to hear the suggestion that worlds shape themselves from star-mist. It does not trouble them at all to see the watery spheres that round themselves into being out of the vapors floating over us; they are nothing but raindrops. But if a planet can grow as a rain-drop grows, why then. It was a great comfort to these timid folk when Lord Rosse's telescope resolved certain nebula into star-clusters. Sir John Herschel would have told them that this made little difference in accounting for the formation of worlds by aggregation, but at any rate it was a comfort to them.

These people have always been afraid of the astronomers, said the Master. They were shy, you know, of the Copernican system, for a long while; well they might be with an oubliette waiting for them if they ventured to think that the earth moved round the sun. Science settled that point finally for them, at length, and then it was all right, when there was no use in disputing the fact any longer. By and by geology began turning up fossils that told extraordinary stories about the duration of life upon our planet. What subterfuges were not used to get rid of their evidence! Think of a man seeing the fossilized skeleton of an animal split out of a quarry, his teeth worn down by mastication, and the remains of food still visible in his interior, and, in order to get rid of a piece of evidence contrary to the traditions he holds to, seriously maintaining that this skeleton never belonged to a living creature, but was created with just these appearances; a make-believe, a sham, a Barnum's-mermaid contrivance to amuse its Creator and impose upon his intelligent children! And now people talk about geological epochs and hundreds of millions of years in the planet's history as calmly as if they were discussing the age of their deceased great-grandmothers. Ten or a dozen years ago people said Sh! Sh! if you ventured to meddle with any question supposed to involve a doubt of the generally accepted Hebrew traditions. To-day such questions are recognized as perfectly fair subjects for general conversation; not in the basement story, perhaps, or among the rank and file of the curbstone congregations, but among intelligent and educated persons. You may preach about them in your pulpit, you may lecture about them, you may talk about them with the first sensible-looking person you happen to meet, you may write magazine articles about them, and the editor need not expect to receive remonstrances from angry subscribers and withdrawals of subscriptions, as he would have been sure to not a great many years ago. Why, you may go to a tea-party where the clergyman's wife shows her best cap and his daughters display their shining ringlets, and you will hear the company discussing the Darwinian theory of the origin of the human race as if it were as harmless a question as that of the lineage of a spinster's lapdog. You may see a fine lady who is as particular in her genuflections as any Buddhist or Mahometan saint in his manifestations of reverence, who will talk over the anthropoid ape, the supposed founder of the family to which we belong, and even go back with you to the acephalous mollusk, first cousin to the clams and mussels, whose rudimental spine was the hinted prophecy of humanity; all this time never dreaming, apparently, that what she takes for a matter of curious speculation involves the whole future of human progress and destiny.

I can't help thinking that if we had talked as freely as we can and do now in the days of the first boarder at this table, I mean the one who introduced it to the public, it would have sounded a good deal more aggressively than it does now. The old Master got rather warm in talking; perhaps the consciousness of having a number of listeners had something to do with it.

This whole business is an open question, he said, and there is no use in saying, "Hush! don't talk about such things!" People do talk about 'em everywhere; and if they don't talk about 'em they think about 'em, and that is worse, if there is anything bad about such questions, that is. If for the Fall of man, science comes to substitute the RISE of man, sir, it means the utter disintegration of all the spiritual pessimisms which have been like a spasm in the heart and a cramp in the intellect of men for so many centuries. And yet who dares to say that it is not a perfectly legitimate and proper question to be discussed, without the slightest regard to the fears or the threats of Pope or prelate?

Sir, I believe, the Master rose from his chair as he spoke, and said in a deep and solemn tone, but without any declamatory vehemence, sir, I believe that we are at this moment in what will be recognized not many centuries hence as one of the late watches in the night of the dark ages. There is a twilight ray, beyond question. We know something of the universe, a very little, and, strangely enough, we know most of what is farthest from us. We have weighed the planets and analyzed the flames of the sun and stars. We predict their movements as if they were machines we ourselves had made and regulated. We know a good deal about the earth on which we live. But the study of man has been so completely subjected to our preconceived opinions, that we have got to begin all over again. We have studied anthropology through theology; we have now to begin the study of theology through anthropology. Until we have exhausted the human element in every form of belief, and that can only be done by what we may call comparative spiritual anatomy, we cannot begin to deal with the alleged extra-human elements without blundering into all imaginable puerilities. If you think for one moment that there is not a single religion in the world which does not come to us through the medium of a preexisting language; and if you remember that this language embodies absolutely nothing but human conceptions and human passions, you will see at once that every religion presupposes its own elements as already existing in those to whom it is addressed. I once went to a church in London and heard the famous Edward Irving preach, and heard some of his congregation speak in the strange words characteristic of their miraculous gift of tongues. I had a respect for the logical basis of this singular phenomenon. I have always thought it was natural that any celestial message should demand a language of its own, only to be understood by divine illumination. All human words tend, of course, to stop short in human meaning. And the more I hear the most sacred terms employed, the more I am satisfied that they have entirely and radically different meanings in the minds of those who use them. Yet they deal with them as if they were as definite as mathematical quantities or geometrical figures. What would become of arithmetic if the figure 2 meant three for one man and five for another and twenty for a third, and all the other numerals were in the same way variable quantities? Mighty intelligent correspondence business men would have with each other! But how is this any worse than the difference of opinion which led a famous clergyman to say to a brother theologian, "Oh, I see, my dear sir, your God is my Devil."

Man has been studied proudly, contemptuously, rather, from the point of view supposed to be authoritatively settled. The self-sufficiency of egotistic natures was never more fully shown than in the expositions of the worthlessness and wretchedness of their fellow-creatures given by the dogmatists who have "gone back," as the vulgar phrase is, on their race, their own flesh and blood. Did you ever read what Mr. Bancroft says about Calvin in his article on Jonathan

Edwards? and mighty well said it is too, in my judgment. Let me remind you of it, whether you have read it or not. "Setting himself up over against the privileged classes, he, with a loftier pride than theirs, revealed the power of a yet higher order of nobility, not of a registered ancestry of fifteen generations, but one absolutely spotless in its escutcheon, preordained in the council chamber of eternity." I think you'll find I have got that sentence right, word for word, and there's a great deal more in it than many good folks who call themselves after the reformer seem to be aware of. The Pope put his foot on the neck of kings, but Calvin and his cohort crushed the whole human race under their heels in the name of the Lord of Hosts. Now, you see, the point that people don't understand is the absolute and utter humility of science, in opposition to this doctrinal self-sufficiency. I don't doubt this may sound a little paradoxical at first, but I think you will find it is all right. You remember the courtier and the monarch, Louis the Fourteenth, wasn't it? never mind, give the poor fellows that live by setting you right a chance. "What o'clock is it?" says the king. "Just whatever o'clock your Majesty pleases," says the courtier. I venture to say the monarch was a great deal more humble than the follower, who pretended that his master was superior to such trifling facts as the revolution of the planet. It was the same thing, you remember, with King Canute and the tide on the sea-shore. The king accepted the scientific fact of the tide's rising. The loyal hangers-on, who believed in divine right, were too proud of the company they found themselves in to make any such humiliating admission. But there are people, and plenty of them, to-day, who will dispute facts just as clear to those who have taken the pains to learn what is known about them, as that of the tide's rising. They don't like to admit these facts, because they throw doubt upon some of their cherished opinions. We are getting on towards the last part of this nineteenth century. What we have gained is not so much in positive knowledge, though that is a good deal, as it is in the freedom of discussion of every subject that comes within the range of observation and inference. How long is it since Mrs. Piozzi wrote, "Let me hope that you will not pursue geology till it leads you into doubts destructive of all comfort in this world and all happiness in the next"?

The Master paused and I remained silent, for I was thinking things I could not say.

It is well always to have a woman near by when one is talking on this class of subjects. Whether there will be three or four women to one man in heaven is a question which I must leave to those who talk as if they knew all about the future condition of the race to answer. But very certainly there is much more of hearty faith, much more of spiritual life, among women than among men, in this world. They need faith to support them more than men do, for they have a great deal less to call them out of themselves, and it comes easier to them, for their habitual state of dependence teaches them to trust in others. When they become voters, if they ever do, it may be feared that the pews will lose what the ward-rooms gain. Relax a woman's hold on man, and her knee-joints will soon begin to stiffen. Self-assertion brings out many fine qualities, but it does not promote devotional habits.

I remember some such thoughts as this were passing through my mind while the Master was talking. I noticed that the Lady was listening to the conversation with a look of more than usual interest. We men have the talk mostly to ourselves at this table; the Master, as you have found out, is fond of monologues, and I myself, well, I suppose I must own to a certain love for the reverberated music of my own accents; at any rate, the Master and I do most of the talking. But others help us do the listening. I think I can show that they listen to some purpose. I am going to surprise my reader with a letter which I received very shortly after the conversation took place which I have just reported. It is of course by a special license, such as belongs to the supreme prerogative of an author, that I am enabled to present it to him. He need ask no questions: it is not his affair how I obtained the right to give publicity to a private communication. I have become somewhat more intimately acquainted with the writer of it than in the earlier period of my connection with this establishment, and I think I may say have gained her confidence to a very considerable degree.

MY DEAR SIR: The conversations I have had with you, limited as they have been, have convinced me that I am quite safe in addressing you with freedom on a subject which interests me, and others more than myself. We at our end of the table have been listening, more or less intelligently, to the discussions going on between two or three of you gentlemen on matters of solemn import to us all. This is nothing very new to me. I have been used, from an early period of my life, to hear the discussion of grave questions, both in politics and religion. I have seen gentlemen at my father's table get as warm over a theological point of dispute as in talking over their political differences. I rather think it has always been very much so, in bad as well as in good company; for you remember how Milton's fallen angels amused themselves with disputing on "providence, foreknowledge, will, and fate," and it was the same thing in that club Goldsmith writes so pleasantly about. Indeed, why should not people very often come, in the course of conversation, to the one subject which lies beneath all else about which our thoughts are occupied? And what more natural than that one should be inquiring about what another has accepted and ceased to have any doubts concerning? It seems to me all right that at the proper time, in the proper place, those who are less easily convinced than their neighbors should have the fullest liberty of calling to account all the opinions which others receive without question. Somebody must stand sentry at the outposts of belief, and it is a sentry's business, I believe, to challenge every one who comes near him, friend or foe.

I want you to understand fully that I am not one of those poor nervous creatures who are frightened out of their wits when any question is started that implies the disturbance of their old beliefs. I manage to see some of the periodicals, and now and then dip a little way into a new book which deals with these curious questions you were talking about, and others like them. You know they find their way almost everywhere. They do not worry me in the least. When I was a little girl, they used to say that if you put a horsehair into a tub of water it would turn into a snake in the course of a few days. That did not seem to me so very much stranger than it was that an egg should turn into a chicken. What can I say to that? Only that it is the Lord's doings, and marvellous in my eyes; and if our philosophical friend should find some little live creatures, or what seem to be live creatures, in any of his messes, I should say as much, and no more. You do not think I would shut up my Bible and Prayer-Book because there is one more thing I do not understand in a world where I understand so very little of all the wonders that surround me?

It may be very wrong to pay any attention to those speculations about the origin of mankind which seem to conflict with the Sacred Record. But perhaps there is some way of reconciling them, as there is of making the seven days of creation harmonize with modern geology. At least, these speculations are curious enough in themselves; and I have seen so many good and handsome children come of parents who were anything but virtuous and comely, that I can believe in almost any amount of improvement taking place in a tribe of living beings, if time and opportunity favor it. I have read in books of natural history that dogs came originally from wolves. When I remember my little Flora, who, as I used to think, could do everything but talk, it does not seem to me that she was much nearer her savage ancestors than some of the horrid cannibal wretches are to their neighbors the great apes.

You see that I am tolerably liberal in my habit of looking at all these questions. We women drift along with the current of the times, listening, in our quiet way, to the discussions going on round us in books and in conversation, and shift the phrases in which we think and talk with something of the same ease as that with which we change our style of dress from year to year. I doubt if you of the other sex know what an effect this habit of accommodating our tastes to changing standards has upon us. Nothing is fixed in them, as you know; the very law of fashion is change. I suspect we learn from our dressmakers to shift the costume of our minds, and slip on the new fashions of thinking all the more easily because we have been accustomed to new styles of dressing every season.

It frightens me to see how much I have written without having yet said a word of what I began this letter on purpose to say. I have taken so much space in "defining my position," to borrow the politicians' phrase, that I begin to fear you will be out of patience before you come to the part of my letter I care most about your reading.

What I want to say is this. When these matters are talked about before persons of different ages and various shades of intelligence, I think one ought to be very careful that his use of language does not injure the sensibilities, perhaps blunt the reverential feelings, of those who are listening to him. You of the sterner sex say that we women have intuitions, but not logic, as our birthright. I shall not commit my sex by conceding this to be true as a whole, but I will accept the first half of it, and I will go so far as to say that we do not always care to follow out a train of thought until it ends in a blind cul de sac, as some of what are called the logical people are fond of doing.

Now I want to remind you that religion is not a matter of intellectual luxury to those of us who are interested in it, but something very different. It is our life, and more than our life; for that is measured by pulse-beats, but our religious consciousness partakes of the Infinite, towards which it is constantly yearning. It is very possible that a hundred or five hundred years from now the forms of religious belief may be so altered that we should hardly know them. But the sense of dependence on Divine influence and the need of communion with the unseen and eternal will be then just what they are now. It is not the geologist's hammer, or the astronomer's telescope, or the naturalist's microscope, that is going to take away the need of the human soul for that Rock to rest upon which is higher than itself, that Star which never sets, that all-pervading Presence which gives life to all the least moving atoms of the immeasurable universe.

I have no fears for myself, and listen very quietly to all your debates. I go from your philosophical discussions to the reading of Jeremy Taylor's "Rule and Exercises of Holy Dying" without feeling that I have unfitted myself in the least degree for its solemn reflections. And, as I have mentioned his name, I cannot help saying that I do not believe that good man himself would have ever shown the bitterness to those who seem to be at variance with the received doctrines which one may see in some of the newspapers that call themselves "religious." I have kept a few old books from my honored father's library, and among them is another of his which I always thought had more true Christianity in its title than there is in a good many whole volumes. I am going to take the book down, or up, for it is not a little one, and write out the title, which, I dare say, you remember, and very likely you have the book. "Discourse of the Liberty of Prophesying, showing the Unreasonableness of prescribing to other Men's Faith, and the Iniquity of persecuting Different Opinions."

Now, my dear sir, I am sure you believe that I want to be liberal and reasonable, and not to act like those weak alarmists who, whenever the silly sheep begin to skip as if something was after them, and huddle together in their fright, are sure there must be a bear or a lion coming to eat them up. But for all that, I want to beg you to handle some of these points, which are so involved in the creed of a good many well-intentioned persons that you cannot separate them from it without picking their whole belief to pieces, with more thought for them than you might think at first they were entitled to. I have no doubt you gentlemen are as wise as serpents, and I want you to be as harmless as doves.

The Young Girl who sits by me has, I know, strong religious instincts. Instead of setting her out to ask all sorts of questions, I would rather, if I had my way, encourage her to form a habit of attending to religious duties, and make the most of the simple faith in which she was bred. I think there are a good many questions young persons may safely postpone to a more convenient season; and as this young creature is overworked, I hate to have her excited by the fever of doubt which it cannot be denied is largely prevailing in our time.

I know you must have looked on our other young friend, who has devoted himself to the sublimest of the sciences, with as much interest as I do. When I was a little girl I used to write out a line of Young's as a copy in my writing-book,

"An undevout astronomer is mad";

but I do not now feel quite so sure that the contemplation of all the multitude of remote worlds does not tend to weaken the idea of a personal Deity. It is not so much that nebular theory which worries me, when I think about this subject, as a kind of bewilderment when I try to conceive of a consciousness filling all those frightful blanks of space they talk about. I sometimes doubt whether that young man worships anything but the stars. They tell me that many young students of science like him never see the inside of a church. I cannot help wishing they did. It humanizes people, quite apart from any higher influence it exerts upon them. One reason, perhaps, why they do not care to go to places of worship is that they are liable to hear the questions they know something about handled in sermons by those who know very much less about them. And so they lose a great deal. Almost every human being, however vague his notions of the Power addressed, is capable of being lifted and solemnized by the exercise of public prayer. When I was a young girl we travelled in Europe, and I visited Ferney with my parents; and I remember we all stopped before a chapel, and I read upon its front, I knew Latin enough to understand it, I am pleased to say, Deo erexit Voltaire. I never forgot it; and knowing what a sad scoffer he was at most sacred things, I could not but be impressed with the fact that even he was not satisfied with himself, until he had shown his devotion in a public and lasting form.

We all want religion sooner or later. I am afraid there are some who have no natural turn for it, as there are persons without an ear for music, to which, if I remember right, I heard one of you comparing what you called religious genius. But sorrow and misery bring even these to know what it means, in a great many instances. May I not say to you, my friend, that I am one who has learned the secret of the inner life by the discipline of trials in the life of outward circumstance? I can remember the time when I thought more about the shade of color in a ribbon, whether it matched my complexion or not, than I did about my spiritual interests in this world or the next. It was needful that I should learn the meaning of that text, "Whom the Lord loveth he chasteneth."

Since I have been taught in the school of trial I have felt, as I never could before, how precious an inheritance is the smallest patrimony of faith. When everything seemed gone from me, I found I had still one possession. The bruised reed that I had never leaned on became my staff. The smoking flax which had been a worry to my eyes burst into flame, and I lighted the taper at it which has since guided all my footsteps. And I am but one of the thousands who have had the same experience. They have been through the depths of affliction, and know the needs of the human soul. It will find its God in the unseen, Father, Saviour, Divine Spirit, Virgin Mother, it must and will breathe its longings and its griefs into the heart of a Being capable of understanding all its necessities and sympathizing with all its woes.

I am jealous, yes, I own I am jealous of any word, spoken or written, that would tend to impair that birthright of reverence which becomes for so many in after years the basis of a deeper religious sentiment. And yet, as I have said, I cannot and will not shut my eyes to the problems which may seriously affect our modes of conceiving the eternal truths on which, and by which, our souls must live. What a fearful time is this into which we poor sensitive and timid creatures are born! I suppose the life of every century has more or less special resemblance to that of some particular Apostle. I cannot help thinking this century has Thomas for its model. How do you suppose the other Apostles felt when that experimental philosopher explored the wounds of the Being who to them was divine with his inquisitive forefinger? In our time that finger has multiplied itself into ten thousand thousand implements of research, challenging all mysteries, weighing the world as in a balance, and sifting through its prisms and spectroscopes the light that comes from the throne of the Eternal.

Pity us, dear Lord, pity us! The peace in believing which belonged to other ages is not for us. Again Thy wounds are opened that we may know whether it is the blood of one like ourselves which flows from them, or whether it is a Divinity that is bleeding for His creatures. Wilt Thou not take the doubt of Thy children whom the time commands to try all things in the place of the unquestioning faith of earlier and simpler-hearted generations? We too have need of Thee. Thy martyrs in other ages were cast into the flames, but no fire could touch their immortal and indestructible faith. We sit in safety and in peace, so far as these poor bodies are concerned; but our cherished beliefs, the hopes, the trust that stayed the hearts of those we loved who have gone before us, are cast into the fiery furnace of an age which is fast turning to dross the certainties and the sanctities once prized as our most precious inheritance. You will understand me, my dear sir, and all my solicitudes and apprehensions. Had I never been assailed by the questions that meet all thinking persons in our time, I might not have thought so anxiously about the risk of perplexing others. I know as well as you must that there are many articles of belief clinging to the skirts of our time which are the bequests of the ages of ignorance that God winked at. But for all that I would train a child in the nurture and admonition of the Lord, according to the simplest and best creed I could disentangle from those barbarisms, and I would in every way try to keep up in young persons that standard of reverence for all sacred subjects which may, without any violent transition, grow and ripen into the devotion of later years. Believe me,

Very sincerely yours,

I have thought a good deal about this letter and the writer of it lately. She seemed at first removed to a distance from all of us, but here I find myself in somewhat near relations with her. What has surprised me more than that, however, is to find that she is becoming so much acquainted with the Register of Deeds. Of all persons in the world, I should least have thought of him as like to be interested in her, and still less, if possible, of her fancying him. I can only say they have been in pretty close conversation several times of late, and, if I dared to think it of so very calm and dignified a personage, I should say that her color was a little heightened after one or more of these interviews. No! that would be too absurd! But I begin to think nothing is absurd in the matter of the relations of the two sexes; and if this high-bred woman fancies the attentions of a piece of human machinery like this elderly individual, it is none of my business.

I have been at work on some more of the Young Astronomer's lines. I find less occasion for meddling with them as he grows more used to versification. I think I could analyze the processes going on in his mind, and the conflict of instincts which he cannot in the nature of things understand. But it is as well to give the reader a chance to find out for himself what is going on in the young man's heart and intellect.

WIND-CLOUDS AND STAR-DRIFTS.

III

The snows that glittered on the disk of Mars
Have melted, and the planet's fiery orb
Rolls in the crimson summer of its year;
But what to me the summer or the snow
Of worlds that throb with life in forms unknown,
If life indeed be theirs; I heed not these.
My heart is simply human; all my care
For them whose dust is fashioned like mine own;

These ache with cold and hunger, live in pain,
And shake with fear of worlds more full of woe;
There may be others worthier of my love,
But such I know not save through these I know.

There are two veils of language, hid beneath
Whose sheltering folds, we dare to be ourselves;
And not that other self which nods and smiles
And babbles in our name; the one is Prayer,
Lending its licensed freedom to the tongue
That tells our sorrows and our sins to Heaven;
The other, Verse, that throws its spangled web
Around our naked speech and makes it bold.
I, whose best prayer is silence; sitting dumb
In the great temple where I nightly serve
Him who is throned in light, have dared to claim
The poet's franchise, though I may not hope
To wear his garland; hear me while I tell
My story in such form as poets use,
But breathed in fitful whispers, as the wind
Sighs and then slumbers, wakes and sighs again.

Thou Vision, floating in the breathless air
Between me and the fairest of the stars,
I tell my lonely thoughts as unto thee.
Look not for marvels of the scholar's pen
In my rude measure; I can only show
A slender-margined, unillumined page,
And trust its meaning to the flattering eye
That reads it in the gracious light of love.
Ah, wouldst thou clothe thyself in breathing shape
And nestle at my side, my voice should lend
Whate'er my verse may lack of tender rhythm
To make thee listen.

I have stood entranced
When, with her fingers wandering o'er the keys,
The white enchantress with the golden hair
Breathed all her soul through some unvalued rhyme;
Some flower of song that long had lost its bloom;
Lo! its dead summer kindled as she sang!
The sweet contralto, like the ringdove's coo,
Thrilled it with brooding, fond, caressing tones,
And the pale minstrel's passion lived again,
Tearful and trembling as a dewy rose
The wind has shaken till it fills the air
With light and fragrance. Such the wondrous charm
A song can borrow when the bosom throbs
That lends it breath.

So from the poet's lips
His verse sounds doubly sweet, for none like him
Feels every cadence of its wave-like flow;
He lives the passion over, while he reads,

That shook him as he sang his lofty strain,
And pours his life through each resounding line,
As ocean, when the stormy winds are hushed,
Still rolls and thunders through his billowy caves.

Let me retrace the record of the years
That made me what I am. A man most wise,
But overworn with toil and bent with age,
Sought me to be his scholar, me, run wild
From books and teachers, kindled in my soul
The love of knowledge; led me to his tower,
Showed me the wonders of the midnight realm
His hollow sceptre ruled, or seemed to rule,
Taught me the mighty secrets of the spheres,
Trained me to find the glimmering specks of light
Beyond the unaided sense, and on my chart
To string them one by one, in order due,
As on a rosary a saint his beads.

I was his only scholar; I became
The echo to his thought; whate'er he knew
Was mine for asking; so from year to year
We wrought together, till there came a time
When I, the learner, was the master half
Of the twinned being in the dome-crowned tower.

Minds roll in paths like planets; they revolve
This in a larger, that a narrower ring,
But round they come at last to that same phase,
That self-same light and shade they showed before.
I learned his annual and his monthly tale,
His weekly axiom and his daily phrase,
I felt them coming in the laden air,
And watched them laboring up to vocal breath,
Even as the first-born at his father's board
Knows ere he speaks the too familiar jest
Is on its way, by some mysterious sign
Forewarned, the click before the striking bell.

He shrivelled as I spread my growing leaves,
Till trust and reverence changed to pitying care;
He lived for me in what he once had been,
But I for him, a shadow, a defence,
The guardian of his fame, his guide, his staff,
Leaned on so long he fell if left alone.
I was his eye, his ear, his cunning hand,
Love was my spur and longing after fame,
But his the goading thorn of sleepless age
That sees its shortening span, its lengthening shades,
That clutches what it may with eager grasp,
And drops at last with empty, outstretched hands.

All this he dreamed not. He would sit him down
Thinking to work his problems as of old,

And find the star he thought so plain a blur,
The columned figures labyrinthine wilds
Without my comment, blind and senseless scrawls
That vexed him with their riddles; he would strive
And struggle for a while, and then his eye
Would lose its light, and over all his mind
The cold gray mist would settle; and erelong
The darkness fell, and I was left alone.

Alone! no climber of an Alpine cliff,
No Arctic venturer on the waveless sea,
Feels the dread stillness round him as it chills
The heart of him who leaves the slumbering earth
To watch the silent worlds that crowd the sky.

Alone! And as the shepherd leaves his flock
To feed upon the hillside, he meanwhile
Finds converse in the warblings of the pipe
Himself has fashioned for his vacant hour,
So have I grown companion to myself,
And to the wandering spirits of the air
That smile and whisper round us in our dreams.
Thus have I learned to search if I may know
The whence and why of all beneath the stars
And all beyond them, and to weigh my life
As in a balance, poising good and ill
Against each other,-asking of the Power
That flung me forth among the whirling worlds,
If I am heir to any inborn right,
Or only as an atom of the dust
That every wind may blow where'er it will.

I am not humble; I was shown my place,
Clad in such robes as Nature had at hand;
Took what she gave, not chose; I know no shame,
No fear for being simply what I am.
I am not proud, I hold my every breath
At Nature's mercy. I am as a babe
Borne in a giant's arms, he knows not where;
Each several heart-beat, counted like the coin
A miser reckons, is a special gift
As from an unseen hand; if that withhold
Its bounty for a moment, I am left
A clod upon the earth to which I fall.

Something I find in me that well might claim
The love of beings in a sphere above
This doubtful twilight world of right and wrong;
Something that shows me of the self-same clay
That creeps or swims or flies in humblest form.
Had I been asked, before I left my bed
Of shapeless dust, what clothing I would wear,
I would have said, More angel and less worm;
But for their sake who are even such as I,

Of the same mingled blood, I would not choose
To hate that meaner portion of myself
Which makes me brother to the least of men.

I dare not be a coward with my lips
Who dare to question all things in my soul;
Some men may find their wisdom on their knees,
Some prone and grovelling in the dust like slaves;
Let the meek glow-worm glisten in the dew;
I ask to lift my taper to the sky
As they who hold their lamps above their heads,
Trusting the larger currents up aloft,
Rather than crossing eddies round their breast,
Threatening with every puff the flickering blaze.

My life shall be a challenge, not a truce!
This is my homage to the mightier powers,
To ask my boldest question, undismayed
By muttered threats that some hysteric sense
Of wrong or insult will convulse the throne
Where wisdom reigns supreme; and if I err,
They all must err who have to feel their way
As bats that fly at noon; for what are we
But creatures of the night, dragged forth by day,
Who needs must stumble, and with stammering steps
Spell out their paths in syllables of pain?

Thou wilt not hold in scorn the child who dares
Look up to Thee, the Father, dares to ask
More than Thy wisdom answers. From Thy hand
The worlds were cast; yet every leaflet claims
From that same hand its little shining sphere
Of star-lit dew; thine image, the great sun,
Girt with his mantle of tempestuous flame,

Glares in mid-heaven; but to his noontide blaze
The slender violet lifts its lidless eye,
And from his splendor steals its fairest hue,
Its sweetest perfume from his scorching fire.

I may just as well stop here as anywhere, for there is more of the manuscript to come, and I can only give it in instalments.

The Young Astronomer had told me I might read any portions of his manuscript I saw fit to certain friends. I tried this last extract on the old Master.

It's the same story we all have to tell, said he, when I had done reading. We are all asking questions nowadays. I should like to hear him read some of his verses himself, and I think some of the other boarders would like to. I wonder if he wouldn't do it, if we asked him! Poets read their own compositions in a singsong sort of way; but they do seem to love 'em so, that I always enjoy it. It makes me laugh a little inwardly to see how they dandle their poetical babies, but I don't let them know it. We must get up a select party of the boarders to hear him read. We'll send him a regular invitation. I will put my name at the head of it, and you shall write it.

That was neatly done. How I hate writing such things! But I suppose I must do it.

CHAPTER VIII

The Master and I had been thinking for some time of trying to get the Young Astronomer round to our side of the table. There are many subjects on which both of us like to talk with him, and it would be convenient to have him nearer to us. How to manage it was not quite so clear as it might have been. The Scarabee wanted to sit with his back to the light, as it was in his present position. He used his eyes so much in studying minute objects, that he wished to spare them all fatigue, and did not like facing a window. Neither of us cared to ask the Man of Letters, so called, to change his place, and of course we could not think of making such a request of the Young Girl or the Lady. So we were at a stand with reference to this project of ours.

But while we were proposing, Fate or Providence disposed everything for us. The Man of Letters, so called, was missing one morning, having folded his tent, that is, packed his carpet-bag with the silence of the Arabs, and encamped, that is, taken lodgings in some locality which he had forgotten to indicate.

The Landlady bore this sudden bereavement remarkably well. Her remarks and reflections; though borrowing the aid of homely imagery and doing occasional violence to the nicer usages of speech, were not without philosophical discrimination.

I like a gentleman that is a gentleman. But there's a difference in what folks call gentlemen as there is in what you put on table. There is cabbages and there is cauliflowers. There is clams and there is oysters. There is mackerel and there is salmon. And there is some that knows the difference and some that doos n't. I had a little account with that boarder that he forgot to settle before he went off, so all of a suddin. I sha'n't say anything about it. I've seen the time when I should have felt bad about losing what he owed me, but it was no great matter; and if he 'll only stay away now he 's gone, I can stand losing it, and not cry my eyes out nor lay awake all night neither. I never had ought to have took him. Where he come from and where he's gone to is unbeknown to me. If he'd only smoked good tobacco, I wouldn't have said a word; but it was such dreadful stuff, it 'll take a week to get his chamber sweet enough to show them that asks for rooms. It doos smell like all possest.

Left any goods? asked the Salesman.

Or dockermunts? added the Member of the Haouse.

The Landlady answered with a faded smile, which implied that there was no hope in that direction. Dr. Benjamin, with a sudden recurrence of youthful feeling, made a fan with the fingers of his right hand, the second phalanx of the thumb resting on the tip of the nose, and the remaining digits diverging from each other, in the plane of the median line of the face, I suppose this is the way he would have described the gesture, which is almost a specialty of the Parisian gamin. That Boy immediately copied it, and added greatly to its effect by extending the fingers of the other hand in a line with those of the first, and vigorously agitating those of the two hands, a gesture which acts like a puncture on the distended self-esteem of one to whom it is addressed, and cheapens the memory of the absent to a very low figure.

I wish the reader to observe that I treasure up with interest all the words uttered by the Salesman. It must have been noticed that he very rarely speaks. Perhaps he has an inner life, with its own deep emotional, and lofty contemplative elements, but as we see him, he is the boarder reduced to the simplest expression of that term. Yet, like most human creatures, he has generic and specific characters not unworthy of being studied. I notice particularly a certain electrical briskness of movement, such as one may see in a squirrel, which clearly belongs to his calling. The dry-goodsman's life behind his counter is a succession of sudden, snappy perceptions and brief series of coordinate spasms; as thus:

"Purple calico, three quarters wide, six yards."

Up goes the arm; bang! tumbles out the flat roll and turns half a dozen somersets, as if for the fun of the thing; the six yards of calico hurry over the measuring nails, hunching their backs up, like six cankerworms; out jump the scissors; snip, clip, rip; the stuff is wisped up, brown papered, tied, labelled, delivered, and the man is himself again, like a child just come out of a convulsion-fit. Think of a man's having some hundreds of these semi-epileptic seizures every day, and you need not wonder that he does not say much; these fits take the talk all out of him.

But because he, or any other man, does not say much, it does not follow that he may not have, as I have said, an exalted and intense inner life. I have known a number of cases where a man who seemed thoroughly commonplace and unemotional has all at once surprised everybody by telling the story of his hidden life far more pointedly and dramatically than any playwright or novelist or poet could have told it for him. I will not insult your intelligence, Beloved, by saying how he has told it.

We had been talking over the subjects touched upon in the Lady's letter.

I suppose one man in a dozen said the Master ought to be born a skeptic. That was the proportion among the Apostles, at any rate.

So there was one Judas among them, I remarked.

Well, said the Master, they 've been whitewashing Judas of late. But never mind him. I did not say there was not one rogue on the average among a dozen men. I don't see how that would interfere with my proposition. If I say that among a dozen men you ought to find one that weighs over a hundred and fifty pounds, and you tell me that there were twelve men in your club, and one of 'em had red hair, I don't see that you have materially damaged my statement.

I thought it best to let the old Master have his easy victory, which was more apparent than real, very evidently, and he went on.

When the Lord sends out a batch of human beings, say a hundred. Did you ever read my book, the new edition of it, I mean?

It is rather awkward to answer such a question in the negative, but I said, with the best grace I could, "No, not the last edition."

Well, I must give you a copy of it. My book and I are pretty much the same thing. Sometimes I steal from my book in my talk without mentioning it, and then I say to myself, "Oh, that won't do; everybody has read my book and knows it by heart." And then the other I says, you know there are two of us, right and left, like a pair of shoes, the other I says, "You're a something or other fool. They have n't read your confounded old book; besides, if they have, they have forgotten all about it." Another time, I say, thinking I will be very honest, "I have said something about that in my book"; and then the other I says, "What a Balaam's quadruped you are to tell 'em it's in your book; they don't care whether it is or not, if it's anything worth saying; and if it isn't worth saying, what are you braying for?" That is a rather sensible fellow, that other chap we talk with, but an impudent whelp. I never got such abuse from any blackguard in my life as I have from that No. 2 of me, the one that answers the other's questions and makes the comments, and does what in demotic phrase is called the "sarsing."

I laughed at that. I have just such a fellow always with me, as wise as Solomon, if I would only heed him; but as insolent as Shimei, cursing, and throwing stones and dirt, and behaving as if he had the traditions of the "ape-like human being" born with him rather than civilized instincts. One does not have to be a king to know what it is to keep a king's jester.

I mentioned my book, the Master said, because I have something in it on the subject we were talking about. I should like to read you a passage here and there out of it, where I have expressed myself a little more freely on some of those matters we handle in conversation. If you don't quarrel with it, I must give you a copy of the book. It's a rather serious thing to get a copy of a book from the writer of it. It has made my adjectives sweat pretty hard, I know, to put together an answer returning thanks and not lying beyond the twilight of veracity, if one may use a figure. Let me try a little of my book on you, in divided doses, as my friends the doctors say.

Fiat experimentum in corpore vili, I said, laughing at my own expense. I don't doubt the medicament is quite as good as the patient deserves, and probably a great deal better, I added, reinforcing my feeble compliment.

[When you pay a compliment to an author, don't qualify it in the next sentence so as to take all the goodness out of it. Now I am thinking of it, I will give you one or two pieces of advice. Be careful to assure yourself that the person you are talking with wrote the article or book you praise. It is not very pleasant to be told, "Well, there, now! I always liked your writings, but you never did anything half so good as this last piece," and then to have to tell the blunderer that this last piece is n't yours, but t' other man's. Take care that the phrase or sentence you commend is not one that is in quotation-marks. "The best thing in your piece, I think, is a line I do not remember meeting before; it struck me as very true and well expressed:

"'An honest man's the noblest work of God.'

"But, my dear lady, that line is one which is to be found in a writer of the last century, and not original with me." One ought not to have undeceived her, perhaps, but one is naturally honest, and cannot bear to be credited with what is not his own. The lady blushes, of course, and says she has not read much ancient literature, or some such thing. The pearl upon the Ethiop's arm is very pretty in verse, but one does not care to furnish the dark background for other persons' jewelry.]

I adjourned from the table in company with the old Master to his apartments. He was evidently in easy circumstances, for he had the best accommodations the house afforded. We passed through a reception room to his library, where everything showed that he had ample means for indulging the modest tastes of a scholar.

The first thing, naturally, when one enters a scholar's study or library, is to look at his books. One gets a notion very speedily of his tastes and the range of his pursuits by a glance round his bookshelves.

Of course, you know there are many fine houses where the library is a part of the upholstery, so to speak. Books in handsome binding kept locked under plate-glass in showy dwarf bookcases are as important to stylish establishments as servants in livery; who sit with folded arms, are to stylish equipages. I suppose those wonderful statues with the folded arms do sometimes change their attitude, and I suppose those books with the gilded backs do sometimes get opened, but it is nobody's business whether they do or not, and it is not best to ask too many questions.

This sort of thing is common enough, but there is another case that may prove deceptive if you undertake to judge from appearances. Once in a while you will come on a house where you will find a family of readers and almost no library. Some of the most indefatigable devourers of literature have very few books. They belong to book clubs, they haunt the public libraries, they borrow of friends, and somehow or other get hold of everything they want, scoop out all it holds for them, and have done with it. When I want a book, it is as a tiger wants a sheep. I must have it with one spring, and, if I miss it, go away defeated and hungry. And my experience with public libraries is that the first volume of the book I inquire for is out, unless I happen to want the second, when that is out.

I was pretty well prepared to understand the Master's library and his account of it. We seated ourselves in two very comfortable chairs, and I began the conversation.

I see you have a large and rather miscellaneous collection of books. Did you get them together by accident or according to some preconceived plan?

Both, sir, both, the Master answered. When Providence throws a good book in my way, I bow to its decree and purchase it as an act of piety, if it is reasonably or unreasonably cheap. I adopt a certain number of books every year, out of a love for the foundlings and stray children of other people's brains that nobody seems to care for. Look here.

He took down a Greek Lexicon finely bound in calf, and spread it open.

Do you see that Hedericus? I had Greek dictionaries enough and to spare, but I saw that noble quarto lying in the midst of an ignoble crowd of cheap books, and marked with a price which I felt to be an insult to scholarship, to the memory of Homer, sir, and the awful shade of AEschylus. I paid the mean price asked for it, and I wanted to double it, but I suppose it would have been a foolish sacrifice of coin to sentiment: I love that book for its looks and behavior. None of your "half-calf" economies in that volume, sir! And see how it lies open anywhere! There is n't a book in my library that has such a generous way of laying its treasures before you. From Alpha to Omega, calm, assured rest at any page that your choice or accident may light on. No lifting of a rebellious leaf like an upstart servant that does not know his place and can never be taught manners, but tranquil, well-bred repose. A book may be a perfect gentleman in its aspect and demeanor, and this book would be good company for personages like Roger Ascham and his pupils the Lady Elizabeth and the Lady Jane Grey.

The Master was evidently riding a hobby, and what I wanted to know was the plan on which he had formed his library. So I brought him back to the point by asking him the question in so many words.

Yes, he said, I have a kind of notion of the way in which a library ought to be put together, no, I don't mean that, I mean ought to grow. I don't pretend to say that mine is a model, but it serves my turn well enough, and it represents me pretty accurately. A scholar must shape his own shell, secrete it one might almost say, for secretion is only separation, you know, of certain elements derived from the materials of the world about us. And a scholar's study, with the books lining its walls, is his shell. It is n't a mollusk's shell, either; it 's a caddice-worm's shell. You know about the caddice-worm?

More or less; less rather than more, was my humble reply.

Well, sir, the caddice-worm is the larva of a fly, and he makes a case for himself out of all sorts of bits of everything that happen to suit his particular fancy, dead or alive, sticks and stones and small shells with their owners in 'em, living as comfortable as ever. Every one of these caddiceworms has his special fancy as to what he will pick up and glue together, with a kind of natural cement he provides himself, to make his case out of. In it he lives, sticking his head and shoulders out once in a while, that is all. Don't you see that a student in his library is a caddice-worm in his case? I've told you that I take an interest in pretty much everything, and don't mean to fence out any human interests from the private grounds of my intelligence. Then, again, there is a subject, perhaps I may say there is more than one, that I want to exhaust, to know to the very bottom. And besides, of course I must have my literary harem, my pare aux cerfs, where my favorites await my moments of leisure and pleasure, my scarce and precious editions, my luxurious typographical masterpieces; my Delilahs, that take my head in their lap: the pleasant story-tellers and the like; the books I love because they are fair to look upon, prized by collectors, endeared by old associations, secret treasures that nobody else knows anything about; books, in short, that I like for insufficient reasons it may be, but peremptorily, and mean to like and to love and to cherish till death us do part.

Don't you see I have given you a key to the way my library is made up, so that you can apriorize the plan according to which I have filled my bookcases? I will tell you how it is carried out.

In the first place, you see, I have four extensive cyclopaedias. Out of these I can get information enough to serve my immediate purpose on almost any subject. These, of course, are supplemented by geographical, biographical, bibliographical, and other dictionaries, including of course lexicons to all the languages I ever meddle with. Next to these come the works relating to my one or two specialties, and these collections I make as perfect as I can. Every library should try to be complete on something, if it were only on the history of pin-heads. I don't mean that I buy all the trashy compilations on my special subjects, but I try to have all the works of any real importance relating to them, old as well as new. In the following compartment you will find the great authors in all the languages I have mastered, from Homer and Hesiod downward to the last great English name.

This division, you see, you can make almost as extensive or as limited as you choose. You can crowd the great representative writers into a small compass; or you can make a library consisting only of the different editions of Horace, if you have space and money enough. Then comes the Harem, the shelf or the bookcase of Delilahs, that you have paid wicked prices for, that you love without pretending to be reasonable about it, and would bag in case of fire before all the rest, just as Mr. Townley took the Clytie to his carriage when the anti-Catholic mob threatened his house in 1780. As for the foundlings like my Hedericus, they go among their peers; it is a pleasure to take them, from the dusty stall where they were elbowed by plebeian school-books and battered odd volumes, and give them Alduses and Elzevirs for companions.

Nothing remains but the Infirmary. The most painful subjects are the unfortunates that have lost a cover. Bound a hundred years ago, perhaps, and one of the rich old browned covers gone, what a pity! Do you know what to do about it? I'll tell you, no, I'll show you. Look at this volume. M. T. Ciceronis Opera, a dozen of 'em, one of 'em minus half his cover, a poor one-legged cripple, six months ago, now see him.

He looked very respectably indeed, both covers dark, ancient, very decently matched; one would hardly notice the fact that they were not twins.

I'll tell you what I did. You poor devil, said I, you are a disgrace to your family. We must send you to a surgeon and have some kind of a Taliacotian operation performed on you. (You remember the operation as described in Hudibras, of course.) The first thing was to find a subject of similar age and aspect ready to part with one of his members. So I went to Quidlibet's, you know Quidlibet and that hieroglyphic sign of his with the omniscient-looking eye as its most prominent feature, and laid my case before him. I want you, said I, to look up an old book of mighty little value, one of your ten-cent vagabonds would be the sort of thing, but an old beggar, with a cover like this, and lay it by for me.

And Quidlibet, who is a pleasant body to deal with, only he has insulted one or two gentlemanly books by selling them to me at very low-bred and shamefully insufficient prices, Quidlibet, I say, laid by three old books for me to help myself from, and did n't take the trouble even to make me pay the thirty cents for 'em. Well, said I to myself, let us look at our three books that have undergone the last insult short of the trunkmaker's or the paper-mills, and see what they are. There may be something worth looking at in one or the other of 'em.

Now do you know it was with a kind of a tremor that I untied the package and looked at these three unfortunates, too humble for the companionable dime to recognize as its equal in value. The same sort of feeling you know if you ever tried the Bible-and-key, or the Sortes Virgiliance. I think you will like to know what the three books were which had been bestowed upon me gratis, that I might tear away one of the covers of the one that best matched my Cicero, and give it to the binder to cobble my crippled volume with.

The Master took the three books from a cupboard and continued.

No. I. An odd volume of The Adventurer. It has many interesting things enough, but is made precious by containing Simon Browne's famous Dedication to the Queen of his Answer to Tindal's "Christianity as old as the Creation." Simon Browne was the Man without a Soul. An excellent person, a most worthy dissenting minister, but lying under a strange delusion.

Here is a paragraph from his Dedication:

"He was once a man; and of some little name; but of no worth, as his present unparalleled case makes but too manifest; for by the immediate hand of an avenging GOD, his very thinking substance has, for more than seven years, been continually wasting away, till it is wholly perished out of him, if it be not utterly come to nothing. None, no, not the least remembrance of its very ruins, remains, not the shadow of an idea is left, nor any sense that so much as one single one, perfect or imperfect, whole or diminished, ever did appear to a mind within him, or was perceived by it."

Think of this as the Dedication of a book "universally allowed to be the best which that controversy produced," and what a flood of light it pours on the insanities of those self-analyzing diarists whose morbid reveries have been so often mistaken for piety! No. I. had something for me, then, besides the cover, which was all it claimed to have worth offering.

No. II. was "A View of Society and Manners in Italy." Vol. III. By John Moore, M. D. (Zeluco Moore.) You know his pleasant book. In this particular volume what interested me most, perhaps, was the very spirited and intelligent account of the miracle of the liquefaction of the blood of Saint Januarius, but it gave me an hour's mighty agreeable reading. So much for Number Two.

No. III. was "An ESSAY On the Great EFFECTS of Even Languid and Unheeded LOCAL MOTION." By the Hon. Robert Boyle. Published in 1685, and, as appears from other sources, "received with great and general applause." I confess I was a little startled to find how near this earlier philosopher had come to the modern doctrines, such as are illustrated in Tyndall's "Heat considered as a Mode of Motion." He speaks of "Us, who endeavor to resolve the Phenomena of Nature into Matter and Local motion." That sounds like the nineteenth century, but what shall we say to this? "As when a bar of iron or silver, having been well hammered, is newly taken off of the anvil; though the eye can discern no motion in it, yet the touch will readily perceive it to be very hot, and if you spit upon it, the brisk agitation of the insensible parts will become visible in that which they will produce in the liquor." He takes a bar of tin, and tries whether by bending it to and fro two or three times he cannot "procure a considerable internal commotion among the parts "; and having by this means broken or cracked it in the middle, finds, as he expected, that the middle parts had considerably heated each other. There are many other curious and interesting observations in the volume which I should like to tell you of, but these will serve my purpose.

Which book furnished you the old cover you wanted? said I.

Did he kill the owl? said the Master, laughing. [I suppose you, the reader, know the owl story.] It was Number Two that lent me one of his covers. Poor wretch! He was one of three, and had lost his two brothers. From him that hath not shall be taken even that which he hath. The Scripture had to be fulfilled in his case. But I couldn't help saying to myself, What do you keep writing books for, when the stalls are covered all over with 'em, good books, too, that nobody will give ten cents apiece for, lying there like so many dead beasts of burden, of no account except to strip off their hides? What is the use, I say? I have made a book or two in my time, and I am making another that perhaps will see the light one of these days. But if I had my life to live over again, I think I should go in for silence, and get as near to Nirvana as I could. This language is such a paltry tool! The handle of it cuts and the blade doesn't. You muddle yourself by not knowing what you mean by a word, and send out your unanswered riddles and rebuses to clear up other people's difficulties. It always seems to me that talk is a ripple and thought is a ground swell. A string of words, that mean pretty much anything, helps you in a certain sense to get hold of a thought, just as a string of syllables that mean nothing helps you to a word; but it's a poor business, it's a poor business, and the more you study definition the more you find out how poor it is. Do you know I sometimes think our little entomological neighbor is doing a sounder business than we people that make books about ourselves and our slippery abstractions? A man can see the spots on a bug and count 'em, and tell what their color is, and put another bug alongside of him and see whether the two are alike or different. And when he uses a word he knows just what he means. There is no mistake as to the meaning and identity of pulex irritans, confound him!

What if we should look in, some day, on the Scarabeeist, as he calls himself? said I. The fact is the Master had got agoing at such a rate that I was willing to give a little turn to the conversation.

Oh, very well, said the Master, I had some more things to say, but I don't doubt they'll keep. And besides, I take an interest in entomology, and have my own opinion on the meloe question.

You don't mean to say you have studied insects as well as solar systems and the order of things generally?

He looked pleased. All philosophers look pleased when people say to them virtually, "Ye are gods." The Master says he is vain constitutionally, and thanks God that he is. I don't think he has enough vanity to make a fool of himself with it, but the simple truth is he cannot help knowing that he has a wide and lively intelligence, and it pleases him to know it, and to be reminded of it, especially in an oblique and tangential sort of way, so as not to look like downright flattery.

Yes, yes, I have amused a summer or two with insects, among other things. I described a new tabanus, horsefly, you know, which, I think, had escaped notice. I felt as grand when I showed up my new discovery as if I had created the beast. I don't doubt Herschel felt as if he had made a planet when he first showed the astronomers Georgium Sidus, as he called it. And that reminds me of something. I was riding on the outside of a stagecoach from London to Windsor in the year, never mind the year, but it must have been in June, I suppose, for I bought some strawberries. England owes me a sixpence with interest from date, for I gave the woman a shilling, and the coach contrived to start or the woman timed it so that I just missed getting my change. What an odd thing memory is, to be sure, to have kept such a triviality, and have lost so much that was invaluable! She is a crazy wench, that Mnemosyne; she throws her jewels out of the window and locks up straws and old rags in her strong box.

[De profundis! said I to myself, the bottom of the bushel has dropped out! Sancta Maria, ora pro nobis!]

But as I was saying, I was riding on the outside of a stage-coach from London to Windsor, when all at once a picture familiar to me from my New England village childhood came upon me like a reminiscence rather than a revelation. It was a mighty bewilderment of slanted masts and spars and ladders and ropes, from the midst of which a vast tube, looking as if it might be a piece of ordnance such as the revolted angels battered the walls of Heaven with, according to Milton, lifted its muzzle defiantly towards the sky. Why, you blessed old rattletrap, said I to myself, I know you as well as I know my father's spectacles and snuff-box! And that same crazy witch of a Memory, so divinely wise and foolish, travels thirty-five hundred miles or so in a single pulse-beat, makes straight for an old house and an old library and an old corner of it, and whisks out a volume of an old cyclopaedia, and there is the picture of which this is the original. Sir William Herschel's great telescope! It was just about as big, as it stood there by the roadside, as it was in the picture, not much different any way. Why should it be? The pupil of your eye is only a gimlet-hole, not so very much bigger than the eye of a sail-needle, and a camel has to go through it before you can see him. You look into a stereoscope and think you see a miniature of a building or a mountain; you don't, you're made a fool of by your lying intelligence, as you call it; you see the building and the mountain just as large as with your naked eye looking straight at the real objects. Doubt it, do you? Perhaps you'd like to doubt it to the music of a couple of gold five-dollar pieces. If you would, say the word, and man and money, as Messrs. Heenan and Morrissey have it, shall be forthcoming; for I will make you look at a real landscape with your right eye, and a stereoscopic view of it with your left eye, both at once, and you can slide one over the other by a little management and see how exactly the picture overlies the true landscape. We won't try it now, because I want to read you something out of my book.

I have noticed that the Master very rarely fails to come back to his original proposition, though he, like myself, is fond of zigzagging in order to reach it. Men's minds are like the pieces on a chess-board in their way of moving. One mind creeps from the square it is on to the next, straight forward, like the pawns. Another sticks close to its own line of thought and follows it as far as it goes, with no heed for others' opinions, as the bishop sweeps the board in the line of his own color. And another class of minds break through everything that lies before them, ride over argument and opposition, and go to the end of the board, like the castle. But there is still another sort of intellect which is very apt to jump over the thought that stands next and come down in the unexpected way of the knight. But that same knight, as the chess manuals will show you, will contrive to get on to every square of the board in a pretty series of moves that looks like a pattern of embroidery, and so these zigzagging minds like the Master's, and I suppose my own is something like it, will sooner or later get back to the square next the one they started from.

The Master took down a volume from one of the shelves. I could not help noticing that it was a shelf near his hand as he sat, and that the volume looked as if he had made frequent use of it. I saw, too, that he handled it in a loving sort of way; the tenderness he would have bestowed on a wife and children had to find a channel somewhere, and what more natural than that he should look fondly on the volume which held the thoughts that had rolled themselves smooth and round in his mind like pebbles on a beach, the dreams which, under cover of the simple artifices such as all writers use, told the little world of readers his secret hopes and aspirations, the fancies which had pleased him and which he could not bear to let die without trying to please others with them? I have a great sympathy with authors, most of all with unsuccessful ones. If one had a dozen lives or so, it would all be very well, but to have only a single ticket in the great lottery, and have that drawn a blank, is a rather sad sort of thing. So I was pleased to see the affectionate kind of pride with which the Master handled his book; it was a success, in its way, and he looked on it with a cheerful sense that he had a right to be proud of it. The Master opened the volume, and, putting on his large round glasses, began reading, as authors love to read that love their books.

The only good reason for believing in the stability of the moral order of things is to be found in the tolerable steadiness of human averages. Out of a hundred human beings fifty-one will be found in the long run on the side of the right, so far as they know it, and against the wrong. They will be organizers rather than disorganizers, helpers and not hinderers in the upward movement of the race. This is the main fact we have to depend on. The right hand of the great organism is a little stronger than the left, that is all.

Now and then we come across a left-handed man. So now and then we find a tribe or a generation, the subject of what we may call moral left-handedness, but that need not trouble us about our formula. All we have to do is to spread the average over a wider territory or a longer period of time. Any race or period that insists on being left-handed must go under if it comes in contact with a right-handed one. If there were, as a general rule, fifty-one rogues in the hundred instead of forty-nine, all other qualities of mind and body being equally distributed between the two sections, the order of things would sooner or later end in universal disorder. It is the question between the leak and the pumps.

It does not seem very likely that the Creator of all things is taken by surprise at witnessing anything any of his creatures do or think. Men have sought out many inventions, but they can have contrived nothing which did not exist as an idea in the omniscient consciousness to which past, present, and future are alike Now.

We read what travellers tell us about the King of Dahomey, or the Fejee Island people, or the short and simple annals of the celebrities recorded in the Newgate Calendar, and do not know just what to make of these brothers and sisters of the race; but I do not suppose an intelligence even as high as the angelic beings, to stop short there, would see anything very peculiar or wonderful about them, except as everything is wonderful and unlike everything else.

It is very curious to see how science, that is, looking at and arranging the facts of a case with our own eyes and our own intelligence, without minding what somebody else has said, or how some old majority vote went in a pack of intriguing ecclesiastics, I say it is very curious to see how science is catching up with one superstition after another.

There is a recognized branch of science familiar to all those who know anything of the studies relating to life, under the name of Teratology. It deals with all sorts of monstrosities which are to be met with in living beings, and more especially in animals. It is found that what used to be called lusus naturae, or freaks of nature, are just as much subject to laws as the naturally developed forms of living creatures.

The rustic looks at the Siamese twins, and thinks he is contemplating an unheard-of anomaly; but there are plenty of cases like theirs in the books of scholars, and though they are not quite so common as double cherries, the mechanism of their formation is not a whit more mysterious than that of the twinned fruits. Such cases do not disturb the average arrangement; we have Changs and Engs at one pole, and Cains and Abels at the other. One child is born with six fingers on each hand, and another falls short by one or more fingers of his due allowance; but the glover puts his faith in the great law of averages, and makes his gloves with five fingers apiece, trusting nature for their counterparts.

Thinking people are not going to be scared out of explaining or at least trying to explain things by the shrieks of persons whose beliefs are disturbed thereby. Comets were portents to Increase

Mather, President of Harvard College; "preachers of Divine wrath, heralds and messengers of evil tidings to the world." It is not so very long since Professor Winthrop was teaching at the same institution. I can remember two of his boys very well, old boys, it is true, they were, and one of them wore a three-cornered cocked hat; but the father of these boys, whom, as I say, I can remember, had to defend himself against the minister of the Old South Church for the impiety of trying to account for earthquakes on natural principles. And his ancestor, Governor Winthrop, would probably have shaken his head over his descendant's dangerous audacity, if one may judge by the solemn way in which he mentions poor Mrs. Hutchinson's unpleasant experience, which so grievously disappointed her maternal expectations. But people used always to be terribly frightened by those irregular vital products which we now call "interesting specimens" and carefully preserve in jars of alcohol. It took next to nothing to make a panic; a child was born a few centuries ago with six teeth in its head, and about that time the Turks began gaining great advantages over the Christians. Of course there was an intimate connection between the prodigy and the calamity. So said the wise men of that day.

All these out-of-the-way cases are studied connectedly now, and are found to obey very exact rules. With a little management one can even manufacture living monstrosities. Malformed salmon and other fish can be supplied in quantity, if anybody happens to want them. Now, what all I have said is tending to is exactly this, namely, that just as the celestial movements are regulated by fixed laws, just as bodily monstrosities are produced according to rule, and with as good reason as normal shapes, so obliquities of character are to be accounted for on perfectly natural principles; they are just as capable of classification as the bodily ones, and they all diverge from a certain average or middle term which is the type of its kind. If life had been a little longer I would have written a number of essays for which, as it is, I cannot expect to have time. I have set down the titles of a hundred or more, and I have often been tempted to publish these, for according to my idea, the title of a book very often renders the rest of it unnecessary. "Moral Teratology," for instance, which is marked No. 67 on my list of "Essays Potential, not Actual," suggests sufficiently well what I should be like to say in the pages it would preface. People hold up their hands at a moral monster as if there was no reason for his existence but his own choice. That was a fine specimen we read of in the papers a few years ago, the Frenchman, it may be remembered, who used to waylay and murder young women, and after appropriating their effects, bury their bodies in a private cemetery he kept for that purpose. It is very natural, and I do not say it is not very proper, to hang such eccentric persons as this; but it is not clear whether his vagaries produce any more sensation at Headquarters than the meek enterprises of the mildest of city missionaries. For the study of Moral Teratology will teach you that you do not get such a malformed character as that without a long chain of causes to account for it; and if you only knew those causes, you would know perfectly well what to expect.

You may feel pretty sure that our friend of the private cemetery was not the child of pious and intelligent parents; that he was not nurtured by the best of mothers, and educated by the most judicious teachers; and that he did not come of a lineage long known and honored for its intellectual and moral qualities. Suppose that one should go to the worst quarter of the city and pick out the worst-looking child of the worst couple he could find, and then train him up successively at the School for Infant Rogues, the Academy for Young Scamps, and the College for Complete Criminal Education, would it be reasonable to expect a Francois Xavier or a Henry Martyn to be the result of such a training? The traditionists, in whose presumptuous hands the science of anthropology has been trusted from time immemorial, have insisted on eliminating cause and effect from the domain of morals. When they have come across a moral monster they have seemed to think that he put himself together, having a free choice of all the constituents which make up manhood, and that consequently no punishment could be too bad for him.

I say, hang him and welcome, if that is the best thing for society; hate him, in a certain sense, as you hate a rattlesnake, but, if you pretend to be a philosopher, recognize the fact that what you hate in him is chiefly misfortune, and that if you had been born with his villanous low forehead and poisoned instincts, and bred among creatures of the Races Maudites whose natural history has to be studied like that of beasts of prey and vermin, you would not have been sitting there in your gold-bowed spectacles and passing judgment on the peccadilloes of your fellow-creatures.

I have seen men and women so disinterested and noble, and devoted to the best works, that it appeared to me if any good and faithful servant was entitled to enter into the joys of his Lord, such as these might be. But I do not know that I ever met with a human being who seemed to me to have a stronger claim on the pitying consideration and kindness of his Maker than a wretched, puny, crippled, stunted child that I saw in Newgate, who was pointed out as one of the most notorious and inveterate little thieves in London. I have no doubt that some of those who were looking at this pitiable morbid secretion of the diseased social organism thought they were very virtuous for hating him so heartily.

It is natural, and in one sense is all right enough. I want to catch a thief and put the extinguisher on an incendiary as much as my neighbors do; but I have two sides to my consciousness as I have two sides to my heart, one carrying dark, impure blood, and the other the bright stream which has been purified and vivified by the great source of life and death, the oxygen of the air which gives all things their vital heat, and burns all things at last to ashes.

One side of me loves and hates; the other side of me judges, say rather pleads and suspends judgment. I think, if I were left to myself, I should hang a rogue and then write his apology and subscribe to a neat monument, commemorating, not his virtues, but his misfortunes. I should, perhaps, adorn the marble with emblems, as is the custom with regard to the more regular and normally constituted members of society. It would not be proper to put the image of a lamb upon the stone which marked the resting-place of him of the private cemetery. But I would not hesitate to place the effigy of a wolf or a hyena upon the monument. I do not judge these animals, I only kill them or shut them up. I presume they stand just as well with their Maker as lambs and kids, and the existence of such beings is a perpetual plea for God Almighty's poor, yelling, scalping Indians, his weasand-stopping Thugs, his despised felons, his murdering miscreants, and all the unfortunates whom we, picked individuals of a picked class of a picked race, scrubbed, combed, and catechized from our cradles upward, undertake to find accommodations for in another state of being where it is to be hoped they will have a better chance than they had in this.

The Master paused, and took off his great round spectacles. I could not help thinking that he looked benevolent enough to pardon Judas Iscariot just at that moment, though his features can knot themselves up pretty, formidably on occasion.

You are somewhat of a phrenologist, I judge, by the way you talk of instinctive and inherited tendencies I said.

They tell me I ought to be, he answered, parrying my question, as I thought. I have had a famous chart made out of my cerebral organs, according to which I ought to have been, something more than a poor Magister Artaum.

I thought a shade of regret deepened the lines on his broad, antique-looking forehead, and I began talking about all the sights I had seen in the way of monstrosities, of which I had a considerable list, as you will see when I tell you my weakness in that direction. This, you understand, Beloved, is private and confidential.

I pay my quarter of a dollar and go into all the side-shows that follow the caravans and circuses round the country. I have made friends of all the giants and all the dwarfs. I became acquainted with Monsieur Bihin, le plus bel homme du monde, and one of the biggest, a great many years ago, and have kept up my agreeable relations with him ever since. He is a most interesting giant, with a softness of voice and tenderness of feeling which I find very engaging. I was on friendly terms with Mr. Charles Freeman, a very superior giant of American birth, seven feet four, I think, in height, "double-jointed," of mylodon muscularity, the same who in a British prize-ring tossed the Tipton Slasher from one side of the rope to the other, and now lies stretched, poor fellow! in a mighty grave in the same soil which holds the sacred ashes of Cribb, and the honored dust of Burke, not the one "commonly called the sublime," but that other Burke to whom Nature had denied the sense of hearing lest he should be spoiled by listening to the praises of the admiring circles which looked on his dear-bought triumphs. Nor have I despised those little ones whom that devout worshipper of Nature in her exceptional forms, the distinguished Barnum, has introduced to the notice of mankind. The General touches his chapeau to me, and the Commodore gives me a sailor's greeting. I have had confidential interviews with the double-headed daughter of Africa, so far, at least, as her twofold personality admitted of private confidences. I have listened to the touching experiences of the Bearded Lady, whose rough cheeks belie her susceptible heart. Miss Jane Campbell has allowed me to question her on the delicate subject of avoirdupois equivalents; and the armless fair one, whose embrace no monarch could hope to win, has wrought me a watch-paper with those despised digits which have been degraded from gloves to boots in our evolution from the condition of quadrumana.

I hope you have read my experiences as good-naturedly as the old Master listened to them. He seemed to be pleased with my whim, and promised to go with me to see all the side-shows of the next caravan. Before I left him he wrote my name in a copy of the new edition of his book, telling me that it would not all be new to me by a great deal, for he often talked what he had printed to make up for having printed a good deal of what he had talked.

Here is the passage of his Poem the Young Astronomer read to us.

WIND-CLOUDS AND STAR-DRIFTS.

IV

From my lone turret as I look around
O'er the green meadows to the ring of blue,
From slope, from summit, and from half-hid vale
The sky is stabbed with dagger-pointed spires,
Their gilded symbols whirling in the wind,
Their brazen tongues proclaiming to the world,
Here truth is sold, the only genuine ware;
See that it has our trade-mark!
You will buy Poison instead of food across the way,
The lies of this or that, each several name
The standard's blazon and the battle-cry
Of some true-gospel faction, and again
The token of the Beast to all beside.
And grouped round each I see a huddling crowd
Alike in all things save the words they use;
In love, in longing, hate and fear the same.

Whom do we trust and serve? We speak of one
And bow to many; Athens still would find
The shrines of all she worshipped safe within
Our tall barbarian temples, and the thrones
That crowned Olympus mighty as of old.
The god of music rules the Sabbath choir;
The lyric muse must leave the sacred nine

To help us please the dilettante's ear;
Plutus limps homeward with us, as we leave
The portals of the temple where we knelt
And listened while the god of eloquence
(Hermes of ancient days, but now disguised
In sable vestments) with that other god
Somnus, the son of Erebus and Nog,
Fights in unequal contest for our souls;
The dreadful sovereign of the under world
Still shakes his sceptre at us, and we hear
The baying of the triple-throated hound;
Eros-is young as ever, and as fair
The lovely Goddess born of ocean's foam.

These be thy gods, O Israel! Who is he,
The one ye name and tell us that ye serve,
Whom ye would call me from my lonely tower
To worship with the many-headed throng?
Is it the God that walked in Eden's grove
In the cool hour to seek our guilty sire?
The God who dealt with Abraham as the sons
Of that old patriarch deal with other men?
The jealous God of Moses, one who feels
An image as an insult, and is wroth
With him who made it and his child unborn?
The God who plagued his people for the sin
Of their adulterous king, beloved of him,
The same who offers to a chosen few
The right to praise him in eternal song
While a vast shrieking world of endless woe
Blends its dread chorus with their rapturous hymn?
Is this the God ye mean, or is it he
Who heeds the sparrow's fall, whose loving heart
Is as the pitying father's to his child,
Whose lesson to his children is, "Forgive,"
Whose plea for all, "They know not what they do"

I claim the right of knowing whom I serve,
Else is my service idle; He that asks
My homage asks it from a reasoning soul.
To crawl is not to worship; we have learned
A drill of eyelids, bended neck and knee,
Hanging our prayers on binges, till we ape
The flexures of the many-jointed worm.
Asia has taught her Aliabs and salaams
To the world's children, we have grown to men!
We who have rolled the sphere beneath our feet
To find a virgin forest, as we lay
The beams of our rude temple, first of all
Must frame its doorway high enough for man
To pass unstooping; knowing as we do
That He who shaped us last of living forms
Has long enough been served by creeping things,
Reptiles that left their foot-prints in the sand

Of old sea-margins that have turned to stone,
And men who learned their ritual; we demand
To know him first, then trust him and then love
When we have found him worthy of our love,
Tried by our own poor hearts and not before;
He must be truer than the truest friend,
He must be tenderer than a woman's love,
A father better than the best of sires;
Kinder than she who bore us, though we sin
Oftener than did the brother we are told,
We-poor ill-tempered mortals-must forgive,
Though seven times sinning threescore times and ten.

This is the new world's gospel: Be ye men!
Try well the legends of the children's time;
Ye are the chosen people, God has led
Your steps across the desert of the deep
As now across the desert of the shore;
Mountains are cleft before you as the sea
Before the wandering tribe of Israel's sons;
Still onward rolls the thunderous caravan,
Its coming printed on the western sky,
A cloud by day, by night a pillared flame;
Your prophets are a hundred unto one
Of them of old who cried, "Thus saith the Lord";
They told of cities that should fall in heaps,
But yours of mightier cities that shall rise
Where yet the lonely fishers spread their nets,
Where hides the fox and hoots the midnight owl;
The tree of knowledge in your garden grows
Not single, but at every humble door;
Its branches lend you their immortal food,
That fills you with the sense of what ye are,
No servants of an altar hewed and carved
From senseless stone by craft of human hands,
Rabbi, or dervish, Brahmin, bishop, bonze,
But masters of the charm with which they work
To keep your hands from that forbidden tree!

Ye that have tasted that divinest fruit,
Look on this world of yours with opened eyes!
Ye are as gods! Nay, makers of your gods,
Each day ye break an image in your shrine
And plant a fairer image where it stood
Where is the Moloch of your fathers' creed,
Whose fires of torment burned for span-long babes?
Fit object for a tender mother's love!
Why not? It was a bargain duly made
For these same infants through the surety's act
Intrusted with their all for earth and heaven,
By Him who chose their guardian, knowing well
His fitness for the task, this, even this,
Was the true doctrine only yesterday
As thoughts are reckoned, and to-day you hear

In words that sound as if from human tongues
Those monstrous, uncouth horrors of the past
That blot the blue of heaven and shame the earth
As would the saurians of the age of slime,
Awaking from their stony sepulchres
And wallowing hateful in the eye of day!

Four of us listened to these lines as the young man read them, the Master and myself and our two ladies. This was the little party we got up to hear him read. I do not think much of it was very new to the Master or myself. At any rate, he said to me when we were alone, That is the kind of talk the "natural man," as the theologians call him, is apt to fall into.

I thought it was the Apostle Paul, and not the theologians, that used the term "natural man", I ventured to suggest.

I should like to know where the Apostle Paul learned English? said the Master, with the look of one who does not mean to be tripped up if he can help himself. But at any rate, he continued, the "natural man," so called, is worth listening to now and then, for he didn't make his nature, and the Devil did n't make it; and if the Almighty made it, I never saw or heard of anything he made that wasn't worth attending to.

The young man begged the Lady to pardon anything that might sound harshly in these crude thoughts of his. He had been taught strange things, he said, from old theologies, when he was a child, and had thought his way out of many of his early superstitions. As for the Young Girl, our Scheherezade, he said to her that she must have got dreadfully tired (at which she colored up and said it was no such thing), and he promised that, to pay for her goodness in listening, he would give her a lesson in astronomy the next fair evening, if she would be his scholar, at which she blushed deeper than before, and said something which certainly was not No.

CHAPTER IX

There was no sooner a vacancy on our side of the table, than the Master proposed a change of seats which would bring the Young Astronomer into our immediate neighborhood. The Scarabee was to move into the place of our late unlamented associate, the Man of Letters, so called. I was to take his place, the Master to take mine, and the young man that which had been occupied by the Master. The advantages of this change were obvious. The old Master likes an audience, plainly enough; and with myself on one side of him, and the young student of science, whose speculative turn is sufficiently shown in the passages from his poem, on the other side, he may feel quite sure of being listened to. There is only one trouble in the arrangement, and that is that it brings this young man not only close to us, but also next to our Scheherezade.

I am obliged to confess that he has shown occasional marks of inattention even while the Master was discoursing in a way that I found agreeable enough. I am quite sure it is no intentional disrespect to the old Master. It seems to me rather that he has become interested in the astronomical lessons he has been giving the Young Girl. He has studied so much alone, that it is naturally a pleasure to him to impart some of his knowledge. As for his young pupil, she has often thought of being a teacher herself, so that she is of course very glad to acquire any accomplishment that may be useful to her in that capacity. I do not see any reason why some of the boarders should have made such remarks as they have done. One cannot teach astronomy to advantage, without going out of doors, though I confess that when two young people go out by daylight to study the stars, as these young folks have done once or twice, I do not so much wonder at a remark or suggestion from those who have nothing better to do than study their neighbors.

I ought to have told the reader before this that I found, as I suspected, that our innocent-looking Scheherezade was at the bottom of the popgun business. I watched her very closely, and one day, when the little monkey made us all laugh by stopping the Member of the Haouse in the middle of a speech he was repeating to us, it was his great effort of the season on a bill for the protection of horn-pout in Little Muddy River, I caught her making the signs that set him going. At a slight tap of her knife against her plate, he got all ready, and presently I saw her cross her knife and fork upon her plate, and as she did so, pop! went the small piece of artillery. The Member of the Haouse was just saying that this bill hit his constitooents in their most vital, when a pellet hit him in the feature of his countenance most exposed to aggressions and least tolerant of liberties. The Member resented this unparliamentary treatment by jumping up from his chair and giving the small aggressor a good shaking, at the same time seizing the implement which had caused his wrath and breaking it into splinters. The Boy blubbered, the Young Girl changed color, and looked as if she would cry, and that was the last of these interruptions.

I must own that I have sometimes wished we had the popgun back, for it answered all the purpose of "the previous question" in a deliberative assembly. No doubt the Young Girl was capricious in setting the little engine at work, but she cut short a good many disquisitions that threatened to be tedious. I find myself often wishing for her and her small fellow-conspirator's intervention, in company where I am supposed to be enjoying myself. When my friend the politician gets too far into the personal details of the quorum pars magna fui, I find myself all at once exclaiming in mental articulation, Popgun! When my friend the story-teller begins that protracted narrative which has often emptied me of all my voluntary laughter for the evening, he has got but a very little way when I say to myself, What wouldn't I give for a pellet from that popgun! In short, so useful has that trivial implement proved as a jaw-stopper and a boricide, that I never go to a club or a dinner-party, without wishing the company included our Scheherezade and That Boy with his popgun.

How clearly I see now into the mechanism of the Young Girl's audacious contrivance for regulating our table-talk! Her brain is tired half the time, and she is too nervous to listen patiently to what a quieter person would like well enough, or at least would not be annoyed by. It amused her to invent a scheme for managing the headstrong talkers, and also let off a certain spirit of mischief which in some of these nervous girls shows itself in much more questionable forms. How cunning these half-hysteric young persons are, to be sure! I had to watch a long time before I detected the telegraphic communication between the two conspirators. I have no doubt she had sedulously schooled the little monkey to his business, and found great delight in the task of instruction.

But now that our Scheherezade has become a scholar instead of a teacher, she seems to be undergoing a remarkable transformation. Astronomy is indeed a noble science. It may well kindle the enthusiasm of a youthful nature. I fancy at times that I see something of that starry light which I noticed in the young man's eyes gradually kindling in hers. But can it be astronomy alone that does it? Her color comes and goes more readily than when the old Master sat next her on the left. It is having this young man at her side, I suppose. Of course it is. I watch her with great, I may say tender interest. If he would only fall in love with her, seize upon her wandering affections and fancies as the Romans seized the Sabine virgins, lift her out of herself and her listless and weary drudgeries, stop the outflow of this young life which is draining itself away in forced literary labor dear me, dear me if, if, if

"If I were God
An' ye were Martin Elginbrod!"

I am afraid all this may never be. I fear that he is too much given to lonely study, to self-companionship, to all sorts of questionings, to looking at life as at a solemn show where he is only a spectator. I dare not build up a romance on what I have yet seen. My reader may, but I will answer for nothing. I shall wait and see.

The old Master and I have at last made that visit to the Scarabee which we had so long promised ourselves.

When we knocked at his door he came and opened it, instead of saying, Come in. He was surprised, I have no doubt, at the sound of our footsteps; for he rarely has a visitor, except the little monkey of a boy, and he may have thought a troop of marauders were coming to rob him of his treasures. Collectors feel so rich in the possession of their rarer specimens, that they forget how cheap their precious things seem to common eyes, and are as afraid of being robbed as if they were dealers in diamonds. They have the name of stealing from each other now and then, it is true, but many of their priceless possessions would hardly tempt a beggar. Values are artificial: you will not be able to get ten cents of the year 1799 for a dime.

The Scarabee was reassured as soon as he saw our faces, and he welcomed us not ungraciously into his small apartment. It was hard to find a place to sit down, for all the chairs were already occupied by cases and boxes full of his favorites. I began, therefore, looking round the room. Bugs of every size and aspect met my eyes wherever they turned. I felt for the moment as I suppose a man may feel in a fit of delirium tremens. Presently my attention was drawn towards a very odd-looking insect on the mantelpiece. This animal was incessantly raising its arms as if towards heaven and clasping them together, as though it were wrestling in prayer.

Do look at this creature, I said to the Master, he seems to be very hard at work at his devotions.

Mantas religiosa, said the Master, I know the praying rogue. Mighty devout and mighty cruel; crushes everything he can master, or impales it on his spiny shanks and feeds upon it, like a gluttonous wretch as he is. I have seen the Mantis religiosa on a larger scale than this, now and then. A sacred insect, sir, sacred to many tribes of men; to the Hottentots, to the Turks, yes, sir, and to the Frenchmen, who call the rascal prie dieu, and believe him to have special charge of children that have lost their way.

Doesn't it seem as if there was a vein of satire as well as of fun that ran through the solemn manifestations of creative wisdom? And of deception too, do you see how nearly those dried leaves resemble an insect?

They do, indeed, I answered, but not so closely as to deceive me. They remind me of an insect, but I could not mistake them for one.

Oh, you couldn't mistake those dried leaves for an insect, hey? Well, how can you mistake that insect for dried leaves? That is the question; for insect it is, phyllum siccifolium, the "walking leaf," as some have called it. The Master had a hearty laugh at my expense.

The Scarabee did not seem to be amused at the Master's remarks or at my blunder. Science is always perfectly serious to him; and he would no more laugh over anything connected with his study, than a clergyman would laugh at a funeral.

They send me all sorts of trumpery, he said, Orthoptera and Lepidoptera; as if a coleopterist, a scarabeeist, cared for such things. This business is no boy's play to me. The insect population of the world is not even catalogued yet, and a lifetime given to the scarabees is a small contribution enough to their study. I like your men of general intelligence well enough, your Linnwuses and your Buffons and your Cuviers; but Cuvier had to go to Latreille for his insects, and if Latreille had been able to consult me, yes, me, gentlemen! he would n't have made the blunders he did about some of the coleoptera.

The old Master, as I think you must have found out by this time, you, Beloved, I mean, who read every word, has a reasonably good opinion, as perhaps he has a right to have, of his own intelligence and acquirements. The Scarabee's exultation and glow as he spoke of the errors of the great entomologist which he himself could have corrected, had the effect on the old Master which a lusty crow has upon the feathered champion of the neighboring barnyard. He too knew something about insects. Had he not discovered a new tabanus? Had he not made preparations of the very coleoptera the Scarabee studied so exclusively, preparations which the illustrious Swammerdam would not have been ashamed of, and dissected a melolontha as exquisitely as Strauss Durckheim himself ever did it? So the Master, recalling these studies of his and certain difficult and disputed points at which he had labored in one of his entomological paroxysms, put a question which there can be little doubt was intended to puzzle the Scarabee, and perhaps, for the best of us is human (I am beginning to love the old Master, but he has his little weaknesses, thank Heaven, like the rest of us), I say perhaps, was meant to show that some folks knew as much about some things as some other folks.

The little dried-up specialist did not dilate into fighting dimensions as, perhaps, again, the Master may have thought he would. He looked a mild surprise, but remained as quiet as one of his own beetles when you touch him and he makes believe he is dead. The blank silence became oppressive. Was the Scarabee crushed, as so many of his namesakes are crushed, under the heel of this trampling omniscient?

At last the Scarabee creaked out very slowly, "Did I understand you to ask the following question, to wit?" and so forth; for I was quite out of my depth, and only know that he repeated the Master's somewhat complex inquiry, word for word.

That was exactly my question, said the Master, and I hope it is not uncivil to ask one which seems to me to be a puzzler.

Not uncivil in the least, said the Scarabee, with something as much like a look of triumph as his dry face permitted, not uncivil at all, but a rather extraordinary question to ask at this date of entomological history. I settled that question some years ago, by a series of dissections, six-and-thirty in number, reported in an essay I can show you and would give you a copy of, but that I am a little restricted in my revenue, and our Society has to be economical, so I have but this one. You see, sir, and he went on with elytra and antennae and tarsi and metatarsi and tracheae and stomata and wing-muscles and leg-muscles and ganglions, all plain enough, I do not doubt, to those accustomed to handling dor-bugs and squash-bugs and such undesirable objects of affection to all but naturalists.

He paused when he got through, not for an answer, for there evidently was none, but to see how the Master would take it. The Scarabee had had it all his own way.

The Master was loyal to his own generous nature. He felt as a peaceful citizen might feel who had squared off at a stranger for some supposed wrong, and suddenly discovered that he was undertaking to chastise Mr. Dick Curtis, "the pet of the Fancy," or Mr. Joshua Hudson; "the John Bull fighter."

He felt the absurdity of his discomfiture, for he turned to me good-naturedly, and said,

"Poor Johnny Raw! What madness could impel
So rum a flat to face so prime a swell?"

To tell the truth, I rather think the Master enjoyed his own defeat. The Scarabee had a right to his victory; a man does not give his life to the study of a single limited subject for nothing, and the moment we come across a first-class expert we begin to take a pride in his superiority. It cannot offend us, who have no right at all to be his match on his own ground. Besides, there is a very curious sense of satisfaction in getting a fair chance to sneer at ourselves and scoff at our own pretensions. The first person of our dual consciousness has been smirking and rubbing his hands and felicitating himself on his innumerable superiorities, until we have grown a little tired of him. Then, when the other fellow, the critic, the cynic, the Shimei, who has been quiet, letting self-love and self-glorification have their perfect work, opens fire upon the first half of our personality and overwhelms it with that wonderful vocabulary of abuse of which he is the unrivalled master, there is no denying that he enjoys it immensely; and as he is ourself for the moment, or at least the chief portion of ourself (the other half-self retiring into a dim corner of semiconsciousness and cowering under the storm of sneers and contumely, you follow me perfectly, Beloved, the way is as plain as the path of the babe to the maternal fount), as, I say, the abusive fellow is the chief part of us for the time, and he likes to exercise his slanderous vocabulary, we on the whole enjoy a brief season of self-depreciation and self-scolding very heartily.

It is quite certain that both of us, the Master and myself, conceived on the instant a respect for the Scarabee which we had not before felt. He had grappled with one difficulty at any rate and mastered it. He had settled one thing, at least, so it appeared, in such a way that it was not to be brought up again. And now he was determined, if it cost him the effort of all his remaining days, to close another discussion and put forever to rest the anxious doubts about the larva of meloe.

Your thirty-six dissections must have cost you a deal of time and labor, the Master said.

What have I to do with time, but to fill it up with labor? answered the Scarabee. It is my meat and drink to work over my beetles. My holidays are when I get a rare specimen. My rest is to watch the habits of insects, those that I do not pretend to study. Here is my muscarium, my home for house-flies; very interesting creatures; here they breed and buzz and feed and enjoy themselves, and die in a good old age of a few months. My favorite insect lives in this other case; she is at home, but in her private-chamber; you shall see her.

He tapped on the glass lightly, and a large, gray, hairy spider came forth from the hollow of a funnel-like web.

And this is all the friend you have to love? said the Master, with a tenderness in his voice which made the question very significant.

Nothing else loves me better than she does, that I know of, he answered.

To think of it! Not even a dog to lick his hand, or a cat to purr and rub her fur against him! Oh, these boarding-houses, these boarding-houses! What forlorn people one sees stranded on their desolate shores! Decayed gentlewomen with the poor wrecks of what once made their households beautiful, disposed around them in narrow chambers as they best may be, coming down day after day, poor souls! to sit at the board with strangers; their hearts full of sad memories which have no language but a sigh, no record but the lines of sorrow on their features; orphans, creatures with growing tendrils and nothing to cling to; lonely rich men, casting about them what to do with the wealth they never knew how to enjoy, when they shall no longer worry over keeping and increasing it; young men and young women, left to their instincts, unguarded, unwatched, save by malicious eyes, which are sure to be found and to find occupation in these miscellaneous collections of human beings; and now and then a shred of humanity like this little adust specialist, with just the resources needed to keep the "radical moisture" from entirely exhaling from his attenuated organism, and busying himself over a point of science, or compiling a hymn-book, or editing a grammar or a dictionary; such are the tenants of boarding-houses whom we cannot think of without feeling how sad it is when the wind is not tempered to the shorn lamb; when the solitary, whose hearts are shrivelling, are not set in families!

The Master was greatly interested in the Scarabee's Muscarium.

I don't remember, he said, that I have heard of such a thing as that before. Mighty curious creatures, these same house-flies! Talk about miracles! Was there ever anything more miraculous, so far as our common observation goes, than the coming and the going of these creatures? Why didn't Job ask where the flies come from and where they go to? I did not say that you and I don't know, but how many people do know anything about it? Where are the cradles of the young flies? Where are the cemeteries of the dead ones, or do they die at all except when we kill them? You think all the flies of the year are dead and gone, and there comes a warm day and all at once there is a general resurrection of 'em; they had been taking a nap, that is all.

I suppose you do not trust your spider in the Muscarium? said I, addressing the Scarabee.

Not exactly, he answered, she is a terrible creature. She loves me, I think, but she is a killer and a cannibal among other insects. I wanted to pair her with a male spider, but it wouldn't do.

Wouldn't do? said I, why not? Don't spiders have their mates as well as other folks?

Oh yes, sometimes; but the females are apt to be particular, and if they don't like the mate you offer them they fall upon him and kill him and eat him up. You see they are a great deal bigger and stronger than the males, and they are always hungry and not always particularly anxious to have one of the other sex bothering round.

Woman's rights! said I, there you have it! Why don't those talking ladies take a spider as their emblem? Let them form arachnoid associations, spinsters and spiders would be a good motto.

The Master smiled. I think it was an eleemosynary smile, for my pleasantry seems to me a particularly basso rilievo, as I look upon it in cold blood. But conversation at the best is only a thin sprinkling of occasional felicities set in platitudes and commonplaces. I never heard people talk like the characters in the "School for Scandal," I should very much like to. I say the Master smiled. But the Scarabee did not relax a muscle of his countenance.

There are persons whom the very mildest of faecetiae sets off into such convulsions of laughter, that one is afraid lest they should injure themselves. Even when a jest misses fire completely, so that it is no jest at all, but only a jocular intention, they laugh just as heartily. Leave out the point of your story, get the word wrong on the duplicity of which the pun that was to excite hilarity depended, and they still honor your abortive attempt with the most lusty and vociferous merriment.

There is a very opposite class of persons whom anything in the nature of a joke perplexes, troubles, and even sometimes irritates, seeming to make them think they are trifled with, if not insulted. If you are fortunate enough to set the whole table laughing, one of this class of persons will look inquiringly round, as if something had happened, and, seeing everybody apparently amused but himself, feel as if he was being laughed at, or at any rate as if something had been said which he was not to hear. Often, however, it does not go so far as this, and there is nothing more than mere insensibility to the cause of other people's laughter, a sort of joke-blindness, comparable to the well-known color-blindness with which many persons are afflicted as a congenital incapacity.

I have never seen the Scarabee smile. I have seen him take off his goggles, he breakfasts in these occasionally, I suppose when he has been tiring his poor old eyes out over night gazing through his microscope, I have seen him take his goggles off, I say, and stare about him, when the rest of us were laughing at something which amused us, but his features betrayed nothing more than a certain bewilderment, as if we had been foreigners talking in an unknown tongue. I do not think it was a mere fancy of mine that he bears a kind of resemblance to the tribe of insects he gives his life to studying. His shiny black coat; his rounded back, convex with years of stooping over his minute work; his angular movements, made natural to him by his habitual style of manipulation; the aridity of his organism, with which his voice is in perfect keeping; all these marks of his special sedentary occupation are so nearly what might be expected, and indeed so much, in accordance with the more general fact that a man's aspect is subdued to the look of what he works in, that I do not feel disposed to accuse myself of exaggeration in my account of the Scarabee's appearance. But I think he has learned something else of his coleopterous friends. The beetles never smile. Their physiognomy is not adapted to the display of the emotions; the lateral movement of their jaws being effective for alimentary purposes, but very limited in its gamut of expression. It is with these unemotional beings that the Scarabee passes his life. He has but one object, and that is perfectly serious, to his mind, in fact, of absorbing interest and importance. In one aspect of the matter he is quite right, for if the Creator has taken the trouble to make one of His creatures in just such a way and not otherwise, from the beginning of its existence on our planet in ages of unknown remoteness to the present time, the man who first explains His idea to us is charged with a revelation. It is by no means impossible that there may be angels in the celestial hierarchy to whom it would be new and interesting. I have often thought that spirits of a higher order than man might be willing to learn something from a human mind like that of Newton, and I see no reason why an angelic being might not be glad to hear a lecture from Mr. Huxley, or Mr. Tyndall, or one of our friends at Cambridge.

I have been sinuous as the Links of Forth seen from Stirling Castle, or as that other river which threads the Berkshire valley and runs, a perennial stream, through my memory, from which I please myself with thinking that I have learned to wind without fretting against the shore, or forgetting cohere I am flowing, sinuous, I say, but not jerky, no, not jerky nor hard to follow for a reader of the right sort, in the prime of life and full possession of his or her faculties.

All this last page or so, you readily understand, has been my private talk with you, the Reader. The cue of the conversation which I interrupted by this digression is to be found in the words "a good motto;" from which I begin my account of the visit again.

Do you receive many visitors, I mean vertebrates, not articulates? said the Master.

I thought this question might perhaps bring il disiato riso, the long-wished-for smile, but the Scarabee interpreted it in the simplest zoological sense, and neglected its hint of playfulness with the most absolute unconsciousness, apparently, of anything not entirely serious and literal.

You mean friends, I suppose, he answered. I have correspondents, but I have no friends except this spider. I live alone, except when I go to my subsection meetings; I get a box of insects now and then, and send a few beetles to coleopterists in other entomological districts; but science is exacting, and a man that wants to leave his record has not much time for friendship. There is no great chance either for making friends among naturalists. People that are at work on different things do not care a great deal for each other's specialties, and people that work on the same thing are always afraid lest one should get ahead of the other, or steal some of his ideas before he has made them public. There are none too many people you can trust in your laboratory. I thought I had a friend once, but he watched me at work and stole the discovery of a new species from me, and, what is more, had it named after himself. Since that time I have liked spiders better than men. They are hungry and savage, but at any rate they spin their own webs out of their own insides. I like very well to talk with gentlemen that play with my branch of entomology; I do not doubt it amused you, and if you want to see anything I can show you, I shall have no scruple in letting you see it. I have never had any complaint to make of amatoors.

Upon my honor, I would hold my right hand up and take my Bible-oath, if it was not busy with the pen at this moment, I do not believe the Scarabee had the least idea in the world of the satire on the student of the Order of Things implied in his invitation to the "amatoor." As for the Master, he stood fire perfectly, as he always does; but the idea that he, who had worked a considerable part of several seasons at examining and preparing insects, who believed himself to have given a new tabanus to the catalogue of native diptera, the idea that he was playing with science, and might be trusted anywhere as a harmless amateur, from whom no expert could possibly fear any anticipation of his unpublished discoveries, went beyond anything set down in that book of his which contained so much of the strainings of his wisdom.

The poor little Scarabee began fidgeting round about this time, and uttering some half-audible words, apologetical, partly, and involving an allusion to refreshments. As he spoke, he opened a small cupboard, and as he did so out bolted an uninvited tenant of the same, long in person, sable in hue, and swift of movement, on seeing which the Scarabee simply said, without emotion, blatta, but I, forgetting what was due to good manners, exclaimed cockroach!

We could not make up our minds to tax the Scarabee's hospitality, already levied upon by the voracious articulate. So we both alleged a state of utter repletion, and did not solve the mystery of the contents of the cupboard, not too luxurious, it may be conjectured, and yet kindly offered, so that we felt there was a moist filament of the social instinct running like a nerve through that exsiccated and almost anhydrous organism.

We left him with professions of esteem and respect which were real. We had gone, not to scoff, but very probably to smile, and I will not say we did not. But the Master was more thoughtful than usual.

If I had not solemnly dedicated myself to the study of the Order of Things, he said, I do verily believe I would give what remains to me of life to the investigation of some single point I could utterly eviscerate and leave finally settled for the instruction and, it may be, the admiration of all coming time. The keel ploughs ten thousand leagues of ocean and leaves no trace of its deep-graven furrows. The chisel scars only a few inches on the face of a rock, but the story it has traced is read by a hundred generations. The eagle leaves no track of his path, no memory of the place where he built his nest; but a patient mollusk has bored a little hole in a marble column of the temple of Serapis, and the monument of his labor outlasts the altar and the statue of the divinity.

Whew! said I to myself, that sounds a little like what we college boys used to call a "squirt." The Master guessed my thought and said, smiling,

That is from one of my old lectures. A man's tongue wags along quietly enough, but his pen begins prancing as soon as it touches paper. I know what you are thinking, you're thinking this is a squirt. That word has taken the nonsense out of a good many high-stepping fellows. But it did a good deal of harm too, and it was a vulgar lot that applied it oftenest.

I am at last perfectly satisfied that our Landlady has no designs on the Capitalist, and as well convinced that any fancy of mine that he was like to make love to her was a mistake. The good woman is too much absorbed in her children, and more especially in "the Doctor," as she delights to call her son, to be the prey of any foolish desire of changing her condition. She is doing very well as it is, and if the young man succeeds, as I have little question that he will, I think it probable enough that she will retire from her position as the head of a boarding-house. We have all liked the good woman who have lived with her, I mean we three friends who have put ourselves on record. Her talk, I must confess, is a little diffuse and not always absolutely correct, according to the standard of the great Worcester; she is subject to lachrymose cataclysms and semiconvulsive upheavals when she reverts in memory to her past trials, and especially when she recalls the virtues of her deceased spouse, who was, I suspect, an adjunct such as one finds not rarely annexed to a capable matron in charge of an establishment like hers; that is to say, an easy-going, harmless, fetch-and-carry, carve-and-help, get-out-of-the-way kind of neuter, who comes up three times (as they say drowning people do) every day, namely, at breakfast, dinner, and tea, and disappears, submerged beneath the waves of life, during the intervals of these events.

It is a source of genuine delight to me, who am of a kindly nature enough, according to my own reckoning, to watch the good woman, and see what looks of pride and affection she bestows upon her Benjamin, and how, in spite of herself, the maternal feeling betrays its influence in her dispensations of those delicacies which are the exceptional element in our entertainments. I will not say that Benjamin's mess, like his Scripture namesake's, is five times as large as that of any of the others, for this would imply either an economical distribution to the guests in general or heaping the poor young man's plate in a way that would spoil the appetite of an Esquimau, but you may be sure he fares well if anybody does; and I would have you understand that our Landlady knows what is what as well as who is who.

I begin really to entertain very sanguine expectations of young Doctor Benjamin Franklin. He has lately been treating a patient of whose good-will may prove of great importance to him. The Capitalist hurt one of his fingers somehow or other, and requested our young doctor to take a look at it. The young doctor asked nothing better than to take charge of the case, which proved more serious than might have been at first expected, and kept him in attendance more than a week. There was one very odd thing about it. The Capitalist seemed to have an idea that he was like to be ruined in the matter of bandages, small strips of worn linen which any old woman could have spared him from her rag-bag, but which, with that strange perversity which long habits of economy give to a good many elderly people, he seemed to think were as precious as if they had been turned into paper and stamped with promises to pay in thousands, from the national treasury. It was impossible to get this whim out of him, and the young doctor had tact enough to humor him in it. All this did not look very promising for the state of mind in which the patient was like to receive his bill for attendance when that should be presented. Doctor Benjamin was man enough, however, to come up to the mark, and sent him in such an account as it was becoming to send a man of ample means who had been diligently and skilfully cared for. He looked forward with some uncertainty as to how it would be received. Perhaps his patient would try to beat him down, and Doctor Benjamin made up his mind to have the whole or nothing. Perhaps he would pay the whole amount, but with a look, and possibly a word, that would make every dollar of it burn like a blister.

Doctor Benjamin's conjectures were not unnatural, but quite remote from the actual fact. As soon as his patient had got entirely well, the young physician sent in his bill. The Capitalist requested him to step into his room with him, and paid the full charge in the handsomest and most gratifying way, thanking him for his skill and attention, and assuring him that he had had great satisfaction in submitting himself to such competent hands, and should certainly apply to him again in case he should have any occasion for a medical adviser. We must not be too sagacious in judging people by the little excrescences of their character. Ex pede Herculem may often prove safe enough, but ex verruca Tullium is liable to mislead a hasty judge of his fellow-men.

I have studied the people called misers and thought a good deal about them. In former years I used to keep a little gold by me in order to ascertain for myself exactly the amount of pleasure to be got out of handling it; this being the traditional delight of the old-fashioned miser. It is by no means to be despised. Three or four hundred dollars in double-eagles will do very well to experiment on. There is something very agreeable in the yellow gleam, very musical in the metallic clink, very satisfying in the singular weight, and very stimulating in the feeling that all the world over these same yellow disks are the master-keys that let one in wherever he wants to go, the servants that bring him pretty nearly everything he wants, except virtue, and a good deal of what passes for that. I confess, then, to an honest liking for the splendors and the specific gravity and the manifold potentiality of the royal metal, and I understand, after a certain imperfect fashion, the delight that an old ragged wretch, starving himself in a crazy hovel, takes in stuffing guineas into old stockings and filling earthen pots with sovereigns, and every now and then visiting his hoards and fingering the fat pieces, and thinking ever all that they represent of earthly and angelic and diabolic energy. A miser pouring out his guineas into his palm and bathing his shrivelled and trembling hands in the yellow heaps before him, is not the prosaic being we are in the habit of thinking him. He is a dreamer, almost a poet. You and I read a novel or a poem to help our imaginations to build up palaces, and transport us into the emotional states and the felicitous conditions of the ideal characters pictured in the book we are reading. But think of him and the significance of the symbols he is handling as compared with the empty syllables and words we are using to build our aerial edifices with! In this hand he holds the smile of beauty and in that the dagger of revenge. The contents of that old glove will buy him the willing service of many an adroit sinner, and with what that coarse sack contains he can purchase the prayers of holy men for all succeeding time. In this chest is a castle in Spain, a real one, and not only in Spain, but anywhere he will choose to have it. If he would know what is the liberality of judgment of any of the straiter sects, he has only to hand over that box of rouleaux to the trustees of one of its educational institutions for the endowment of two or three professorships. If he would dream of being remembered by coming generations, what monument so enduring as a college building that shall bear his name, and even when its solid masonry shall crumble give place to another still charged with the same sacred duty of perpetuating his remembrance. Who was Sir Matthew Holworthy, that his name is a household word on the lips of thousands of scholars, and will be centuries hence, as that of Walter de Merton, dead six hundred years ago, is to-day at Oxford? Who was Mistress Holden, that she should be blessed among women by having her name spoken gratefully and the little edifice she caused to be erected preserved as her monument from generation to generation? All these possibilities, the lust of the eye, the lust of the flesh, the pride of life; the tears of grateful orphans by the gallon; the prayers of Westminster Assembly's Catechism divines by the thousand; the masses of priests by the century; all these things, and more if more there be that the imagination of a lover of gold is likely to range over, the miser hears and sees and feels and hugs and enjoys as he paddles with his lean hands among the sliding, shining, ringing, innocent-looking bits of yellow metal, toying with them as the lion-tamer handles the great carnivorous monster, whose might and whose terrors are child's play to the latent forces and power of harm-doing of the glittering counters played with in the great game between angels and devils.

I have seen a good deal of misers, and I think I understand them as well as most persons do. But the Capitalist's economy in rags and his liberality to the young doctor are very oddly contrasted with each other. I should not be surprised at any time to hear that he had endowed a scholarship or professorship or built a college dormitory, in spite of his curious parsimony in old linen.

I do not know where our Young Astronomer got the notions that he expresses so freely in the lines that follow. I think the statement is true, however, which I see in one of the most popular Cyclopaedias, that "the non-clerical mind in all ages is disposed to look favorably upon the doctrine of the universal restoration to holiness and happiness of all fallen intelligences, whether human or angelic." Certainly, most of the poets who have reached the heart of men, since Burns dropped the tear for poor "auld Nickie-ben" that softened the stony-hearted theology of Scotland, have had "non-clerical" minds, and I suppose our young friend is in his humble way an optimist like them. What he says in verse is very much the same thing as what is said in prose in all companies, and thought by a great many who are thankful to anybody that will say it for them, not a few clerical as wall as "non-clerical" persons among them.

WIND-CLOUDS AND STAR-DRIFTS.

V

What am I but the creature Thou hast made?
What have I save the blessings Thou hast lent?
What hope I but Thy mercy and Thy love?
Who but myself shall cloud my soul with fear?
Whose hand protect me from myself but Thine?

I claim the rights of weakness, I, the babe,
Call on my sire to shield me from the ills
That still beset my path, not trying me
With snares beyond my wisdom or my strength,
He knowing I shall use them to my harm,
And find a tenfold misery in the sense
That in my childlike folly I have sprung
The trap upon myself as vermin use
Drawn by the cunning bait to certain doom.
Who wrought the wondrous charm that leads us on
To sweet perdition, but the self-same power
That set the fearful engine to destroy
His wretched offspring (as the Rabbis tell),
And hid its yawning jaws and treacherous springs
In such a show of innocent sweet flowers
It lured the sinless angels and they fell?

Ah! He who prayed the prayer of all mankind
Summed in those few brief words the mightiest plea
For erring souls before the courts of heaven,
Save us from being tempted, lest we fall!
If we are only as the potter's clay
Made to be fashioned as the artist wills,
And broken into shards if we offend
The eye of Him who made us, it is well;
Such love as the insensate lump of clay
That spins upon the swift-revolving wheel
Bears to the hand that shapes its growing form,
Such love, no more, will be our hearts' return
To the great Master-workman for his care,
Or would be, save that this, our breathing clay,
Is intertwined with fine innumerous threads
That make it conscious in its framer's hand;
And this He must remember who has filled
These vessels with the deadly draught of life,
Life, that means death to all it claims. Our love
Must kindle in the ray that streams from heaven,
A faint reflection of the light divine;
The sun must warm the earth before the rose
Can show her inmost heart-leaves to the sun.

He yields some fraction of the Maker's right
Who gives the quivering nerve its sense of pain;
Is there not something in the pleading eye
Of the poor brute that suffers, which arraigns
The law that bids it suffer? Has it not
A claim for some remembrance in the book
That fills its pages with the idle words
Spoken of men? Or is it only clay,
Bleeding and aching in the potter's hand,
Yet all his own to treat it as he will
And when he will to cast it at his feet,
Shattered, dishonored, lost forevermore?
My dog loves me, but could he look beyond
His earthly master, would his love extend
To Him who, Hush! I will not doubt that He
Is better than our fears, and will not wrong
The least, the meanest of created things!

He would not trust me with the smallest orb
That circles through the sky; he would not give
A meteor to my guidance; would not leave
The coloring of a cloudlet to my hand;
He locks my beating heart beneath its bars
And keeps the key himself; he measures out
The draughts of vital breath that warm my blood,
Winds up the springs of instinct which uncoil,
Each in its season; ties me to my home,
My race, my time, my nation, and my creed
So closely that if I but slip my wrist
Out of the band that cuts it to the bone,
Men say, "He hath a devil"; he has lent
All that I hold in trust, as unto one
By reason of his weakness and his years
Not fit to hold the smallest shred in fee
Of those most common things he calls his own
And yet, my Rabbi tells me, he has left
The care of that to which a million worlds.
Filled with unconscious life were less than naught,
Has left that mighty universe, the Soul,
To the weak guidance of our baby hands,
Turned us adrift with our immortal charge,
Let the foul fiends have access at their will,
Taking the shape of angels, to our hearts,
Our hearts already poisoned through and through
With the fierce virus of ancestral sin.
If what my Rabbi tells me is the truth,
Why did the choir of angels sing for joy?
Heaven must be compassed in a narrow space,
And offer more than room enough for all
That pass its portals; but the underworld,
The godless realm, the place where demons forge
Their fiery darts and adamantine chains,
Must swarm with ghosts that for a little while
Had worn the garb of flesh, and being heirs

Of all the dulness of their stolid sires,
And all the erring instincts of their tribe,
Nature's own teaching, rudiments of "sin,"
Fell headlong in the snare that could not fail
To trap the wretched creatures shaped of clay
And cursed with sense enough to lose their souls!

Brother, thy heart is troubled at my word;
Sister, I see the cloud is on thy brow.
He will not blame me, He who sends not peace,
But sends a sword, and bids us strike amain
At Error's gilded crest, where in the van
Of earth's great army, mingling with the best
And bravest of its leaders, shouting loud
The battle-cries that yesterday have led
The host of Truth to victory, but to-day
Are watchwords of the laggard and the slave,
He leads his dazzled cohorts. God has made
This world a strife of atoms and of spheres;
With every breath I sigh myself away
And take my tribute from the wandering wind
To fan the flame of life's consuming fire;
So, while my thought has life, it needs must burn,
And burning, set the stubble-fields ablaze,
Where all the harvest long ago was reaped
And safely garnered in the ancient barns,
But still the gleaners, groping for their food,
Go blindly feeling through the close-shorn straw,
While the young reapers flash their glittering steel
Where later suns have ripened nobler grain!

We listened to these lines in silence. They were evidently written honestly, and with feeling, and no doubt meant to be reverential. I thought, however, the Lady looked rather serious as he finished reading. The Young Girl's cheeks were flushed, but she was not in the mood for criticism.

As we came away the Master said to me: The stubble-fields are mighty slow to take fire. These young fellows catch up with the world's ideas one after another, they have been tamed a long while, but they find them running loose in their minds, and think they are ferae naturae. They remind me of young sportsmen who fire at the first feathers they see, and bring down a barnyard fowl. But the chicken may be worth bagging for all that, he said, good-humoredly.

CHAPTER X

Caveat Lector. Let the reader look out for himself. The old Master, whose words I have so frequently quoted and shall quote more of, is a dogmatist who lays down the law, ex cathedra, from the chair of his own personality. I do not deny that he has the ambition of knowing something about a greater number of subjects than any one man ought to meddle with, except in a very humble and modest way. And that is not his way. There was no doubt something of, humorous bravado in his saying that the actual "order of things" did not offer a field sufficiently ample for his intelligence. But if I found fault with him, which would be easy enough, I should say that he holds and expresses definite opinions about matters that he could afford to leave open questions, or ask the judgment of others about. But I do not want to find fault with him. If he does not settle all the points he speaks of so authoritatively, he sets me thinking about them, and I like a man as a companion who is not afraid of a half-truth. I know he says some things peremptorily that he may inwardly debate with himself. There are two ways of dealing with assertions of this kind. One may attack them on the false side and perhaps gain a conversational victory. But I like better to take them up on the true side and see how much can be made of that aspect of the dogmatic assertion. It is the only comfortable way of dealing with persons like the old Master.

There have been three famous talkers in Great Britain, either of whom would illustrate what I say about dogmatists well enough for my purpose. You cannot doubt to what three I refer: Samuel the First, Samuel the Second, and Thomas, last of the Dynasty. (I mean the living Thomas and not Thomas B.)

I say the last of the Dynasty, for the conversational dogmatist on the imperial scale becomes every year more and more an impossibility. If he is in intelligent company he will be almost sure to find some one who knows more about some of the subjects he generalizes upon than any wholesale thinker who handles knowledge by the cargo is like to know. I find myself, at certain intervals, in the society of a number of experts in science, literature, and art, who cover a pretty wide range, taking them all together, of human knowledge. I have not the least doubt that if the great Dr. Samuel Johnson should come in and sit with this company at one of their Saturday dinners, he would be listened to, as he always was, with respect and attention. But there are subjects upon which the great talker could speak magisterially in his time and at his club, upon which so wise a man would express himself guardedly at the meeting where I have supposed him a guest. We have a scientific man or two among us, for instance, who would be entitled to smile at the good Doctor's estimate of their labors, as I give it here:

"Of those that spin out life in trifles and die without a memorial, many flatter themselves with high opinion of their own importance and imagine that they are every day adding some improvement to human life." - "Some turn the wheel of electricity, some suspend rings to a loadstone, and find that what they did yesterday they can do again to-day. Some register the changes of the wind, and die fully convinced that the wind is changeable.

"There are men yet more profound, who have heard that two colorless liquors may produce a color by union, and that two cold bodies will grow hot if they are mingled; they mingle them, and produce the effect expected, say it is strange, and mingle them again."

I cannot transcribe this extract without an intense inward delight in its wit and a full recognition of its thorough half-truthfulness. Yet if while the great moralist is indulging in these vivacities, he can be imagined as receiving a message from Mr. Boswell or Mrs. Thrale flashed through the depths of the ocean, we can suppose he might be tempted to indulge in another oracular utterance, something like this: A wise man recognizes the convenience of a general statement, but he bows to the authority of a particular fact. He who would bound the possibilities of human knowledge by the limitations of present acquirements would take the dimensions of the infant in ordering the habiliments of the adult. It is the province of knowledge to speak and it is the privilege of wisdom to listen. Will the Professor have the kindness to inform me by what steps of gradual development the ring and the loadstone, which were but yesterday the toys of children and idlers, have become the means of approximating the intelligences of remote continents, and wafting emotions unchilled through the abysses of the no longer unfathomable deep?

This, you understand, Beloved, is only a conventional imitation of the Doctor's style of talking. He wrote in grand balanced phrases, but his conversation was good, lusty, off-hand familiar talk. He used very often to have it all his own way. If he came back to us we must remember that to treat him fairly we must suppose him on a level with the knowledge of our own time. But that knowledge is more specialized, a great deal, than knowledge was in his day. Men cannot talk about things they have seen from the outside with the same magisterial authority the talking dynasty pretended to. The sturdy old moralist felt grand enough, no doubt, when he said, "He that is growing great and happy by electrifying a bottle wonders how the world can be engaged by trifling prattle about war or peace." Benjamin Franklin was one of these idlers who were electrifying bottles, but he also found time to engage in the trifling prattle about war and peace going on in those times. The talking Doctor hits him very hard in "Taxation no Tyranny": "Those who wrote the Address (of the American Congress in 1775), though they have shown no great extent or profundity of mind, are yet probably wiser than to believe it: but they have been taught by some master of mischief how to put in motion the engine of political electricity; to attract by the sounds of Liberty and Property, to repel by those of Popery and Slavery; and to give the great stroke by the name of Boston." The talking dynasty has always been hard upon us Americans. King Samuel II. says: "It is, I believe, a fact verified beyond doubt, that some years ago it was impossible to obtain a copy of the Newgate Calendar, as they had all been bought up by the Americans, whether to suppress the blazon of their forefathers or to assist in their genealogical researches I could never learn satisfactorily." As for King Thomas, the last of the monological succession, he made such a piece of work with his prophecies and his sarcasms about our little trouble with some of the Southern States, that we came rather to pity him for his whims and crotchets than to get angry with him for calling us bores and other unamiable names.

I do not think we believe things because considerable people say them, on personal authority, that is, as intelligent listeners very commonly did a century ago. The newspapers have lied that belief out of us. Any man who has a pretty gift of talk may hold his company a little while when there is nothing better stirring. Every now and then a man who may be dull enough prevailingly has a passion of talk come over him which makes him eloquent and silences the rest. I have a great respect for these divine paroxysms, these half-inspired moments of influx when they seize one whom we had not counted among the luminaries of the social sphere. But the man who cangive us a fresh experience on anything that interests us overrides everybody else. A great peril escaped makes a great story-teller of a common person enough. I remember when a certain vessel was wrecked long ago, that one of the survivors told the story as well as Defoe could have told it. Never a word from him before; never a word from him since. But when it comes to talking one's common thoughts, those that come and go as the breath does; those that tread the mental areas and corridors with steady, even foot-fall, an interminable procession of every hue and garb, there are few, indeed, that can dare to lift the curtain which hangs before the window in the breast and throw open the window, and let us look and listen. We are all loyal enough to our sovereign when he shows himself, but sovereigns are scarce. I never saw the absolute homage of listeners but once, that I remember, to a man's common talk, and that was to the conversation of an old man, illustrious by his lineage and the exalted honors he had won, whose experience had lessons for the wisest, and whose eloquence had made the boldest tremble.

All this because I told you to look out for yourselves and not take for absolute truth everything the old Master of our table, or anybody else at it sees fit to utter. At the same time I do not think that he, or any of us whose conversation I think worth reporting, says anything for the mere sake of saying it and without thinking that it holds some truth, even if it is not unqualifiedly true.

I suppose a certain number of my readers wish very heartily that the Young Astronomer whose poetical speculations I am recording would stop trying by searching to find out the Almighty, and sign the thirty-nine articles, or the Westminster Confession of Faith, at any rate slip his neck into some collar or other, and pull quietly in the harness, whether it galled him or not. I say, rather, let him have his talk out; if nobody else asks the questions he asks, some will be glad to hear them, but if you, the reader, find the same questions in your own mind, you need not be afraid to see how they shape themselves in another's intelligence. Do you recognize the fact that we are living in a new time? Knowledge, it excites prejudices to call it science, is advancing as irresistibly, as majestically, as remorselessly as the ocean moves in upon the shore. The courtiers of King Canute (I am not afraid of the old comparison), represented by the adherents of the traditional beliefs of the period, move his chair back an inch at a time, but not until his feet are pretty damp, not to say wet. The rock on which he sat securely awhile ago is completely under water. And now people are walking up and down the beach and judging for themselves how far inland the chair of King Canute is like to be moved while they and their children are looking on, at the rate in which it is edging backward. And it is quite too late to go into hysterics about it.

The shore, solid, substantial, a great deal more than eighteen hundred years old, is natural humanity. The beach which the ocean of knowledge, you may call it science if you like, is flowing over, is theological humanity. Somewhere between the Sermon on the Mount and the teachings of Saint Augustine sin was made a transferable chattel. (I leave the interval wide for others to make narrow.)

The doctrine of heritable guilt, with its mechanical consequences, has done for our moral nature what the doctrine of demoniac possession has done in barbarous times and still does among barbarous tribes for disease. Out of that black cloud came the lightning which struck the compass of humanity. Conscience, which from the dawn of moral being had pointed to the poles of right and wrong only as the great current of will flowed through the soul, was demagnetized, paralyzed, and knew henceforth no fixed meridian, but stayed where the priest or the council placed it. There is nothing to be done but to polarize the needle over again. And for this purpose we must study the lines of direction of all the forces which traverse our human nature.

We must study man as we have studied stars and rocks. We need not go, we are told, to our sacred books for astronomy or geology or other scientific knowledge. Do not stop there! Pull Canute's chair back fifty rods at once, and do not wait until he is wet to the knees! Say now, bravely, as you will sooner or later have to say, that we need not go to any ancient records for our anthropology. Do we not all hold, at least, that the doctrine of man's being a blighted abortion, a miserable disappointment to his Creator, and hostile and hateful to him from his birth, may give way to the belief that he is the latest terrestrial manifestation of an ever upward-striving movement of divine power? If there lives a man who does not want to disbelieve the popular notions about the condition and destiny of the bulk of his race, I should like to have him look me in the face and tell me so.

I am not writing for the basement story or the nursery, and I do not pretend to be, but I say nothing in these pages which would not be said without fear of offence in any intelligent circle, such as clergymen of the higher castes are in the habit of frequenting. There are teachers in type for our grandmothers and our grandchildren who vaccinate the two childhoods with wholesome doctrine, transmitted harmlessly from one infant to another. But we three men at our table have taken the disease of thinking in the natural way. It is an epidemic in these times, and those who are afraid of it must shut themselves up close or they will catch it.

I hope none of us are wanting in reverence. One at least of us is a regular church-goer, and believes a man may be devout and yet very free in the expression of his opinions on the gravest subjects. There may be some good people who think that our young friend who puts his thoughts in verse is going sounding over perilous depths, and are frightened every time he throws the lead. There is nothing to be frightened at. This is a manly world we live in. Our reverence is good for nothing if it does not begin with self-respect. Occidental manhood springs from that as its basis; Oriental manhood finds the greatest satisfaction in self-abasement. There is no use in trying to graft the tropical palm upon the Northern pine. The same divine forces underlie the growth of both, but leaf and flower and fruit must follow the law of race, of soil, of climate. Whether the questions which assail my young friend have risen in my reader's mind or not, he knows perfectly well that nobody can keep such questions from springing up in every young mind of any force or honesty. As for the excellent little wretches who grow up in what they are taught, with never a scruple or a query, Protestant or Catholic, Jew or Mormon, Mahometan or Buddhist, they signify nothing in the intellectual life of the race. If the world had been wholly peopled with such half-vitalized mental negatives, there never would have been a creed like that of Christendom.

I entirely agree with the spirit of the verses I have looked over, in this point at least, that a true man's allegiance is given to that which is highest in his own nature. He reverences truth, he loves kindness, he respects justice. The two first qualities he understands well enough. But the last, justice, at least as between the Infinite and the finite, has been so utterly dehumanized, disintegrated, decomposed, and diabolized in passing through the minds of the half-civilized banditti who have peopled and unpeopled the world for some scores of generations, that it has become a mere algebraic x, and has no fixed value whatever as a human conception.

As for power, we are outgrowing all superstition about that. We have not the slightest respect for it as such, and it is just as well to remember this in all our spiritual adjustments. We fear power when we cannot master it; but just as far as we can master it, we make a slave and a beast of burden of it without hesitation. We cannot change the ebb and flow of the tides, or the course of the seasons, but we come as near it as we can. We dam out the ocean, we make roses bloom in winter and water freeze in summer. We have no more reverence for the sun than we have for a fish-tail gas-burner; we stare into his face with telescopes as at a ballet-dancer with opera-glasses; we pick his rays to pieces with prisms as if they were so many skeins of colored yarn; we tell him we do not want his company and shut him out like a troublesome vagrant. The gods of the old heathen are the servants of to-day. Neptune, Vulcan, Aolus, and the bearer of the thunderbolt himself have stepped down from their pedestals and put on our livery. We cannot always master them, neither can we always master our servant, the horse, but we have put a bridle on the wildest natural agencies. The mob of elemental forces is as noisy and turbulent as ever, but the standing army of civilization keeps it well under, except for an occasional outbreak.

When I read the Lady's letter printed some time since, I could not help honoring the feeling which prompted her in writing it. But while I respect the innocent incapacity of tender age and the limitations of the comparatively uninstructed classes, it is quite out of the question to act as if matters of common intelligence and universal interest were the private property of a secret society, only to be meddled with by those who know the grip and the password.

We must get over the habit of transferring the limitations of the nervous temperament and of hectic constitutions to the great Source of all the mighty forces of nature, animate and inanimate. We may confidently trust that we have over us a Being thoroughly robust and grandly magnanimous, in distinction from the Infinite Invalid bred in the studies of sickly monomaniacs, who corresponds to a very common human type, but makes us blush for him when we contrast him with a truly noble man, such as most of us have had the privilege of knowing both in public and in private life.

I was not a little pleased to find that the Lady, in spite of her letter, sat through the young man's reading of portions of his poem with a good deal of complacency. I think I can guess what is in her mind. She believes, as so many women do, in that great remedy for discontent, and doubts about humanity, and questionings of Providence, and all sorts of youthful vagaries, I mean the love-cure. And she thinks, not without some reason, that these astronomical lessons, and these readings of poetry and daily proximity at the table, and the need of two young hearts that have been long feeling lonely, and youth and nature and "all impulses of soul and sense," as Coleridge has it, will bring these two young people into closer relations than they perhaps have yet thought of; and so that sweet lesson of loving the neighbor whom he has seen may lead him into deeper and more trusting communion with the Friend and Father whom he has not seen.

The Young Girl evidently did not intend that her accomplice should be a loser by the summary act of the Member of the Haouse: I took occasion to ask That Boy what had become of all the popguns. He gave me to understand that popguns were played out, but that he had got a squirt and a whip, and considered himself better off than before.

This great world is full of mysteries. I can comprehend the pleasure to be got out of the hydraulic engine; but what can be the fascination of a whip, when one has nothing to flagellate but the calves of his own legs, I could never understand. Yet a small riding-whip is the most popular article with the miscellaneous New-Englander at all great gatherings, cattle-shows and Fourth-of-July celebrations. If Democritus and Heraclitus could walk arm in arm through one of these crowds, the first would be in a broad laugh to see the multitude of young persons who were rejoicing in the possession of one of these useless and worthless little commodities; happy himself to see how easily others could purchase happiness. But the second would weep bitter tears to think what a rayless and barren life that must be which could extract enjoyment from the miserable flimsy wand that has such magic attraction for sauntering youths and simpering maidens. What a dynamometer of happiness are these paltry toys, and what a rudimentary vertebrate must be the freckled adolescent whose yearning for the infinite can be stayed even for a single hour by so trifling a boon from the venal hands of the finite!

Pardon these polysyllabic reflections, Beloved, but I never contemplate these dear fellow-creatures of ours without a delicious sense of superiority to them and to all arrested embryos of intelligence, in which I have no doubt you heartily sympathize with me. It is not merely when I look at the vacuous countenances of the mastigophori, the whip-holders, that I enjoy this luxury (though I would not miss that holiday spectacle for a pretty sum of money, and advise you by all means to make sure of it next Fourth of July, if you missed it this), but I get the same pleasure from many similar manifestations.

I delight in Regalia, so called, of the kind not worn by kings, nor obtaining their diamonds from the mines of Golconda. I have a passion for those resplendent titles which are not conferred by a sovereign and would not be the open sesame to the courts of royalty, yet which are as opulent in impressive adjectives as any Knight of the Garter's list of dignities. When I have recognized in the every-day name of His Very Worthy High Eminence of some cabalistic association, the inconspicuous individual whose trifling indebtedness to me for value received remains in a quiescent state and is likely long to continue so, I confess to having experienced a thrill of pleasure. I have smiled to think how grand his magnificent titular appendages sounded in his own ears and what a feeble tintinnabulation they made in mine. The crimson sash, the broad diagonal belt of the mounted marshal of a great procession, so cheap in themselves, yet so entirely satisfactory to the wearer, tickle my heart's root.

Perhaps I should have enjoyed all these weaknesses of my infantile fellow-creatures without an afterthought, except that on a certain literary anniversary when I tie the narrow blue and pink ribbons in my button-hole and show my decorated bosom to the admiring public, I am conscious of a certain sense of distinction and superiority in virtue of that trifling addition to my personal adornments which reminds me that I too have some embryonic fibres in my tolerably well-matured organism.

I hope I have not hurt your feelings, if you happen to be a High and Mighty Grand Functionary in any illustrious Fraternity. When I tell you that a bit of ribbon in my button-hole sets my vanity prancing, I think you cannot be grievously offended that I smile at the resonant titles which make you something more than human in your own eyes. I would not for the world be mistaken for one of those literary roughs whose brass knuckles leave their mark on the foreheads of so many inoffensive people.

There is a human sub-species characterized by the coarseness of its fibre and the acrid nature of its intellectual secretions. It is to a certain extent penetrative, as all creatures are which are provided with stings. It has an instinct which guides it to the vulnerable parts of the victim on which it fastens. These two qualities give it a certain degree of power which is not to be despised. It might perhaps be less mischievous, but for the fact that the wound where it leaves its poison opens the fountain from which it draws its nourishment.

Beings of this kind can be useful if they will only find their appropriate sphere, which is not literature, but that circle of rough-and-tumble political life where the fine-fibred men are at a discount, where epithets find their subjects poison-proof, and the sting which would be fatal to a literary debutant only wakes the eloquence of the pachydermatous ward-room politician to a fiercer shriek of declamation.

The Master got talking the other day about the difference between races and families. I am reminded of what he said by what I have just been saying myself about coarse-fibred and fine-fibred people.

We talk about a Yankee, a New-Englander, he said, as if all of 'em were just the same kind of animal. "There is knowledge and knowledge," said John Bunyan. There are Yankees and Yankees. Do you know two native trees called pitch pine and white pine respectively? Of course you know 'em. Well, there are pitch-pine Yankees and white-pine Yankees. We don't talk about the inherited differences of men quite as freely, perhaps, as they do in the Old World, but republicanism doesn't alter the laws of physiology. We have a native aristocracy, a superior race, just as plainly marked by nature as of a higher and finer grade than the common run of people as the white pine is marked in its form, its stature, its bark, its delicate foliage, as belonging to the nobility of the forest; and the pitch pine, stubbed, rough, coarse-haired, as of the plebeian order. Only the strange thing is to see in what a capricious way our natural nobility is distributed. The last born nobleman I have seen, I saw this morning; he was pulling a rope that was fastened to a Maine schooner loaded with lumber. I should say he was about twenty years old, as fine a figure of a young man as you would ask to see, and with a regular Greek outline of countenance, waving hair, that fell as if a sculptor had massed it to copy, and a complexion as rich as a red sunset. I have a notion that the State of Maine breeds the natural nobility in a larger proportion than some other States, but they spring up in all sorts of out-of-the-way places. The young fellow I saw this morning had on an old flannel shirt, a pair of trowsers that meant hard work, and a cheap cloth cap pushed back on his head so as to let the large waves of hair straggle out over his forehead; he was tugging at his rope with the other sailors, but upon my word I don't think I have seen a young English nobleman of all those whom I have looked upon that answered to the notion of "blood" so well as this young fellow did. I suppose if I made such a levelling confession as this in public, people would think I was looking towards being the labor-reform candidate for President. But I should go on and spoil my prospects by saying that I don't think the white-pine Yankee is the more generally prevailing growth, but rather the pitch-pine Yankee.

The Member of the Haouse seemed to have been getting a dim idea that all this was not exactly flattering to the huckleberry districts. His features betrayed the growth of this suspicion so clearly that the Master replied to his look as if it had been a remark. [I need hardly say that this particular member of the General Court was a pitch-pine Yankee of the most thoroughly characterized aspect and flavor.]

Yes, Sir, the Master continued, Sir being anybody that listened, there is neither flattery nor offence in the views which a physiological observer takes of the forms of life around him. It won't do to draw individual portraits, but the differences of natural groups of human beings are as proper subjects of remark as those of different breeds of horses, and if horses were Houyhnhnms I don't think they would quarrel with us because we made a distinction between a

"Morgan" and a "Messenger." The truth is, Sir, the lean sandy soil and the droughts and the long winters and the east-winds and the cold storms, and all sorts of unknown local influences that we can't make out quite so plainly as these, have a tendency to roughen the human organization and make it coarse, something as it is with the tree I mentioned. Some spots and some strains of blood fight against these influences, but if I should say right out what I think, it would be that the finest human fruit, on the whole; and especially the finest women that we get in New England are raised under glass.

Good gracious! exclaimed the Landlady, under glass!

Give me cowcumbers raised in the open air, said the Capitalist, who was a little hard of hearing.

Perhaps, I remarked, it might be as well if you would explain this last expression of yours. Raising human beings under glass I take to be a metaphorical rather than a literal statement of your meaning.

No, Sir! replied the Master, with energy, I mean just what I say, Sir. Under glass, and with a south exposure. During the hard season, of course, for in the heats of summer the tenderest hot-house plants are not afraid of the open air. Protection is what the transplanted Aryan requires in this New England climate. Keep him, and especially keep her, in a wide street of a well-built city eight months of the year; good solid brick walls behind her, good sheets of plate-glass, with the sun shining warm through them, in front of her, and you have put her in the condition of the pine-apple, from the land of which, and not from that of the other kind of pine, her race started on its travels. People don't know what a gain there is to health by living in cities, the best parts of them of course, for we know too well what the worst parts are. In the first place you get rid of the noxious emanations which poison so many country localities with typhoid fever and dysentery, not wholly rid of them, of course, but to a surprising degree. Let me tell you a doctor's story. I was visiting a Western city a good many years ago; it was in the autumn, the time when all sorts of malarious diseases are about. The doctor I was speaking of took me to see the cemetery just outside the town, I don't know how much he had done to fill it, for he didn't tell me, but I'll tell you what he did say.

"Look round," said the doctor. "There isn't a house in all the ten-mile circuit of country you can see over, where there isn't one person, at least, shaking with fever and ague. And yet you need n't be afraid of carrying it away with you, for as long as your home is on a paved street you are safe."

I think it likely, the Master went on to say, that my friend the doctor put it pretty strongly, but there is no doubt at all that while all the country round was suffering from intermittent fever, the paved part of the city was comparatively exempted. What do you do when you build a house on a damp soil, and there are damp soils pretty much everywhere? Why you floor the cellar with cement, don't you? Well, the soil of a city is cemented all over, one may say, with certain qualifications of course. A first-rate city house is a regular sanatorium. The only trouble is, that the little good-for-nothings that come of utterly used-up and worn-out stock, and ought to die, can't die, to save their lives. So they grow up to dilute the vigor of the race with skim-milk vitality. They would have died, like good children, in most average country places; but eight months of shelter in a regulated temperature, in a well-sunned house, in a duly moistened air, with good sidewalks to go about on in all weather, and four months of the cream of summer and the fresh milk of Jersey cows, make the little sham organizations, the worm-eaten wind-falls, for that 's what they look like, hang on to the boughs of life like "froze-n-thaws"; regular struldbrugs they come to be, a good many of 'em.

The Scarabee's ear was caught by that queer word of Swift's, and he asked very innocently what kind of bugs he was speaking of, whereupon That Boy shouted out, Straddlebugs! to his own immense amusement and the great bewilderment of the Scarabee, who only saw that there was one of those unintelligible breaks in the conversation which made other people laugh, and drew back his antennae as usual, perplexed, but not amused.

I do not believe the Master had said all he was going to say on this subject, and of course all these statements of his are more or less one-sided. But that some invalids do much better in cities than in the country is indisputable, and that the frightful dysenteries and fevers which have raged like pestilences in many of our country towns are almost unknown in the better built sections of some of our large cities is getting to be more generally understood since our well-to-do people have annually emigrated in such numbers from the cemented surface of the city to the steaming soil of some of the dangerous rural districts. If one should contrast the healthiest country residences with the worst city ones the result would be all the other way, of course, so that there are two sides to the question, which we must let the doctors pound in their great mortar, infuse and strain, hoping that they will present us with the clear solution when they have got through these processes. One of our chief wants is a complete sanitary map of every State in the Union.

The balance of our table, as the reader has no doubt observed, has been deranged by the withdrawal of the Man of Letters, so called, and only the side of the deficiency changed by the removal of the Young Astronomer into our neighborhood. The fact that there was a vacant chair on the side opposite us had by no means escaped the notice of That Boy. He had taken advantage of his opportunity and invited in a schoolmate whom he evidently looked upon as a great personage. This boy or youth was a good deal older than himself and stood to him apparently in the light of a patron and instructor in the ways of life. A very jaunty, knowing young gentleman he was, good-looking, smartly dressed, smooth-checked as yet, curly-haired, with a roguish eye, a sagacious wink, a ready tongue, as I soon found out; and as I learned could catch a ball on the fly with any boy of his age; not quarrelsome, but, if he had to strike, hit from the shoulder; the pride of his father (who was a man of property and a civic dignitary), and answering to the name of Johnny.

I was a little surprised at the liberty That Boy had taken in introducing an extra peptic element at our table, reflecting as I did that a certain number of avoirdupois ounces of nutriment which the visitor would dispose of corresponded to a very appreciable pecuniary amount, so that he was levying a contribution upon our Landlady which she might be inclined to complain of. For the Caput mortuum (or deadhead, in vulgar phrase) is apt to be furnished with a Venter vivus, or, as we may say, a lively appetite. But the Landlady welcomed the new-comer very heartily.

Why! How do you do Johnny?! with the notes of interrogation and of admiration both together, as here represented.

Johnny signified that he was doing about as well as could be expected under the circumstances, having just had a little difference with a young person whom he spoke of as "Pewter-jaw" (I suppose he had worn a dentist's tooth-straightening contrivance during his second dentition), which youth he had finished off, as he said, in good shape, but at the expense of a slight epistaxis, we will translate his vernacular expression.

The three ladies all looked sympathetic, but there did not seem to be any great occasion for it, as the boy had come out all right, and seemed to be in the best of spirits.

And how is your father and your mother? asked the Landlady.

Oh, the Governor and the Head Centre? A 1, both of 'em. Prime order for shipping, warranted to stand any climate. The Governor says he weighs a hunderd and seventy-five pounds. Got a chin-tuft just like Ed'in Forrest. D'd y' ever see Ed'in Forrest play Metamora? Bully, I tell you! My old gentleman means to be Mayor or Governor or President or something or other before he goes off the handle, you'd better b'lieve. He's smart, and I've heard folks say I take after him.

Somehow or other I felt as if I had seen this boy before, or known something about him. Where did he get those expressions "A 1" and "prime" and so on? They must have come from somebody who has been in the retail dry-goods business, or something of that nature. I have certain vague reminiscences that carry me back to the early times of this boardinghouse. Johnny. Landlady knows his father well.

Boarded with her, no doubt. There was somebody by the name of John, I remember perfectly well, lived with her. I remember both my friends mentioned him, one of them very often. I wonder if this boy isn't a son of his! I asked the Landlady after breakfast whether this was not, as I had suspected, the son of that former boarder.

To be sure he is, she answered, and jest such a good-natur'd sort of creatur' as his father was. I always liked John, as we used to call his father. He did love fun, but he was a good soul, and stood by me when I was in trouble, always. He went into business on his own account after a while, and got married, and settled down into a family man. They tell me he is an amazing smart business man, grown wealthy, and his wife's father left her money. But I can't help calling him John, law, we never thought of calling him anything else, and he always laughs and says, "That's right." This is his oldest son, and everybody calls him Johnny. That Boy of ours goes to the same school with his boy, and thinks there never was anybody like him, you see there was a boy undertook to impose on our boy, and Johnny gave the other boy a good licking, and ever since that he is always wanting to have Johnny round with him and bring him here with him, and when those two boys get together, there never was boys that was so chock full of fun and sometimes mischief, but not very bad mischief, as those two boys be. But I like to have him come once in a while when there is room at the table, as there is now, for it puts me in mind of the old times, when my old boarders was all round me, that I used to think so much of, not that my boarders that I have now a'nt very nice people, but I did think a dreadful sight of the gentleman that made that first book; it helped me on in the world more than ever he knew of, for it was as good as one of them Brandreth's pills advertisements, and did n't cost me a cent, and that young lady he married too, she was nothing but a poor young schoolma'am when she come to my house, and now, and she deserved it all too; for she was always just the same, rich or poor, and she is n't a bit prouder now she wears a camel's-hair shawl, than she was when I used to lend her a woollen one to keep her poor dear little shoulders warm when she had to go out and it was storming, and then there was that old gentleman, I can't speak about him, for I never knew how good he was till his will was opened, and then it was too late to thank him....

I respected the feeling which caused the interval of silence, and found my own eyes moistened as I remembered how long it was since that friend of ours was sitting in the chair where I now sit, and what a tidal wave of change has swept over the world and more especially over this great land of ours, since he opened his lips and found so many kind listeners.

The Young Astronomer has read us another extract from his manuscript. I ran my eye over it, and so far as I have noticed it is correct enough in its versification. I suppose we are getting gradually over our hemispherical provincialism, which allowed a set of monks to pull their hoods over our eyes and tell us there was no meaning in any religious symbolism but our own. If I am mistaken about this advance I am very glad to print the young man's somewhat outspoken lines to help us in that direction.

WIND-CLOUDS AND STAR-DRIFTS.

VI

The time is racked with birth-pangs; every hour
Brings forth some gasping truth, and truth new-born
Looks a misshapen and untimely growth,
The terror of the household and its shame,
A monster coiling in its nurse's lap
That some would strangle, some would only starve;
But still it breathes, and passed from hand to hand,
And suckled at a hundred half-clad breasts,
Comes slowly to its stature and its form,
Calms the rough ridges of its dragon-scales,
Changes to shining locks its snaky hair,
And moves transfigured into angel guise,
Welcomed by all that cursed its hour of birth,
And folded in the same encircling arms
That cast it like a serpent from their hold!

If thou wouldst live in honor, die in peace,
Have the fine words the marble-workers learn
To carve so well, upon thy funeral-stone,
And earn a fair obituary, dressed
In all the many-colored robes of praise,
Be deafer than the adder to the cry
Of that same foundling truth, until it grows
To seemly favor, and at length has won
The smiles of hard-mouthed men and light-upped dames,
Then snatch it from its meagre nurse's breast,
Fold it in silk and give it food from gold;
So shalt thou share its glory when at last
It drops its mortal vesture, and revealed
In all the splendor of its heavenly form,
Spreads on the startled air its mighty wings!

Alas! how much that seemed immortal truth
That heroes fought for, martyrs died to save,
Reveals its earth-born lineage, growing old
And limping in its march, its wings unplumed,
Its heavenly semblance faded like a dream!

Here in this painted casket, just unsealed,
Lies what was once a breathing shape like thine,
Once loved as thou art loved; there beamed the eyes
That looked on Memphis in its hour of pride,
That saw the walls of hundred-gated Thebes,
And all the mirrored glories of the Nile.
See how they toiled that all-consuming time
Might leave the frame immortal in its tomb;
Filled it with fragrant balms and odorous gums
That still diffuse their sweetness through the air,
And wound and wound with patient fold on fold
The flaxen bands thy hand has rudely torn!
Perchance thou yet canst see the faded stain
Of the sad mourner's tear.

But what is this?

The sacred beetle, bound upon the breast
Of the blind heathen! Snatch the curious prize,
Give it a place among thy treasured spoils
Fossil and relic, corals, encrinites,
The fly in amber and the fish in stone,
The twisted circlet of Etruscan gold,
Medal, intaglio, poniard, poison-ring,
Place for the Memphian beetle with thine hoard!

Ah! longer than thy creed has blest the world
This toy, thus ravished from thy brother's breast,
Was to the heart of Mizraim as divine,
As holy, as the symbol that we lay
On the still bosom of our white-robed dead,
And raise above their dust that all may know
Here sleeps an heir of glory. Loving friends,
With tears of trembling faith and choking sobs,
And prayers to those who judge of mortal deeds,
Wrapped this poor image in the cerement's fold
That Isis and Osiris, friends of man,
Might know their own and claim the ransomed soul

An idol? Man was born to worship such!
An idol is an image of his thought;
Sometimes he carves it out of gleaming stone,
And sometimes moulds it out of glittering gold,
Or rounds it in a mighty frescoed dome,
Or lifts it heavenward in a lofty spire,
Or shapes it in a cunning frame of words,
Or pays his priest to make it day by day;
For sense must have its god as well as soul;
A new-born Dian calls for silver shrines,
And Egypt's holiest symbol is our own,
The sign we worship as did they of old
When Isis and Osiris ruled the world.

Let us be true to our most subtle selves,
We long to have our idols like the rest.
Think! when the men of Israel had their God
Encamped among them, talking with their chief,
Leading them in the pillar of the cloud
And watching o'er them in the shaft of fire,
They still must have an image; still they longed
For somewhat of substantial, solid form
Whereon to hang their garlands, and to fix
Their wandering thoughts, and gain a stronger hold
For their uncertain faith, not yet assured
If those same meteors of the day and night
Were not mere exhalations of the soil.

Are we less earthly than the chosen race?
Are we more neighbors of the living God
Than they who gathered manna every morn,
Reaping where none had sown, and heard the voice

Of him who met the Highest in the mount,
And brought them tables, graven with His hand?
Yet these must have their idol, brought their gold,
That star-browed Apis might be god again;
Yea, from their ears the women brake the rings
That lent such splendors to the gypsy brown
Of sunburnt cheeks, what more could woman do
To show her pious zeal? They went astray,
But nature led them as it leads us all.

We too, who mock at Israel's golden calf
And scoff at Egypt's sacred scarabee,
Would have our amulets to clasp and kiss,
And flood with rapturous tears, and bear with us
To be our dear companions in the dust,
Such magic works an image in our souls!

Man is an embryo; see at twenty years
His bones, the columns that uphold his frame
Not yet cemented, shaft and capital,
Mere fragments of the temple incomplete.
At twoscore, threescore, is he then full grown?
Nay, still a child, and as the little maids
Dress and undress their puppets, so he tries
To dress a lifeless creed, as if it lived,
And change its raiment when the world cries shame!
We smile to see our little ones at play
So grave, so thoughtful, with maternal care
Nursing the wisps of rags they call their babes;
Does He not smile who sees us with the toys
We call by sacred names, and idly feign
To be what we have called them?
He is still The Father of this helpless nursery-brood,
Whose second childhood joins so close its first,
That in the crowding, hurrying years between
We scarce have trained our senses to their task
Before the gathering mist has dimmed our eyes,
And with our hollowed palm we help our ear,
And trace with trembling hand our wrinkled names,
And then begin to tell our stories o'er,
And see not hear-the whispering lips that say,
"You know? Your father knew him. This is he,
Tottering and leaning on the hireling's arm,"
And so, at length, disrobed of all that clad
The simple life we share with weed and worm,
Go to our cradles, naked as we came.

CHAPTER XI

I suppose there would have been even more remarks upon the growing intimacy of the Young Astronomer and his pupil, if the curiosity of the boarders had not in the mean time been so much excited at the apparently close relation which had sprung up between the Register of

Deeds and the Lady. It was really hard to tell what to make of it. The Register appeared at the table in a new coat. Suspicious. The Lady was evidently deeply interested in him, if we could judge by the frequency and the length of their interviews. On at least one occasion he has brought a lawyer with him, which naturally suggested the idea that there were some property arrangements to be attended to, in case, as seems probable against all reasons to the contrary, these two estimable persons, so utterly unfitted, as one would say, to each other, contemplated an alliance. It is no pleasure to me to record an arrangement of this kind. I frankly confess I do not know what to make of it. With her tastes and breeding, it is the last thing that I should have thought of, her uniting herself with this most commonplace and mechanical person, who cannot even offer her the elegances and luxuries to which she might seem entitled on changing her condition.

While I was thus interested and puzzled I received an unexpected visit from our Landlady. She was evidently excited, and by some event which was of a happy nature, for her countenance was beaming and she seemed impatient to communicate what she had to tell. Impatient or not, she must wait a moment, while I say a word about her. Our Landlady is as good a creature as ever lived. She is a little negligent of grammar at times, and will get a wrong word now and then; she is garrulous, circumstantial, associates facts by their accidental cohesion rather than by their vital affinities, is given to choking and tears on slight occasions, but she has a warm heart, and feels to her boarders as if they were her blood-relations. She began her conversation abruptly. I expect I'm a going to lose one of my boarders, she said.

You don't seem very unhappy about it, madam, I answered. We all took it easily when the person who sat on our side of the table quitted us in such a hurry, but I do not think there is anybody left that either you or the boarders want to get rid of unless it is myself, I added modestly.

You! said the Landlady, you! No indeed. When I have a quiet boarder that's a small eater, I don't want to lose him. You don't make trouble, you don't find fault with your vit - [Dr. Benjamin had schooled his parent on this point and she altered the word] with your food, and you know when you've had enough.

I really felt proud of this eulogy, which embraces the most desirable excellences of a human being in the capacity of boarder.

The Landlady began again. I'm going to lose, at least, I suppose I shall, one of the best boarders I ever had, that Lady that's been with me so long.

I thought there was something going on between her and the Register, I said.

Something! I should think there was! About three months ago he began making her acquaintance. I thought there was something particular. I did n't quite like to watch 'em very close; but I could n't help overbearing some of the things he said to her, for, you see, he used to follow her up into the parlor, they talked pretty low, but I could catch a word now and then. I heard him say something to her one day about "bettering her condition," and she seemed to be thinking very hard about it, and turning of it over in her mind, and I said to myself, She does n't want to take up with him, but she feels dreadful poor, and perhaps he has been saving and has got money in the bank, and she does n't want to throw away a chance of bettering herself without thinking it over. But dear me, says I to myself, to think of her walking up the broad aisle into meeting alongside of such a homely, rusty-looking creatur' as that! But there's no telling what folks will do when poverty has got hold of 'em.

Well, so I thought she was waiting to make up her mind, and he was hanging on in hopes she'd come round at last, as women do half the time, for they don't know their own minds and the wind blows both ways at once with 'em as the smoke blows out of the tall chimlies, east out of this one and west out of that, so it's no use looking at 'em to know what the weather is.

But yesterday she comes up to me after breakfast, and asks me to go up with her into her little room. Now, says I to myself, I shall hear all about it. I saw she looked as if she'd got some of her trouble off her mind, and I guessed that it was settled, and so, says I to myself, I must wish her joy and hope it's all for the best, whatever I think about it.

Well, she asked me to set down, and then she begun. She said that she was expecting to have a change in her condition of life, and had asked me up so that I might' have the first news of it. I am sure says I - I wish you both joy. Merriage is a blessed thing when folks is well sorted, and it is an honorable thing, and the first meracle was at the merriage in Canaan. It brings a great sight of happiness with it, as I've had a chance of knowing, for my hus -

The Landlady showed her usual tendency to "break" from the conversational pace just at this point, but managed to rein in the rebellious diaphragm, and resumed her narrative.

Merriage! says she, pray who has said anything about merriage? I beg your pardon, ma'am, says I, I thought you had spoke of changing your condition and I - She looked so I stopped right short.

Don't say another word, says she, but jest listen to what I am going to tell you.

My friend, says she, that you have seen with me so often lately, was hunting among his old Record books, when all at once he come across an old deed that was made by somebody that had my family name. He took it into his head to read it over, and he found there was some kind of a condition that if it was n't kept, the property would all go back to them that was the heirs of the one that gave the deed, and that he found out was me. Something or other put it into his head, says she, that the company that owned the property, it was ever so rich a company and owned land all round everywhere, hadn't kept to the conditions. So he went to work, says she, and hunted through his books and he inquired all round, and he found out pretty much all about it, and at last he come to me, it 's my boarder, you know, that says all this and says he, Ma'am, says he, if you have any kind of fancy for being a rich woman you've only got to say so. I didn't know what he meant, and I began to think, says she, he must be crazy. But he explained it all to me, how I'd nothing to do but go to court and I could get a sight of property back. Well, so she went on telling me, there was ever so much more that I suppose was all plain enough, but I don't remember it all, only I know my boarder was a good deal worried at first at the thought of taking money that other people thought was theirs, and the Register he had to talk to her, and he brought a lawyer and he talked to her, and her friends they talked to her, and the upshot of it all was that the company agreed to settle the business by paying her, well, I don't know just how much, but enough to make her one of the rich folks again.

I may as well add here that, as I have since learned, this is one of the most important cases of releasing right of reentry for condition broken which has been settled by arbitration for a considerable period. If I am not mistaken the Register of Deeds will get something more than a new coat out of this business, for the Lady very justly attributes her change of fortunes to his sagacity and his activity in following up the hint he had come across by mere accident.

So my supernumerary fellow-boarder, whom I would have dispensed with as a cumberer of the table, has proved a ministering angel to one of the personages whom I most cared for.

One would have thought that the most scrupulous person need not have hesitated in asserting an unquestioned legal and equitable claim simply because it had lain a certain number of years in abeyance. But before the Lady could make up her mind to accept her good fortune she had been kept awake many nights in doubt and inward debate whether she should avail herself of her rights. If it had been private property, so that another person must be made poor that she should become rich, she would have lived and died in want rather than claim her own. I do not think any of us would like to turn out the possessor of a fine estate enjoyed for two or three generations on the faith of unquestioned ownership by making use of some old forgotten instrument, which accident had thrown in our way.

But it was all nonsense to indulge in any sentiment in a case like this, where it was not only a right, but a duty which she owed herself and others in relation with her, to accept what Providence, as it appeared, had thrust upon her, and when no suffering would be occasioned to anybody. Common sense told her not to refuse it. So did several of her rich friends, who remembered about this time that they had not called upon her for a good while, and among them Mrs. Midas Goldenrod.

Never had that lady's carriage stood before the door of our boarding-house so long, never had it stopped so often, as since the revelation which had come from the Registry of Deeds. Mrs. Midas Goldenrod was not a bad woman, but she loved and hated in too exclusive and fastidious a way to allow us to consider her as representing the highest ideal of womanhood. She hated narrow ill-ventilated courts, where there was nothing to see if one looked out of the window but old men in dressing-gowns and old women in caps; she hated little dark rooms with air-tight stoves in them; she hated rusty bombazine gowns and last year's bonnets; she hated gloves that were not as fresh as new-laid eggs, and shoes that had grown bulgy and wrinkled in service; she hated common crockeryware and teaspoons of slight constitution; she hated second appearances on the dinner-table; she hated coarse napkins and table-cloths; she hated to ride in the horsecars; she hated to walk except for short distances, when she was tired of sitting in her carriage. She loved with sincere and undisguised affection a spacious city mansion and a charming country villa, with a seaside cottage for a couple of months or so; she loved a perfectly appointed household, a cook who was up to all kinds of salmis and vol-au-vents, a French maid, and a stylish-looking coachman, and the rest of the people necessary to help one live in a decent manner; she loved pictures that other people said were first-rate, and which had at least cost first-rate prices; she loved books with handsome backs, in showy cases; she loved heavy and richly wrought plate; fine linen and plenty of it; dresses from Paris frequently, and as many as could be got in without troubling the customhouse; Russia sables and Venetian point-lace; diamonds, and good big ones; and, speaking generally, she loved dear things in distinction from cheap ones, the real article and not the economical substitute.

For the life of me I cannot see anything Satanic in all this. Tell me, Beloved, only between ourselves, if some of these things are not desirable enough in their way, and if you and I could not make up our minds to put up with some of the least objectionable of them without any great inward struggle? Even in the matter of ornaments there is something to be said. Why should we be told that the New Jerusalem is paved with gold, and that its twelve gates are each of them a pearl, and that its foundations are garnished with sapphires and emeralds and all manner of precious stones, if these are not among the most desirable of objects? And is there anything very strange in the fact that many a daughter of earth finds it a sweet foretaste of heaven to wear about her frail earthly tabernacle these glittering reminders of the celestial city?

Mrs. Midas Goldenrod was not so entirely peculiar and anomalous in her likes and dislikes; the only trouble was that she mixed up these accidents of life too much with life itself, which is so often serenely or actively noble and happy without reference to them. She valued persons chiefly according to their external conditions, and of course the very moment her relative, the Lady of our breakfast-table, began to find herself in a streak of sunshine she came forward with a lighted candle to show her which way her path lay before her.

The Lady saw all this, how plainly, how painfully! yet she exercised a true charity for the weakness of her relative. Sensible people have as much consideration for the frailties of the rich as for those of the poor. There is a good deal of excuse for them. Even you and I, philosophers and philanthropists as we may think ourselves, have a dislike for the enforced economies, proper and honorable though they certainly are, of those who are two or three degrees below us in the scale of agreeable living.

These are very worthy persons you have been living with, my dear, said Mrs. Midas [the "My dear" was an expression which had flowered out more luxuriantly than ever before in the new streak of sunshine] eminently respectable parties, I have no question, but then we shall want you to move as soon as possible to our quarter of the town, where we can see more of you than we have been able to in this queer place.

It was not very pleasant to listen to this kind of talk, but the Lady remembered her annual bouquet, and her occasional visits from the rich lady, and restrained the inclination to remind her of the humble sphere from which she herself, the rich and patronizing personage, had worked her way up (if it was up) into that world which she seemed to think was the only one where a human being could find life worth having. Her cheek flushed a little, however, as she said to Mrs. Midas that she felt attached to the place where she had been living so long. She doubted, she was pleased to say, whether she should find better company in any circle she was like to move in than she left behind her at our boarding-house. I give the old Master the credit of this compliment. If one does not agree with half of what he says, at any rate he always has something to say, and entertains and lets out opinions and whims and notions of one kind and another that one can quarrel with if he is out of humor, or carry away to think about if he happens to be in the receptive mood.

But the Lady expressed still more strongly the regret she should feel at leaving her young friend, our Scheherezade. I cannot wonder at this. The Young Girl has lost what little playfulness she had in the earlier months of my acquaintance with her. I often read her stories partly from my interest in her, and partly because I find merit enough in them to deserve something, better than the rough handling they got from her coarse-fibred critic, whoever he was. I see evidence that her thoughts are wandering from her task, that she has fits of melancholy, and bursts of tremulous excitement, and that she has as much as she can do to keep herself at all to her stated, inevitable, and sometimes almost despairing literary labor. I have had some acquaintance with vital phenomena of this kind, and know something of the nervous nature of young women and its "magnetic storms," if I may borrow an expression from the physicists, to indicate the perturbations to which they are liable. She is more in need of friendship and counsel now than ever before, it seems to me, and I cannot bear to think that the Lady, who has become like a mother to her, is to leave her to her own guidance.

It is plain enough what is at the bottom of this disturbance. The astronomical lessons she has been taking have become interesting enough to absorb too much of her thoughts, and she finds them wandering to the stars or elsewhere, when they should be working quietly in the editor's harness.

The Landlady has her own views on this matter which she communicated to me something as follows:

I don't quite like to tell folks what a lucky place my boarding-house is, for fear I should have all sorts of people crowding in to be my boarders for the sake of their chances. Folks come here poor and they go away rich. Young women come here without a friend in the world, and the next thing that happens is a gentleman steps up to 'em and says, "If you'll take me for your pardner for life, I'll give you a good home and love you ever so much besides"; and off goes my young lady-boarder into a fine three-story house, as grand as the governor's wife, with everything to make her comfortable, and a husband to care for her into the bargain. That's the way it is with the young ladies that comes to board with me, ever since the gentleman that wrote the first book that advertised my establishment (and never charged me a cent for it neither) merried the Schoolma'am. And I think but that's between you and me, that it 's going to be the same thing right over again between that young gentleman and this young girl here, if she doos n't kill herself with writing for them news papers, it 's too bad they don't pay her more for writing her stories, for I read one of 'em that made me cry so the Doctor, my Doctor Benjamin, said, "Ma, what makes your eyes look so?" and wanted to rig a machine up and look at 'em, but I told him what the matter was, and that he needn't fix up his peeking contrivances on my account, anyhow she's a nice young woman as ever lived, and as industrious with that pen of hers as if she was at work with a sewing-machine, and there ain't much difference, for that matter, between sewing on shirts and writing on stories, one way you work with your foot, and the other way you work with your fingers, but I rather guess there's more headache in the stories than there is in the stitches, because you don't have to think quite so hard while your foot's going as you do when your fingers is at work, scratch, scratch, scratch, scribble, scribble, scribble.

It occurred to me that this last suggestion of the Landlady was worth considering by the soft-handed, broadcloth-clad spouters to the laboring classes, so called in distinction from the idle people who only contrive the machinery and discover the processes and lay out the work and draw the charts and organize the various movements which keep the world going and make it tolerable. The organ-blower works harder with his muscles, for that matter, than the organ player, and may perhaps be exasperated into thinking himself a downtrodden martyr because he does not receive the same pay for his services.

I will not pretend that it needed the Landlady's sagacious guess about the Young Astronomer and his pupil to open my eyes to certain possibilities, if not probabilities, in that direction. Our Scheherezade kept on writing her stories according to agreement, so many pages for so many dollars, but some of her readers began to complain that they could not always follow her quite so well as in her earlier efforts. It seemed as if she must have fits of absence. In one instance her heroine began as a blonde and finished as a brunette; not in consequence of the use of any cosmetic, but through simple inadvertence. At last it happened in one of her stories that a prominent character who had been killed in an early page, not equivocally, but mortally, definitively killed, done for, and disposed of, reappeared as if nothing had happened towards the close of her narrative. Her mind was on something else, and she had got two stories mixed up and sent her manuscript without having looked it over. She told this mishap to the Lady, as something she was dreadfully ashamed of and could not possibly account for. It had cost her a sharp note from the publisher, and would be as good as a dinner to some half-starved Bohemian of the critical press.

The Lady listened to all this very thoughtfully, looking at her with great tenderness, and said, "My poor child!" Not another word then, but her silence meant a good deal.

When a man holds his tongue it does not signify much. But when a woman dispenses with the office of that mighty member, when she sheathes her natural weapon at a trying moment, it means that she trusts to still more formidable enginery; to tears it may be, a solvent more powerful than that with which Hannibal softened the Alpine rocks, or to the heaving bosom, the sight of which has subdued so many stout natures, or, it may be, to a sympathizing, quieting look which says "Peace, be still!" to the winds and waves of the little inland ocean, in a language that means more than speech.

While these matters were going on the Master and I had many talks on many subjects. He had found me a pretty good listener, for I had learned that the best way of getting at what was worth having from him was to wind him up with a question and let him run down all of himself. It is easy to turn a good talker into an insufferable bore by contradicting him, and putting questions for him to stumble over, that is, if he is not a bore already, as "good talkers" are apt to be, except now and then.

We had been discussing some knotty points one morning when he said all at once:

Come into my library with me. I want to read you some new passages from an interleaved copy of my book. You haven't read the printed part yet. I gave you a copy of it, but nobody reads a book that is given to him. Of course not. Nobody but a fool expects him to. He reads a little in it here and there, perhaps, and he cuts all the leaves if he cares enough about the writer, who will be sure to call on him some day, and if he is left alone in his library for five minutes will have hunted every corner of it until he has found the book he sent, if it is to be found at all, which does n't always happen, if there's a penal colony anywhere in a garret or closet for typographical offenders and vagrants.

What do you do when you receive a book you don't want, from the author? said I.

Give him a good-natured adjective or two if I can, and thank him, and tell him I am lying under a sense of obligation to him.

That is as good an excuse for lying as almost any, I said.

Yes, but look out for the fellows that send you a copy of their book to trap you into writing a bookseller's advertisement for it. I got caught so once, and never heard the end of it and never shall hear it. He took down an elegantly bound volume, on opening which appeared a flourishing and eminently flattering dedication to himself. There, said he, what could I do less than acknowledge such a compliment in polite terms, and hope and expect the book would prove successful, and so forth and so forth? Well, I get a letter every few months from some new locality where the man that made that book is covering the fences with his placards, asking me whether I wrote that letter which he keeps in stereotype and has kept so any time these dozen or fifteen years. Animus tuus oculus, as the freshmen used to say. If her Majesty, the Queen of England, sends you a copy of her "Leaves from the Journal of Our Life in the Highlands," be sure you mark your letter of thanks for it Private!

We had got comfortably seated in his library in the mean time, and the Master had taken up his book. I noticed that every other page was left blank, and that he had written in a good deal of new matter.

I tell you what, he said, there 's so much intelligence about nowadays in books and newspapers and talk that it's mighty hard to write without getting something or other worth listening to into your essay or your volume. The foolishest book is a kind of leaky boat on a sea of wisdom; some of the wisdom will get in anyhow. Every now and then I find something in my book that seems so good to me, I can't help thinking it must have leaked in. I suppose other people discover that it came through a leak, full as soon as I do. You must write a book or two to find out how much and how little you know and have to say. Then you must read some notices of it by somebody that loves you and one or two by somebody that hates you. You 'll find yourself a very odd piece of property after you 've been through these experiences. They 're trying to the constitution; I'm always glad to hear that a friend is as well as can be expected after he 's had a book.

You must n't think there are no better things in these pages of mine than the ones I'm going to read you, but you may come across something here that I forgot to say when we were talking over these matters.

He began, reading from the manuscript portion of his book:

We find it hard to get and to keep any private property in thought. Other people are all the time saying the same things we are hoarding to say when we get ready. [He looked up from his book just here and said, "Don't be afraid, I am not going to quote Pereant."] One of our old boarders, the one that called himself "The Professor" I think it was, said some pretty audacious things about what he called "pathological piety," as I remember, in one of his papers. And here comes along Mr. Galton, and shows in detail from religious biographies that "there is a frequent correlation between an unusually devout disposition and a weak constitution." Neither of them appeared to know that John Bunyan had got at the same fact long before them. He tells us, "The more healthy the lusty man is, the more prone he is unto evil." If the converse is true, no wonder that good people, according to Bunyan, are always in trouble and terror, for he says,

"A Christian man is never long at ease;
When one fright is gone, another doth him seize."

If invalidism and the nervous timidity which is apt to go with it are elements of spiritual superiority, it follows that pathology and toxicology should form a most important part of a theological education, so that a divine might know how to keep a parish in a state of chronic bad health in order that it might be virtuous.

It is a great mistake to think that a man's religion is going to rid him of his natural qualities. "Bishop Hall" (as you may remember to have seen quoted elsewhere) "prefers Nature before Grace in the Election of a wife, because, saith he, it will be a hard Task, where the Nature is peevish and froward, for Grace to make an entire conquest while Life lasteth."

"Nature" and "Grace" have been contrasted with each other in a way not very respectful to the Divine omnipotence. Kings and queens reign "by the Grace of God," but a sweet, docile, pious disposition, such as is born in some children and grows up with them, that congenital gift which good Bishop Hall would look for in a wife, is attributed to "Nature." In fact "Nature" and "Grace," as handled by the scholastics, are nothing more nor less than two hostile Divinities in the Pantheon of post-classical polytheism.

What is the secret of the profound interest which "Darwinism" has excited in the minds and hearts of more persons than dare to confess their doubts and hopes? It is because it restores "Nature" to its place as a true divine manifestation. It is that it removes the traditional curse from that helpless infant lying in its mother's arms. It is that it lifts from the shoulders of man the responsibility for the fact of death. It is that, if it is true, woman can no longer be taunted with having brought down on herself the pangs which make her sex a martyrdom. If development upward is the general law of the race; if we have grown by natural evolution out of the cave-man, and even less human forms of life, we have everything to hope from the future. That the question can be discussed without offence shows that we are entering on a new era, a Revival greater than that of Letters, the Revival of Humanity.

The prevalent view of "Nature" has been akin to that which long reigned with reference to disease. This used to be considered as a distinct entity apart from the processes of life, of which it is one of the manifestations. It was a kind of demon to be attacked with things of odious taste and smell; to be fumigated out of the system as the evil spirit was driven from the bridal-chamber in the story of Tobit. The Doctor of earlier days, even as I can remember him, used to exorcise the demon of disease with recipes of odor as potent as that of the angel's diabolifuge, the smoke from a fish's heart and liver, duly burned, "the which smell when the evil spirit had smelled he fled into the uttermost parts of Egypt." The very moment that disease passes into the category of vital processes, and is recognized as an occurrence absolutely necessary, inevitable, and as one may say, normal under certain given conditions of constitution and circumstance, the medicine-man loses his half-miraculous endowments. The mythical serpent is untwined from the staff of Esculapius, which thenceforth becomes a useful walking-stick, and does not pretend to be anything more.

Sin, like disease, is a vital process. It is a function, and not an entity. It must be studied as a section of anthropology. No preconceived idea must be allowed to interfere with our investigation of the deranged spiritual function, any more than the old ideas of demoniacal possession must be allowed to interfere with our study of epilepsy. Spiritual pathology is a proper subject for direct observation and analysis, like any other subject involving a series of living actions.

In these living actions everything is progressive. There are sudden changes of character in what is called "conversion" which, at first, hardly seem to come into line with the common laws of evolution. But these changes have been long preparing, and it is just as much in the order of nature that certain characters should burst all at once from the rule of evil propensities, as it is that the evening primrose should explode, as it were, into bloom with audible sound, as you may read in Keats's Endymion, or observe in your own garden.

There is a continual tendency in men to fence in themselves and a few of their neighbors who agree with them in their ideas, as if they were an exception to their race. We must not allow any creed or religion whatsoever to confiscate to its own private use and benefit the virtues which belong to our common humanity. The Good Samaritan helped his wounded neighbor simply because he was a suffering fellow-creature. Do you think your charitable act is more acceptable than the Good Samaritan's, because you do it in the name of Him who made the memory of that kind man immortal? Do you mean that you would not give the cup of cold water for the sake simply and solely of the poor, suffering fellow-mortal, as willingly as you now do, professing to give it for the sake of Him who is not thirsty or in need of any help of yours? We must ask questions like this, if we are to claim for our common nature what belongs to it.

The scientific study of man is the most difficult of all branches of knowledge. It requires, in the first place, an entire new terminology to get rid of that enormous load of prejudices with which every term applied to the malformations, the functional disturbances, and the organic diseases of the moral nature is at present burdened. Take that one word Sin, for instance: all those who have studied the subject from nature and not from books know perfectly well that a certain fraction of what is so called is nothing more or less than a symptom of hysteria; that another fraction is the index of a limited degree of insanity; that still another is the result of a congenital tendency which removes the act we sit in judgment upon from the sphere of self-determination, if not entirely, at least to such an extent that the subject of the tendency cannot be judged by any normal standard.

To study nature without fear is possible, but without reproach, impossible. The man who worships in the temple of knowledge must carry his arms with him as our Puritan fathers had to do when they gathered in their first rude meeting-houses. It is a fearful thing to meddle with the ark which holds the mysteries of creation. I remember that when I was a child the tradition was whispered round among us little folks that if we tried to count the stars we should drop down dead. Nevertheless, the stars have been counted and the astronomer has survived. This nursery legend is the child's version of those superstitions which would have strangled in their cradles the young sciences now adolescent and able to take care of themselves, and which, no longer daring to attack these, are watching with hostile aspect the rapid growth of the comparatively new science of man.

The real difficulty of the student of nature at this time is to reconcile absolute freedom and perfect fearlessness with that respect for the past, that reverence, for the spirit of reverence wherever we find it, that tenderness for the weakest fibres by which the hearts of our fellow-creatures hold to their religious convictions, which will make the transition from old belief to a larger light and liberty an interstitial change and not a violent mutilation.

I remember once going into a little church in a small village some miles from a great European capital. The special object of adoration in this humblest of places of worship was a bambino, a holy infant, done in wax, and covered with cheap ornaments such as a little girl would like to beautify her doll with. Many a good Protestant of the old Puritan type would have felt a strong impulse to seize this "idolatrous" figure and dash it to pieces on the stone floor of the little church. But one must have lived awhile among simple-minded pious Catholics to know what this poor waxen image and the whole baby-house of bambinos mean for a humble, unlettered, unimaginative peasantry. He will find that the true office of this eidolon is to fix the mind of the worshipper, and that in virtue of the devotional thoughts it has called forth so often for so many years in the mind of that poor old woman who is kneeling before it, it is no longer a wax doll for her, but has undergone a transubstantiation quite as real as that of the Eucharist. The moral is that we must not roughly smash other people's idols because we know, or think we know, that they are of cheap human manufacture.

Do you think cheap manufactures encourage idleness? said I.

The Master stared. Well he might, for I had been getting a little drowsy, and wishing to show that I had been awake and attentive, asked a question suggested by some words I had caught, but which showed that I had not been taking the slightest idea from what he was reading me. He stared, shook his head slowly, smiled good-humoredly, took off his great round spectacles, and shut up his book.

Sat prates biberunt, he said. A sick man that gets talking about himself, a woman that gets talking about her baby, and an author that begins reading out of his own book, never know when to stop. You'll think of some of these things you've been getting half asleep over by and by. I don't want you to believe anything I say; I only want you to try to see what makes me believe it.

My young friend, the Astronomer, has, I suspect, been making some addition to his manuscript. At any rate some of the lines he read us in the afternoon of this same day had never enjoyed the benefit of my revision, and I think they had but just been written. I noticed that his manner was somewhat more excited than usual, and his voice just towards the close a little tremulous. Perhaps I may attribute his improvement to the effect of my criticisms, but whatever the reason, I think these lines are very nearly as correct as they would have been if I had looked them over.

WIND-CLOUDS AND STAR-DRIFTS.

VII

What if a soul redeemed, a spirit that loved
While yet on earth and was beloved in turn,
And still remembered every look and tone
Of that dear earthly sister who was left
Among the unwise virgins at the gate,
Itself admitted with the bridegroom's train,
What if this spirit redeemed, amid the host
Of chanting angels, in some transient lull
Of the eternal anthem, heard the cry
Of its lost darling, whom in evil hour
Some wilder pulse of nature led astray
And left an outcast in a world of fire,

Condemned to be the sport of cruel fiends,
Sleepless, unpitying, masters of the skill
To wring the maddest ecstasies of pain
From worn-out souls that only ask to die,
Would it not long to leave the bliss of Heaven,
Bearing a little water in its hand
To moisten those poor lips that plead in vain
With Him we call our Father? Or is all
So changed in such as taste celestial joy
They hear unmoved the endless wail of woe,
The daughter in the same dear tones that hushed
Her cradled slumbers; she who once had held
A babe upon her bosom from its voice
Hoarse with its cry of anguish, yet the same?

No! not in ages when the Dreadful Bird
Stamped his huge footprints, and the Fearful Beast
Strode with the flesh about those fossil bones
We build to mimic life with pygmy hands,
Not in those earliest days when men ran wild
And gashed each other with their knives of stone,
When their low foreheads bulged in ridgy brows
And their flat hands were callous in the palm
With walking in the fashion of their sires,
Grope as they might to find a cruel god
To work their will on such as human wrath
Had wrought its worst to torture, and had left
With rage unsated, white and stark and cold,
Could hate have shaped a demon more malign
Than him the dead men mummied in their creed
And taught their trembling children to adore!
Made in his image! Sweet and gracious souls
Dear to my heart by nature's fondest names,
Is not your memory still the precious mould
That lends its form to Him who hears my prayer?
Thus only I behold him, like to them,
Long-suffering, gentle, ever slow to wrath,
If wrath it be that only wounds to heal,
Ready to meet the wanderer ere he reach
The door he seeks, forgetful of his sin,
Longing to clasp him in a father's arms,
And seal his pardon with a pitying tear!

Four gospels tell their story to mankind,
And none so full of soft, caressing words
That bring the Maid of Bethlehem and her Babe
Before our tear-dimmed eyes, as his who learned
In the meek service of his gracious art
The tones which like the medicinal balms
That calm the sufferer's anguish, soothe our souls.
 Oh that the loving woman, she who sat
So long a listener at her Master's feet,
Had left us Mary's Gospel, all she heard
Too sweet, too subtle for the ear of man!

Mark how the tender-hearted mothers read
The messages of love between the lines
Of the same page that loads the bitter tongue
Of him who deals in terror as his trade
With threatening words of wrath that scorch like flame!
They tell of angels whispering round the bed
Of the sweet infant smiling in its dream,
Of lambs enfolded in the Shepherd's arms,
Of Him who blessed the children; of the land
Where crystal rivers feed unfading flowers,
Of cities golden-paved with streets of pearl,
Of the white robes the winged creatures wear,
The crowns and harps from whose melodious strings
One long, sweet anthem flows forevermore!

We too bad human mothers, even as Thou,
Whom we have learned to worship as remote
From mortal kindred, wast a cradled babe.
The milk of woman filled our branching veins,
She lulled us with her tender nursery-song,
And folded round us her untiring arms,
While the first unremembered twilight year
Shaped us to conscious being; still we feel
Her pulses in our own, too faintly feel;
Would that the heart of woman warmed our creeds!

Not from the sad-eyed hermit's lonely cell,
Not from the conclave where the holy men
Glare on each other, as with angry eyes
They battle for God's glory and their own,
Till, sick of wordy strife, a show of hands
Fixes the faith of ages yet unborn,
Ah, not from these the listening soul can hear
The Father's voice that speaks itself divine!
Love must be still our Master; till we learn
What he can teach us of a woman's heart,
We know not His, whose love embraces all.

There are certain nervous conditions peculiar to women in which the common effects of poetry and of music upon their sensibilities are strangely exaggerated. It was not perhaps to be wondered at that Octavia fainted when Virgil in reading from his great poem came to the line beginning Tu Marcellus eris: It is not hard to believe the story told of one of the two Davidson sisters, that the singing of some of Moore's plaintive melodies would so impress her as almost to take away the faculties of sense and motion. But there must have been some special cause for the singular nervous state into which this reading threw the young girl, our Scheherezade. She was doubtless tired with overwork and troubled with the thought that she was not doing herself justice, and that she was doomed to be the helpless prey of some of those corbies who not only pick out corbies' eyes, but find no other diet so nutritious and agreeable.

Whatever the cause may have been, her heart heaved tumultuously, her color came and went, and though she managed to avoid a scene by the exercise of all her self-control, I watched her very anxiously, for I was afraid she would have had a hysteric turn, or in one of her pallid moments that she would have fainted and fallen like one dead before us.

I was very glad, therefore, when evening came, to find that she was going out for a lesson on the stars. I knew the open air was what she needed, and I thought the walk would do her good, whether she made any new astronomical acquisitions or not.

It was now late in the autumn, and the trees were pretty nearly stripped of their leaves. There was no place so favorable as the Common for the study of the heavens. The skies were brilliant with stars, and the air was just keen enough to remind our young friends that the cold season was at hand. They wandered round for a while, and at last found themselves under the Great Elm, drawn thither, no doubt, by the magnetism it is so well known to exert over the natives of its own soil and those who have often been under the shadow of its outstretched arms. The venerable survivor of its contemporaries that flourished in the days when Blackstone rode beneath it on his bull was now a good deal broken by age, yet not without marks of lusty vitality. It had been wrenched and twisted and battered by so many scores of winters that some of its limbs were crippled and many of its joints were shaky, and but for the support of the iron braces that lent their strong sinews to its more infirm members it would have gone to pieces in the first strenuous northeaster or the first sudden and violent gale from the southwest. But there it stood, and there it stands as yet, though its obituary was long ago written after one of the terrible storms that tore its branches, leafing out hopefully in April as if it were trying in its dumb language to lisp "Our Father," and dropping its slender burden of foliage in October as softly as if it were whispering Amen!

Not far from the ancient and monumental tree lay a small sheet of water, once agile with life and vocal with evening melodies, but now stirred only by the swallow as he dips his wing, or by the morning bath of the English sparrows, those high-headed, thick-bodied, full-feeding, hot-tempered little John Bulls that keep up such a swashing and swabbing and spattering round all the water basins, one might think from the fuss they make about it that a bird never took a bath here before, and that they were the missionaries of ablution to the unwashed Western world.

There are those who speak lightly of this small aqueous expanse, the eye of the sacred enclosure, which has looked unwinking on the happy faces of so many natives and the curious features of so many strangers. The music of its twilight minstrels has long ceased, but their memory lingers like an echo in the name it bears. Cherish it, inhabitants of the two-hilled city, once three-hilled; ye who have said to the mountain, "Remove hence," and turned the sea into dry land! May no contractor fill his pockets by undertaking to fill thee, thou granite girdled lakelet, or drain the civic purse by drawing off thy waters! For art thou not the Palladium of our Troy? Didst thou not, like the Divine image which was the safeguard of Ilium, fall from the skies, and if the Trojan could look with pride upon the heaven-descended form of the Goddess of Wisdom, cannot he who dwells by thy shining oval look in that mirror and contemplate Himself, the Native of Boston.

There must be some fatality which carries our young men and maidens in the direction of the Common when they have anything very particular to exchange their views about. At any rate I remember two of our young friends brought up here a good many years ago, and I understand that there is one path across the enclosure which a young man must not ask a young woman to take with him unless he means business, for an action will hold for breach of promise, if she consents to accompany him, and he chooses to forget his obligations:

Our two young people stood at the western edge of the little pool, studying astronomy in the reflected firmament. The Pleiades were trembling in the wave before them, and the three great stars of Orion, for these constellations were both glittering in the eastern sky.

"There is no place too humble for the glories of heaven to shine in," she said.

"And their splendor makes even this little pool beautiful and noble," he answered. "Where is the light to come from that is to do as much for our poor human lives?"

A simple question enough, but the young girl felt her color change as she answered, "From friendship, I think."

Grazing only as-yet, not striking full, hardly hitting at all, but there are questions and answers that come so very near, the wind of them alone almost takes the breath away.

There was an interval of silence. Two young persons can stand looking at water for a long time without feeling the necessity of speaking. Especially when the water is alive with stars and the young persons are thoughtful and impressible. The water seems to do half the thinking while one is looking at it; its movements are felt in the brain very much like thought. When I was in full training as a flaneur, I could stand on the Pont Neuf with the other experts in the great science of passive cerebration and look at the river for half an hour with so little mental articulation that when I moved on it seemed as if my thinking-marrow had been asleep and was just waking up refreshed after its nap.

So the reader can easily account for the interval of silence. It is hard to tell how long it would have lasted, but just then a lubberly intrusive boy threw a great stone, which convulsed the firmament, the one at their feet, I mean. The six Pleiads disappeared as if in search of their lost sister; the belt of Orion was broken asunder, and a hundred worlds dissolved back into chaos. They turned away and strayed off into one of the more open paths, where the view of the sky over them was unobstructed. For some reason or other the astronomical lesson did not get on very fast this evening.

Presently the young man asked his pupil:

Do you know what the constellation directly over our heads is?

Is it not Cassiopea? she asked a little hesitatingly.

No, it is Andromeda. You ought not to have forgotten her, for I remember showing you a double star, the one in her right foot, through the equatorial telescope. You have not forgotten the double star, the two that shone for each other and made a little world by themselves?

No, indeed, she answered, and blushed, and felt ashamed because she had said indeed, as if it had been an emotional recollection.

The double-star allusion struck another dead silence. She would have given a week's pay to any invisible attendant that would have cut her stay-lace.

At last: Do you know the story of Andromeda? he said.

Perhaps I did once, but suppose I don't remember it.

He told her the story of the unfortunate maiden chained to a rock and waiting for a sea-beast that was coming to devour her, and how Perseus came and set her free, and won her love with her life. And then he began something about a young man chained to his rock, which was a star-gazer's tower, a prey by turns to ambition, and lonely self-contempt and unwholesome scorn of the life he looked down upon after the serenity of the firmament, and endless questionings that led him nowhere, and now he had only one more question to ask. He loved her. Would she break his chain? He held both his hands out towards her, the palms together, as if they were fettered at the wrists. She took hold of them very gently; parted them a little; then wider, wider, and found herself all at once folded, unresisting, in her lover's arms.

So there was a new double-star in the living firmament. The constellations seemed to kindle with new splendors as the student and the story-teller walked homeward in their light; Alioth and Algol looked down on them as on the first pair of lovers they shone over, and the autumn air seemed full of harmonies as when the morning stars sang together.

CHAPTER XII

The old Master had asked us, the Young Astronomer and myself, into his library, to hear him read some passages from his interleaved book. We three had formed a kind of little club without knowing it from the time when the young man began reading those extracts from his poetical reveries which I have reproduced in these pages. Perhaps we agreed in too many things, I suppose if we could have had a good hard-headed, old-fashioned New England divine to meet with us it might have acted as a wholesome corrective. For we had it all our own way; the Lady's kindly remonstrance was taken in good part, but did not keep us from talking pretty freely, and as for the Young Girl, she listened with the tranquillity and fearlessness which a very simple trusting creed naturally gives those who hold it. The fewer outworks to the citadel of belief, the fewer points there are to be threatened and endangered.

The reader must not suppose that I even attempt to reproduce everything exactly as it took place in our conversations, or when we met to listen to the Master's prose or to the Young Astronomer's verse. I do not pretend to give all the pauses and interruptions by question or otherwise. I could not always do it if I tried, but I do not want to, for oftentimes it is better to let the speaker or reader go on continuously, although there may have been many breaks in the course of the conversation or reading. When, for instance, I by and by reproduce what the Landlady said to us, I shall give it almost without any hint that it was arrested in its flow from time to time by various expressions on the part of the hearers.

I can hardly say what the reason of it was, but it is very certain that I had a vague sense of some impending event as we took our seats in the Master's library. He seemed particularly anxious that we should be comfortably seated, and shook up the cushions of the arm-chairs himself, and got them into the right places.

Now go to sleep, he said or listen, just which you like best. But I am going to begin by telling you both a secret.

Liberavi animam meam. That is the meaning of my book and of my literary life, if I may give such a name to that party-colored shred of human existence. I have unburdened myself in this book, and in some other pages, of what I was born to say. Many things that I have said in my ripe days have been aching in my soul since I was a mere child. I say aching, because they conflicted with many of my inherited beliefs, or rather traditions. I did not know then that two strains of blood were striving in me for the mastery, two! twenty, perhaps, twenty thousand, for aught I know, but represented to me by two, paternal and maternal. Blind forces in themselves; shaping thoughts as they shaped features and battled for the moulding of constitution and the mingling of temperament.

Philosophy and poetry came, to me before I knew their names.

Je fis mes premiers vers, sans savoir les ecrire.

Not verses so much as the stuff that verses are made of. I don't suppose that the thoughts which came up of themselves in my mind were so mighty different from what come up in the minds of other young folks. And that's the best reason I could give for telling 'em. I don't believe anything I've written is as good as it seemed to me when I wrote it, he stopped, for he was afraid he was lying, not much that I've written, at any rate, he said, with a smile at the honesty which made him qualify his statement. But I do know this: I have struck a good many chords, first and last, in the consciousness of other people. I confess to a tender feeling for my little brood of thoughts. When they have been welcomed and praised it has pleased me, and if at any time they have been rudely handled and despitefully entreated it has cost me a little worry. I don't despise reputation, and I should like to be remembered as having said something worth lasting well enough to last.

But all that is nothing to the main comfort I feel as a writer. I have got rid of something my mind could not keep to itself and rise as it was meant to into higher regions. I saw the aeronauts the other day emptying from the bags some of the sand that served as ballast. It glistened a moment in the sunlight as a slender shower, and then was lost and seen no more as it scattered itself unnoticed. But the airship rose higher as the sand was poured out, and so it seems to me I have felt myself getting above the mists and clouds whenever I have lightened myself of some portion of the mental ballast I have carried with me. Why should I hope or fear when I send out my book? I have had my reward, for I have wrought out my thought, I have said my say, I have freed my soul. I can afford to be forgotten.

Look here! he said. I keep oblivion always before me. He pointed to a singularly perfect and beautiful trilobite which was lying on a pile of manuscripts. Each time I fill a sheet of paper with what I am writing, I lay it beneath this relic of a dead world, and project my thought forward into eternity as far as this extinct crustacean carries it backward. When my heart beats too lustily with vain hopes of being remembered, I press the cold fossil against it and it grows calm. I touch my forehead with it, and its anxious furrows grow smooth. Our world, too, with all its breathing life, is but a leaf to be folded with the other strata, and if I am only patient, by and by I shall be just as famous as imperious Caesar himself, embedded with me in a conglomerate.

He began reading: "There is no new thing under the sun," said the Preacher. He would not say so now, if he should come to life for a little while, and have his photograph taken, and go up in a balloon, and take a trip by railroad and a voyage by steamship, and get a message from General Grant by the cable, and see a man's leg cut off without its hurting him. If it did not take his breath away and lay him out as flat as the Queen of Sheba was knocked over by the splendors of his court, he must have rivalled our Indians in the nil admarari line.

For all that, it is a strange thing to see what numbers of new things are really old. There are many modern contrivances that are of as early date as the first man, if not thousands of centuries older. Everybody knows how all the arrangements of our telescopes and microscopes are anticipated in the eye, and how our best musical instruments are surpassed by the larynx. But there are some very odd things any anatomist can tell, showing how our recent contrivances are anticipated in the human body. In the alimentary canal are certain pointed eminences called villi, and certain ridges called valvuloe conniventes. The makers of heating apparatus have exactly reproduced the first in the "pot" of their furnaces, and the second in many of the radiators to be seen in our public buildings. The object in the body and the heating apparatus is the same; to increase the extent of surface. We mix hair with plaster (as the Egyptians mixed straw with clay to make bricks) so that it shall hold more firmly. But before man had any artificial dwelling the same contrivance of mixing fibrous threads with a cohesive substance had been employed in the jointed fabric of his own spinal column. India-rubber is modern, but the yellow animal substance which is elastic like that, and serves the same purpose in the animal economy which that serves in our mechanical contrivances, is as old as the mammalia. The dome, the round and the Gothic arch, the groined roof, the flying buttress, are all familiar to those who have studied the bony frame of man. All forms of the lever and all the principal kinds of hinges are to be met with in our own frames. The valvular arrangements of the blood-vessels are unapproached by any artificial apparatus, and the arrangements for preventing friction are so perfect that two surfaces will play on each other for fourscore years or more and never once trouble their owner by catching or rubbing so as to be felt or heard.

But stranger than these repetitions are the coincidences one finds in the manners and speech of antiquity and our own time. In the days when Flood Ireson was drawn in the cart by the Maenads of Marblehead, that fishing town had the name of nurturing a young population not over fond of strangers. It used to be said that if an unknown landsman showed himself in the streets, the boys would follow after him, crying, "Rock him! Rock him! He's got a long-tailed coat on!"

Now if one opens the Odyssey, he will find that the Phaeacians, three thousand years ago, were wonderfully like these youthful Marbleheaders. The blue-eyed Goddess who convoys Ulysses, under the disguise of a young maiden of the place, gives him some excellent advice. "Hold your tongue," she says, "and don't look at anybody or ask any questions, for these are seafaring people, and don't like to have strangers round or anybody that does not belong here."

Who would have thought that the saucy question, "Does your mother know you're out?" was the very same that Horace addressed to the bore who attacked him in the Via Sacra?

Interpellandi locus hic erat; Est tibi mater?
Cognati, queis te salvo est opus?

And think of the London cockney's prefix of the letter h to innocent words beginning with a vowel having its prototype in the speech of the vulgar Roman, as may be seen in the verses of Catullus:

Chommoda dicebat, siquando commoda vellet
Dicere, et hinsidias Arrius insidias.
Et tum mirifice sperabat se esse locutum,
Cum quantum poterat, dixerat hinsidias...

Hoc misso in Syriam, requierant omnibus aures...
Cum subito affertur nuncius horribilis;
Ionios fluctus, postquam illue Arrius isset,
Jam non Ionios esse, sed Hionios.

Our neighbors of Manhattan have an excellent jest about our crooked streets which, if they were a little more familiar with a native author of unquestionable veracity, they would strike out from the letter of "Our Boston Correspondent," where it is a source of perennial hilarity. It is worth while to reprint, for the benefit of whom it may concern, a paragraph from the authentic history of the venerable Diedrich Knickerbocker:

"The sage council, as has been mentioned in a preceding chapter, not being able to determine upon any plan for the building of their city, the cows, in a laudable fit of patriotism, took it under their peculiar charge, and as they went to and from pasture, established paths through the bushes, on each side of which the good folks built their houses; which is one cause of the rambling and picturesque turns and labyrinths, which distinguish certain streets of New York at this very day."

When I was a little boy there came to stay with us for a while a young lady with a singularly white complexion. Now I had often seen the masons slacking lime, and I thought it was the whitest thing I had ever looked upon. So I always called this fair visitor of ours Slacked Lime. I think she is still living in a neighboring State, and I am sure she has never forgotten the fanciful name I gave her. But within ten or a dozen years I have seen this very same comparison going the round of the papers, and credited to a Welsh poet, David Ap Gwyllym, or something like that, by name.

I turned a pretty sentence enough in one of my lectures about finding poppies springing up amidst the corn; as if it had been foreseen by nature that wherever there should be hunger that asked for food, there would be pain that needed relief, and many years afterwards. I had the pleasure of finding that Mistress Piozzi had been beforehand with me in suggesting the same moral reflection.

I should like to carry some of my friends to see a giant bee-hive I have discovered. Its hum can be heard half a mile, and the great white swarm counts its tens of thousands. They pretend to call it a planing-mill, but if it is not a bee-hive it is so like one that if a hundred people have not said so before me, it is very singular that they have not. If I wrote verses I would try to bring it in, and I suppose people would start up in a dozen places, and say, "Oh, that bee-hive simile is mine, and besides, did not Mr. Bayard Taylor call the snowflakes 'white bees'?"

I think the old Master had chosen these trivialities on purpose to amuse the Young Astronomer and myself, if possible, and so make sure of our keeping awake while he went on reading, as follows:

How the sweet souls of all time strike the same note, the same because it is in unison with the divine voice that sings to them! I read in the Zend Avesta, "No earthly man with a hundred-fold strength speaks so much evil as Mithra with heavenly strength speaks good. No earthly man with a hundred-fold strength does so much evil as Mithra with heavenly strength does good."

And now leave Persia and Zoroaster, and come down with me to our own New England and one of our old Puritan preachers. It was in the dreadful days of the Salem Witchcraft delusion that one Jonathan Singletary, being then in the prison at Ipswich, gave his testimony as to certain fearful occurrences, a great noise, as of many cats climbing, skipping, and jumping, of throwing about of furniture, and of men walking in the chambers, with crackling and shaking as if the house would fall upon him.

"I was at present," he says, "something affrighted; yet considering what I had lately heard made out by Mr. Mitchel at Cambridge, that there is more good in God than there is evil in sin, and that although God is the greatest good and sin the greatest evil, yet the first Being of evil cannot weave the scales or overpower the first Being of good: so considering that the authour of good was of greater power than the authour of evil, God was pleased of his goodness to keep me from being out of measure frighted."

I shall always bless the memory of this poor, timid creature for saving that dear remembrance of "Matchless Mitchel." How many, like him, have thought they were preaching a new gospel, when they were only reaffirming the principles which underlie the Magna Charta of humanity, and are common to the noblest utterances of all the nobler creeds! But spoken by those solemn lips to those stern, simpleminded hearers, the words I have cited seem to me to have a fragrance like the precious ointment of spikenard with which Mary anointed her Master's feet. I can see the little bare meeting-house, with the godly deacons, and the grave matrons, and the comely maidens, and the sober manhood of the village, with the small group of college students sitting by themselves under the shadow of the awful Presidential Presence, all listening to that preaching, which was, as Cotton Mather says, "as a very lovely song of one that hath a pleasant voice"; and as the holy pastor utters those blessed words, which are not of any one church or age, but of all time, the humble place of worship is filled with their perfume, as the house where Mary knelt was filled with the odor of the precious ointment.

The Master rose, as he finished reading this sentence, and, walking to the window, adjusted a curtain which he seemed to find a good deal of trouble in getting to hang just as he wanted it.

He came back to his arm-chair, and began reading again

If men would only open their eyes to the fact which stares them in the face from history, and is made clear enough by the slightest glance at the condition of mankind, that humanity is of immeasurably greater importance than their own or any other particular belief, they would no more attempt to make private property of the grace of God than to fence in the sunshine for their own special use and enjoyment.

We are all tattoed in our cradles with the beliefs of our tribe; the record may seem superficial, but it is indelible. You cannot educate a man wholly out of the superstitious fears which were early implanted in his imagination; no matter how utterly his reason may reject them, he will still feel as the famous woman did about ghosts, Je n'y crois pas, mais je les crains, "I don't believe in them, but I am afraid of them, nevertheless."

As people grow older they come at length to live so much in memory that they often think with a kind of pleasure of losing their dearest blessings. Nothing can be so perfect while we possess it as it will seem when remembered. The friend we love best may sometimes weary us by his presence or vex us by his infirmities. How sweet to think of him as he will be to us after we have outlived him ten or a dozen years! Then we can recall him in his best moments, bid him stay with us as long as we want his company, and send him away when we wish to be alone again. One might alter Shenstone's well-known epitaph to suit such a case:

Hen! quanto minus est cum to vivo versari

Quam erit (vel esset) tui mortui reminisse!

"Alas! how much less the delight of thy living presence Than will (or would) be that of remembering thee when thou hast left us!"

I want to stop here, I the Poet, and put in a few reflections of my own, suggested by what I have been giving the reader from the Master's Book, and in a similar vein.

How few things there are that do not change their whole aspect in the course of a single generation! The landscape around us is wholly different. Even the outlines of the hills that surround us are changed by the creeping of the villages with their spires and school-houses up their sides. The sky remains the same, and the ocean. A few old churchyards look very much as they used to, except, of course, in Boston, where the gravestones have been rooted up and planted in rows with walks between them, to the utter disgrace and ruin of our most venerated cemeteries. The Registry of Deeds and the Probate Office show us the same old folios, where we can read our grandfather's title to his estate (if we had a grandfather and he happened to own anything) and see how many pots and kettles there were in his kitchen by the inventory of his personal property.

Among living people none remain so long unchanged as the actors. I can see the same Othello to-day, if I choose, that when I was a boy I saw smothering Mrs. Duff-Desdemona with the pillow, under the instigations of Mr. Cooper-Iago. A few stone heavier than he was then, no doubt, but the same truculent blackamoor that took by the thr-r-r-oat the circumcised dog in Aleppo, and told us about it in the old Boston Theatre. In the course of a fortnight, if I care to cross the water, I can see Mademoiselle Dejazet in the same parts I saw her in under Louis Philippe, and be charmed by the same grace and vivacity which delighted my grandmother (if she was in Paris, and went to see her in the part of Fanchon toute seule at the Theatre des Capucines) in the days when the great Napoleon was still only First Consul.

The graveyard and the stage are pretty much the only places where you can expect to find your friends as you left them, five and twenty or fifty years ago. I have noticed, I may add, that old theatre-goers bring back the past with their stories more vividly than men with any other experiences. There were two old New-Yorkers that I used to love to sit talking with about the stage. One was a scholar and a writer of note; a pleasant old gentleman, with the fresh cheek of an octogenarian Cupid. The other not less noted in his way, deep in local lore, large-brained, full-blooded, of somewhat perturbing and tumultuous presence. It was good to hear them talk of George Frederic Cooke, of Kean, and the lesser stars of those earlier constellations. Better still to breakfast with old Samuel Rogers, as some of my readers have done more than once, and hear him answer to the question who was the best actor he remembered, "I think, on the whole, Garrick."

If we did but know how to question these charming old people before it is too late! About ten years, more or less, after the generation in advance of our own has all died off, it occurs to us all at once, "There! I can ask my old friend what he knows of that picture, which must be a Copley; of that house and its legends about which there is such a mystery. He (or she) must know all about that." Too late! Too late!

Still, now and then one saves a reminiscence that means a good deal by means of a casual question. I asked the first of those two old New-Yorkers the following question: "Who, on the whole, seemed to you the most considerable person you ever met?"

Now it must be remembered that this was a man who had lived in a city that calls itself the metropolis, one who had been a member of the State and the National Legislature, who had come in contact with men of letters and men of business, with politicians and members of all the professions, during a long and distinguished public career. I paused for his answer with no little curiosity. Would it be one of the great Ex-Presidents whose names were known to, all the world? Would it be the silver-tongued orator of Kentucky or the "God-like" champion of the Constitution, our New-England Jupiter Capitolinus? Who would it be?

"Take it altogether," he answered, very deliberately, "I should say Colonel Elisha Williams was the most notable personage that I have met with."

Colonel Elisha Williams! And who might he be, forsooth? A gentleman of singular distinction, you may be well assured, even though you are not familiar with his name; but as I am not writing a biographical dictionary, I shall leave it to my reader to find out who and what he was.

One would like to live long enough to witness certain things which will no doubt come to pass by and by. I remember that when one of our good kindhearted old millionnaires was growing very infirm, his limbs failing him, and his trunk getting packed with the infirmities which mean that one is bound on a long journey, he said very simply and sweetly, "I don't care about living a great deal longer, but I should like to live long enough to find out how much old (a many-millioned fellow-citizen) is worth." And without committing myself on the longevity-question, I confess I should like to live long enough to see a few things happen that are like to come, sooner or later.

I want to hold the skull of Abraham in my hand. They will go through the cave of Machpelah at Hebron, I feel sure, in the course of a few generations at the furthest, and as Dr. Robinson knows of nothing which should lead us to question the correctness of the tradition which regards this as the place of sepulture of Abraham and the other patriarchs, there is no reason why we may not find his mummied body in perfect preservation, if he was embalmed after the Egyptian fashion. I suppose the tomb of David will be explored by a commission in due time, and I should like to see the phrenological developments of that great king and divine singer and warm-blooded man. If, as seems probable, the anthropological section of society manages to get round the curse that protects the bones of Shakespeare, I should like to see the dome which rounded itself over his imperial brain. Not that I am what is called a phrenologist, but I am curious as to the physical developments of these fellow-mortals of mine, and a little in want of a sensation.

I should like to live long enough to see the course of the Tiber turned, and the bottom of the river thoroughly dredged. I wonder if they would find the seven-branched golden candlestick brought from Jerusalem by Titus, and said to have been dropped from the Milvian bridge. I have often thought of going fishing for it some year when I wanted a vacation, as some of my friends used to go to Ireland to fish for salmon. There was an attempt of that kind, I think, a few years ago.

We all know how it looks well enough, from the figure of it on the Arch of Titus, but I should like to "heft" it in my own hand, and carry it home and shine it up (excuse my colloquialisms), and sit down and look at it, and think and think and think until the Temple of Solomon built up its walls of hewn stone and its roofs of cedar around me as noiselessly as when it rose, and "there was neither hammer nor axe nor any tool of iron heard in the house while it was in building."

All this, you will remember, Beloved, is a digression on my own account, and I return to the old Master whom I left smiling at his own alteration of Shenstone's celebrated inscription. He now begin reading again:

I want it to be understood that I consider that a certain number of persons are at liberty to dislike me peremptorily, without showing cause, and that they give no offence whatever in so doing.

If I did not cheerfully acquiesce in this sentiment towards myself on the part of others, I should not feel at liberty to indulge my own aversions. I try to cultivate a Christian feeling to all my fellow-creatures, but inasmuch as I must also respect truth and honesty, I confess to myself a certain number of inalienable dislikes and prejudices, some of which may possibly be shared by others. Some of these are purely instinctive, for others I can assign a reason. Our likes and dislikes play so important a part in the Order of Things that it is well to see on what they are founded.

There are persons I meet occasionally who are too intelligent by half for my liking. They know my thoughts beforehand, and tell me what I was going to say. Of course they are masters of all my knowledge, and a good deal besides; have read all the books I have read, and in later editions; have had all the experiences I have been through, and more-too. In my private opinion every mother's son of them will lie at any time rather than confess ignorance.

I have a kind of dread, rather than hatred, of persons with a large excess of vitality; great feeders, great laughers, great story-tellers, who come sweeping over their company with a huge tidal wave of animal spirits and boisterous merriment. I have pretty good spirits myself, and enjoy a little mild pleasantry, but I am oppressed and extinguished by these great lusty, noisy creatures, and feel as if I were a mute at a funeral when they get into full blast.

I cannot get along much better with those drooping, languid people, whose vitality falls short as much as that of the others is in excess. I have not life enough for two; I wish I had. It is not very enlivening to meet a fellow-creature whose expression and accents say, "You are the hair that breaks the camel's back of my endurance, you are the last drop that makes my cup of woe run over"; persons whose heads drop on one side like those of toothless infants, whose voices recall the tones in which our old snuffling choir used to wail out the verses of:

"Life is the time to serve the Lord."

There is another style which does not captivate me. I recognize an attempt at the grand manner now and then, in persons who are well enough in their way, but of no particular importance, socially or otherwise. Some family tradition of wealth or distinction is apt to be at the bottom of it, and it survives all the advantages that used to set it off. I like family pride as well as my neighbors, and respect the high-born fellow-citizen whose progenitors have not worked in their shirt-sleeves for the last two generations full as much as I ought to. But grand pere oblige; a person with a known grandfather is too distinguished to find it necessary to put on airs. The few Royal Princes I have happened to know were very easy people to get along with, and had not half the social knee-action I have often seen in the collapsed dowagers who lifted their eyebrows at me in my earlier years.

My heart does not warm as it should do towards the persons, not intimates, who are always too glad to see me when we meet by accident, and discover all at once that they have a vast deal to unbosom themselves of to me.

There is one blameless person whom I cannot love and have no excuse for hating. It is the innocent fellow-creature, otherwise inoffensive to me, whom I find I have involuntarily joined on turning a corner. I suppose the Mississippi, which was flowing quietly along, minding its own business, hates the Missouri for coming into it all at once with its muddy stream. I suppose the Missouri in like manner hates the Mississippi for diluting with its limpid, but insipid current the rich reminiscences of the varied soils through which its own stream has wandered. I will not compare myself, to the clear or the turbid current, but I will own that my heart sinks when I find all of a sudden I am in for a corner confluence, and I cease loving my neighbor as myself until I can get away from him.

These antipathies are at least weaknesses; they may be sins in the eye of the Recording Angel. I often reproach myself with my wrong-doings. I should like sometimes to thank Heaven for saving me from some kinds of transgression, and even for granting me some qualities that if I dared I should be disposed to call virtues. I should do so, I suppose, if I did not remember the story of the Pharisee. That ought not to hinder me. The parable was told to illustrate a single virtue, humility, and the most unwarranted inferences have been drawn from it as to the whole character of the two parties. It seems not at all unlikely, but rather probable, that the Pharisee was a fairer dealer, a better husband, and a more charitable person than the Publican, whose name has come down to us "linked with one virtue," but who may have been guilty, for aught that appears to the contrary, of "a thousand crimes." Remember how we limit the application of other parables. The lord, it will be recollected, commended the unjust steward because he had done wisely. His shrewdness was held up as an example, but after all he was a miserable swindler, and deserved the state-prison as much as many of our financial operators. The parable of the Pharisee and the Publican is a perpetual warning against spiritual pride. But it must not frighten any one of us out of being thankful that he is not, like this or that neighbor, under bondage to strong drink or opium, that he is not an Erie-Railroad Manager, and that his head rests in virtuous calm on his own pillow. If he prays in the morning to be kept out of temptation as well as for his daily bread, shall he not return thanks at night that he has not fallen into sin as well as that his stomach has been filled? I do not think the poor Pharisee has ever had fair play, and I am afraid a good many people sin with the comforting, half-latent intention of smiting their breasts afterwards and repeating the prayer of the Publican.

(Sensation.)

This little movement which I have thus indicated seemed to give the Master new confidence in his audience. He turned over several pages until he came to a part of the interleaved volume where we could all see he had written in a passage of new matter in red ink as of special interest.

I told you, he said, in Latin, and I repeat it in English, that I have freed my soul in these pages, I have spoken my mind. I have read you a few extracts, most of them of rather slight texture, and some of them, you perhaps thought, whimsical. But I meant, if I thought you were in the right mood for listening to it, to read you some paragraphs which give in small compass the pith, the marrow, of all that my experience has taught me. Life is a fatal complaint, and an eminently contagious one. I took it early, as we all do, and have treated it all along with the best palliatives I could get hold of, inasmuch as I could find no radical cure for its evils, and have so far managed to keep pretty comfortable under it.

It is a great thing for a man to put the whole meaning of his life into a few paragraphs, if he does it so that others can make anything out of it. If he conveys his wisdom after the fashion of the old alchemists, he may as well let it alone. He must talk in very plain words, and that is what I have done. You want to know what a certain number of scores of years have taught me that I think best worth telling. If I had half a dozen square inches of paper, and one penful of ink, and five minutes to use them in for the instruction of those who come after me, what should I put down in writing? That is the question.

Perhaps I should be wiser if I refused to attempt any such brief statement of the most valuable lesson that life has taught me. I am by no means sure that I had not better draw my pen through the page that holds the quintessence of my vital experiences, and leave those who wish to know what it is to distil to themselves from my many printed pages. But I have excited your curiosity, and I see that you are impatient to hear what the wisdom, or the folly, it may be, of a life shows for, when it is crowded into a few lines as the fragrance of a gardenful of roses is concentrated in a few drops of perfume.

By this time I confess I was myself a little excited. What was he going to tell us? The Young Astronomer looked upon him with an eye as clear and steady and brilliant as the evening star, but I could see that he too was a little nervous, wondering what would come next.

The old Master adjusted his large round spectacles, and began:

It has cost me fifty years to find my place in the Order of Things. I had explored all the sciences; I had studied the literature of all ages; I had travelled in many lands; I had learned how to follow the working of thought in men and of sentiment and instinct in women. I had examined for myself all the religions that could make out any claim for themselves. I had fasted and prayed with the monks of a lonely convent; I had mingled with the crowds that shouted glory at camp-meetings; I had listened to the threats of Calvinists and the promises of Universalists; I had been a devout attendant on a Jewish Synagogue; I was in correspondence with an intelligent Buddhist; and I met frequently with the inner circle of Rationalists, who believed in the persistence of Force, and the identity of alimentary substances with virtue, and were reconstructing the universe on this basis, with absolute exclusion of all Supernumeraries. In these pursuits I had passed the larger part of my half-century of existence, as yet with little satisfaction. It was on the morning of my fiftieth birthday that the solution of the great problem I had sought so long came to me as a simple formula, with a few grand but obvious inferences. I will repeat the substance of this final intuition:

The one central fact an the Order of Things which solves all questions is:

At this moment we were interrupted by a knock at the Master's door. It was most inopportune, for he was on the point of the great disclosure, but common politeness compelled him to answer it, and as the step which we had heard was that of one of the softer-footed sex, he chose to rise from his chair and admit his visitor.

This visitor was our Landlady. She was dressed with more than usual nicety, and her countenance showed clearly that she came charged with an important communication.

I did n't low there was company with you, said the Landlady, but it's jest as well. I've got something to tell my boarders that I don't want to tell them, and if I must do it, I may as well tell you all at once as one to a time. I 'm agoing to give up keeping boarders at the end of this year, I mean come the end of December.

She took out a white handkerchief, at hand in expectation of what was to happen, and pressed it to her eyes. There was an interval of silence. The Master closed his book and laid it on the table. The Young Astronomer did not look as much surprised as I should have expected. I was completely taken aback, I had not thought of such a sudden breaking up of our little circle.

When the Landlady had recovered her composure, she began again:

The Lady that's been so long with me is going to a house of her own, one she has bought back again, for it used to belong to her folks. It's a beautiful house, and the sun shines in at the front windows all day long. She's going to be wealthy again, but it doos n't make any difference in her ways. I've had boarders complain when I was doing as well as I knowed how for them, but I never heerd a word from her that wasn't as pleasant as if she'd been talking to the Governor's lady. I've knowed what it was to have women-boarders that find fault, there's some of 'em would quarrel with me and everybody at my table; they would quarrel with the Angel Gabriel if he lived in the house with 'em, and scold at him and tell him he was always dropping his feathers round, if they could n't find anything else to bring up against him.

Two other boarders of mine has given me notice that they was expecting to leave come the first of January. I could fill up their places easy enough, for ever since that first book was wrote that called people's attention to my boarding-house, I've had more wanting to come than I wanted to keep.

But I'm getting along in life, and I ain't quite so rugged as I used to be. My daughter is well settled and my son is making his own living. I've done a good deal of hard work in my time, and I feel as if I had a right to a little rest. There's nobody knows what a woman that has the charge of a family goes through, but God Almighty that made her. I've done my best for them that I loved, and for them that was under my roof. My husband and my children was well cared for when they lived, and he and them little ones that I buried has white marble head-stones and foot-stones, and an iron fence round the lot, and a place left for me betwixt him and the....

Some has always been good to me, some has made it a little of a strain to me to get along. When a woman's back aches with overworking herself to keep her house in shape, and a dozen mouths are opening at her three times a day, like them little young birds that split their heads open so you can a'most see into their empty stomachs, and one wants this and another wants that, and provisions is dear and rent is high, and nobody to look to, then a sharp word cuts, I tell you, and a hard look goes right to your heart. I've seen a boarder make a face at what I set before him, when I had tried to suit him jest as well as I knew how, and I haven't cared to eat a thing myself all the rest of that day, and I've laid awake without a wink of sleep all night. And then when you come down the next morning all the boarders stare at you and wonder what makes you so low-spirited, and why you don't look as happy and talk as cheerful as one of them rich ladies that has dinner-parties, where they've nothing to do but give a few orders, and somebody comes and cooks their dinner, and somebody else comes and puts flowers on the table, and a lot of men dressed up like ministers come and wait on everybody, as attentive as undertakers at a funeral.

And that reminds me to tell you that I'm agoing to live with my daughter. Her husband's a very nice man, and when he isn't following a corpse, he's as good company as if he was a member of the city council. My son, he's agoing into business with the old Doctor he studied with, and he's agoing to board with me at my daughter's for a while, I suppose he'll be getting a wife before long. [This with a pointed look at our young friend, the Astronomer.]

It is n't but a little while longer that we are going to be together, and I want to say to you gentlemen, as I mean to say to the others and as I have said to our two ladies, that I feel more obligated to, you for the way you 've treated me than I know very well how to put into words. Boarders sometimes expect too much of the ladies that provides for them. Some days the meals are better than other days; it can't help being so. Sometimes the provision-market is n't well supplied, sometimes the fire in the cooking-stove does n't burn so well as it does other days; sometimes the cook is n't so lucky as she might be. And there is boarders who is always laying in wait for the days when the meals is not quite so good as they commonly be, to pick a quarrel with the one that is trying to serve them so as that they shall be satisfied. But you've all been good and kind to me. I suppose I'm not quite so spry and quick-sighted as I was a dozen years ago, when my boarder wrote that first book so many have asked me about. But now I'm going to stop taking boarders. I don't believe you'll think much about what I did n't do, because I couldn't, but remember that at any rate I tried honestly to serve you. I hope God will bless all that set at my table, old and young, rich and poor, merried and single, and single that hopes soon to be married. My husband that's dead and gone always believed that we all get to heaven sooner or later, and sence I've grown older and buried so many that I've loved I've come to feel that perhaps I should meet all of them that I've known here or at least as many of 'em as I wanted to in a better world. And though I don't calculate there is any boarding-houses in heaven, I hope I shall some time or other meet them that has set round my table one year after another, all together, where there is no fault-finding with the food and no occasion for it, and if I do meet them and you there or anywhere, if there is anything I can do for you....

.... Poor dear soul! Her ideas had got a little mixed, and her heart was overflowing, and the white handkerchief closed the scene with its timely and greatly needed service.

What a pity, I have often thought, that she came in just at that precise moment! For the old Master was on the point of telling us, and through one of us the reading world, I mean that fraction of it which has reached this point of the record, at any rate, of telling you, Beloved, through my pen, his solution of a great problem we all have to deal with. We were some weeks longer together, but he never offered to continue his reading. At length I ventured to give him a hint that our young friend and myself would both of us be greatly gratified if he would begin reading from his unpublished page where he had left off.

No, sir, he said, better not, better not. That which means so much to me, the writer, might be a disappointment, or at least a puzzle, to you, the listener. Besides, if you'll take my printed book and be at the trouble of thinking over what it says, and put that with what you've heard me say, and then make those comments and reflections which will be suggested to a mind in so many respects like mine as is your own, excuse my good opinion of myself,

(It is a high compliment to me, I replied) you will perhaps find you have the elements of the formula and its consequences which I was about to read you. It's quite as well to crack your own filberts as to borrow the use of other people's teeth. I think we will wait awhile before we pour out the Elixir Vitae.

To tell the honest truth, I suspect the Master has found out that his formula does not hold water quite so perfectly as he was thinking, so long as he kept it to himself, and never thought of imparting it to anybody else. The very minute a thought is threatened with publicity it seems to shrink towards mediocrity, as. I have noticed that a great pumpkin, the wonder of a village, seemed to lose at least a third of its dimensions between the field where it grew and the cattle-show fair-table, where it took its place with other enormous pumpkins from other wondering villages. But however that maybe, I shall always regret that I had not the opportunity of judging for myself how completely the Master's formula, which, for him, at least, seemed to have solved the great problem, would have accomplished that desirable end for me.

The Landlady's announcement of her intention to give up keeping boarders was heard with regret by all who met around her table. The Member of the Haouse inquired of me whether I could tell him if the Lamb Tahvern was kept well abaout these times. He knew that members from his place used to stop there, but he hadn't heerd much abaout it of late years. I had to inform him that that fold of rural innocence had long ceased offering its hospitalities to the legislative, flock. He found refuge at last, I have learned, in a great public house in the northern section of the city, where, as he said, the folks all went up stairs in a rat-trap, and the last I heard of him was looking out of his somewhat elevated attic-window in a northwesterly direction in hopes that he might perhaps get a sight of the Grand Monadnock, a mountain in New Hampshire which I have myself seen from the top of Bunker Hill Monument.

The Member of the Haouse seems to have been more in a hurry to find a new resting-place than the other boarders. By the first of January, however, our whole company was scattered, never to meet again around the board where we had been so long together.

The Lady moved to the house where she had passed many of her prosperous years. It had been occupied by a rich family who had taken it nearly as it stood, and as the pictures had been dusted regularly, and the books had never been handled, she found everything in many respects as she had left it, and in some points improved, for the rich people did not know what else to do, and so they spent money without stint on their house and its adornments, by all of which she could not help profiting. I do not choose to give the street and number of the house where she lives, but a-great many poor people know very well where it is, and as a matter of course the rich ones roll up to her door in their carriages by the dozen every fine Monday while anybody is in town.

It is whispered that our two young folks are to be married before another season, and that the Lady has asked them to come and stay with her for a while. Our Scheherezade is to write no more stories. It is astonishing to see what a change for the better in her aspect a few weeks of brain-rest and heart's ease have wrought in her. I doubt very much whether she ever returns to literary labor. The work itself was almost heart-breaking, but the effect upon her of the sneers and cynical insolences of the literary rough who came at her in mask and brass knuckles was to give her what I fear will be a lifelong disgust against any writing for the public, especially in any of the periodicals. I am not sorry that she should stop writing, but I am sorry that she should have been silenced in such a rude way. I doubt, too, whether the Young Astronomer will pass the rest of his life in hunting for comets and planets. I think he has found an attraction that will call him down from the celestial luminaries to a light not less pure and far less remote. And I am inclined to believe that the best answer to many of those questions which have haunted him and found expression in his verse will be reached by a very different channel from that of lonely contemplation, the duties, the cares, the responsible realities of a life drawn out of itself by the power of newly awakened instincts and affections. The double star was prophetic, I thought it would be.

The Register of Deeds is understood to have been very handsomely treated by the boarder who owes her good fortune to his sagacity and activity. He has engaged apartments at a very genteel boarding-house not far from the one where we have all been living. The Salesman found it a simple matter to transfer himself to an establishment over the way; he had very little to move, and required very small accommodations.

The Capitalist, however, seems to have felt it impossible to move without ridding himself of a part at least of his encumbrances. The community was startled by the announcement that a citizen who did not wish his name to be known had made a free gift of a large sum of money, it was in tens of thousands, to an institution of long standing and high character in the city of which he was a quiet resident. The source of such a gift could not long be kept secret. It, was our economical, not to say parsimonious Capitalist who had done this noble act, and the poor man had to skulk through back streets and keep out of sight, as if he were a show character in a travelling caravan, to avoid the acknowledgments of his liberality, which met him on every hand and put him fairly out of countenance.

That Boy has gone, in virtue of a special invitation, to make a visit of indefinite length at the house of the father of the older boy, whom we know by the name of Johnny. Of course he is having a good time, for Johnny's father is full of fun, and tells first-rate stories, and if neither of the boys gets his brains kicked out by the pony, or blows himself up with gunpowder, or breaks through the ice and gets drowned, they will have a fine time of it this winter.

The Scarabee could not bear to remove his collections, and the old Master was equally unwilling to disturb his books. It was arranged, therefore, that they should keep their apartments until the new tenant should come into the house, when, if they were satisfied with her management, they would continue as her boarders.

The last time I saw the Scarabee he was still at work on the meloe question. He expressed himself very pleasantly towards all of us, his fellow-boarders, and spoke of the kindness and consideration with which the Landlady had treated him when he had been straitened at times for want of means. Especially he seemed to be interested in our young couple who were soon to be united. His tired old eyes glistened as he asked about them, could it be that their little romance recalled some early vision of his own? However that may be, he got up presently and went to a little box in which, as he said, he kept some choice specimens. He brought to me in his hand something which glittered. It was an exquisite diamond beetle.

If you could get that to her, he said, they tell me that ladies sometimes wear them in their hair. If they are out of fashion, she can keep it till after they're married, and then perhaps after a while there may be, you know, you know what I mean, there may be larvae, that's what I'm thinking there may be, and they'll like to look at it.

As he got out the word larvae, a faint sense of the ridiculous seemed to take hold of the Scarabee, and for the first and only time during my acquaintance with him a slight attempt at a smile showed itself on his features. It was barely perceptible and gone almost as soon as seen, yet I am pleased to put it on record that on one occasion at least in his life the Scarabee smiled.

The old Master keeps adding notes and reflections and new suggestions to his interleaved volume, but I doubt if he ever gives them to the public. The study he has proposed to himself does not grow easier the longer it is pursued. The whole Order of Things can hardly be completely unravelled in any single person's lifetime, and I suspect he will have to adjourn the final stage of his investigations to that more luminous realm where the Landlady hopes to rejoin the company of boarders who are nevermore to meet around her cheerful and well-ordered table.

The curtain has now fallen, and I show myself a moment before it to thank my audience and say farewell. The second comer is commonly less welcome than the first, and the third makes but a rash venture. I hope I have not wholly disappointed those who have been so kind to my predecessors.

To you, Beloved, who have never failed to cut the leaves which hold my record, who have never nodded over its pages, who have never hesitated in your allegiance, who have greeted me with unfailing smiles and part from me with unfeigned regrets, to you I look my last adieu as I bow myself out of sight, trusting my poor efforts to your always kind remembrance.

www.ingramcontent.com/pod-product-compliance
Lightning Source LLC
Chambersburg PA
CBHW061656040426
42446CB00010B/1768